The
Second United States Infantry Division
in Korea

The
Second United States Infantry Division
in Korea
1950 — 1951

by

Lieutenant Clark C. Munroe

with illustrations by

Captain Byron Smith

and

Private First Class Robert C. James

Toppan Printing Co., Ltd.
Tokyo, Japan

To our gallant comrades who sacrificed their lives willingly for us, their units, and their country.

May God grant that we like they be "Second to None" in soldierly virtues.

TABLE OF CONTENTS

Foreword

The beginning of the Korean War found the United States Army inadequate in strength to fight a war. As usual and of necessity, it committed its forces in a piecemeal fashion, doing the best it could with what was available. Subsequent events have proved that decision was sound.

This history of the 2d U. S. Infantry Division in Korea has been compiled as the events which it records have occurred. It is realized that such an early narrative of complicated events makes some inaccurracies and some omissions inevitable. These hazards are accepted however, in the desire to deliver to those valiant men who made history in Korea a record of their operations in a readable form.

This volume goes to press before the fighting has ceased and it could be the first in a series. But as a result of the efforts of men like those written about in the following pages, the current peace talks might be successful and this could also be the only volume required to record the Division's campaigns in Korea.

Every effort has been made to include all the units of the Division and to portray accurately and without prejudice the magnificent job which each has done.

An extensive section is devoted to the members of the 2d U. S. Infantry Division whose outstanding achievements in battle were recognized by award of the Congressional Medal of Honor, the Distinguished Service Cross, the Silver Star, the Bronze Star and the Purple Heart.

All awards are those published through 5 November 1951. For those submitted after that date but pending final approval, we have included a special section in the back of the awards and decoration section.

This history was made possible only through painstaking research, effort and assistance on the part of many people. The excellent historical records kept and written by unit historians under very adverse battle and weather conditions and compiled by Major Fred J. Meyer and Captain Carleton F. Robinson, division historians, served as background material for this entire volume.

The photographs reproduced here and those which served as background for the sketches were supplied by the 2d Signal Company and the Far East Command. First Lieutenant William S. Stewart was particularly helpful in compiling and furnishing statistics and copies of awards and decorations. Private First Class Lorin Brown loaned a valuable hand with the illustrating.

The sketch maps which add so much to the battle accounts were done by Private First Class Chris A. Karayan. Sergeant Neil Pritchard devised the map of Korea. Corporal John W. Corey was of immeasurable assistance in typing the many drafts and the final manuscript.

Colonel O. B. Powers of the FEC Printing and Publishing Center was particularly helpful in arranging printing contracts and making many valuable suggestions.

To all these people and to the many others who helped in any way with the compiling of this history go the heartfelt thanks of the production staff.

And, finally, our deep appreciation and respect to the men of the 2d Infantry Division whose story we have tried to tell and because of whose valor and sacrifices this world will one day be a better place in which to live.

Kapyong, Korea
15 November 1951

THE TOP COMMANDERS

13 November 1951

TO THE MEMBERS OF THE UNITED STATES 2ND INFANTRY DIVISION.

Twenty-five years ago it was my privilege to serve in your Division, then stationed at Fort Sam Houston, Texas.

While at much reduced strength, all units of the old "square" organization were active and stationed together. While nearly ten years had elapsed since World War I, there was still a nucleus of veteran non-commissioned officers in the Division who had fought with it in France.

The spirit of the Division was felt from top to bottom. Its commanders of all grades were conscious of the privilege of service in its ranks. It spent a great part of the year under field conditions in field exercises. It trained hard, even during that period when another world war seemed but a remote possibility.

I next served with the Division in the Battle of the Bulge. It was then, not in the Corps I commanded, but the right Division of the 5th Corps on my left, and so its action was closely coordinated with that of my own unit. Finally it was my privilege to have this magnificent Division once again under my command beginning in December of last year.

By study or observation I have known the achievements of this Division thoughout its active service. I count among my proudest and happiest recollections of service those times when I belonged to it or saw it in action.

I send to each of you now privileged to wear the Indian Head my heart-felt best wishes and my earnest hope that you may realize the privilege of service which is yours, and realizing this, may still further enhance its splendid reputation.

M. B. RIDGWAY,
General, United States Army.

17 November 1951

THE COMMANDING GENERAL

Major General Robert N. Young
Commanding General
Second Infantry Division
Korea   And your Officers and Men -

all magnificent in battle - of a great Division:

    ON THE BATTLEFIELDS IN KOREA, THE SECOND DIVISION'S

INDOMITABLE SPIRIT, PROFESSIONAL COMPETENCE, AND SUSTAINED

BRILLIANCE IN ACTION HAVE CONTRIBUTED IMMEASURABLY TO THE

SUCCESS OF THE EIGHTH ARMY.

JAMES A. VAN FLEET
General, U.S. Army

Major General Laurence B. Keiser
8 July 1950 — 6 Dec 1950

Major General Clark L. Ruffner
14 Jan 1951 — 31 Aug 1951

Major General Robert B. McClure
7 Dec 1950 — 13 Jan 1951

Major General Robert N. Young
1 Sept 1951 — date

Assistant Division Commanders

Brig Gen Joseph S. Bradley
8 Jul 50 to 15 Dec 50

Brig Gen George C. Stewart
15 Dec 50 to 18 Aug 51

Brig Gen Haydon L. Boatner
18 Aug 51 to Present

Division Artilley Commanders

Brig Gen Loyal M. Haynes
8 Jul 50 to 18 Mar 51

Brig Gen Thomas E. deShazo
19 Mar 51 to 31 Aug 51

Colonel Edwin A. Walker
1 Sep 51 to 22 Oct 51

Colonel W. C. Bullock
23 Oct 51 to Present

Deputy Assistant Division Commanders

Colonel James P. Barney
16 Dec 50 to 2 Apr 51

Colonel Rupert D. Graves
3 Apr 51 to 24 Jun 51

Chiefs of Staff

Colonel James M. Tully
8 Jul 50 to 6 Sep 50

Colonel Gerald C. Epley
7 Sep 50 to 24 Jun 51

Colonel Rupert D. Graves
25 June 51 to 4 Nov 51

Lt. Colonel Edward L. Rowny
5 Nov 51 to Present

Assistant Chiefs of Staff

G1	*G2*	*G3*	*G4*
Lt Col James D. Tanner 8 Jul 50 to 24 Jun 51	Lt Col Gerald C. Epley 8 Jul 51 to 6 Sep 51	Lt Col Maurice C. Holden 8 Jul 50 to 10 Dec 50	Lt Col Frank C. Sinsel 8 Jul 50 to 7 Aug 51
Lt Col Neil Robinson 25 Jun 51 to 28 Sep 51	Lt Col Ralph L. Foster 7 Sep 50 to 25 May 51	Col John G. Coughlin 11 Dec 50 to 22 Jan 51	Lt Col Arthur J. Cornelson 8 Aug 51 to Present
Major Daniel F. Hughes 29 Sep 51 to Present	Lt Col Albert W. Aykroyd 25 May 51 to Present	Lt Col Claire E. Hutchin 23 Jan 51 to 25 May 51	
		Lt Col Ralph L. Foster 26 May 51 to 3 Aug 51	
		Lt Col Thomas W. Mellen 4 Aug 51 to Present	

Regimental Combat Team Commanders

9th Infantry
Colonel Charles C. Sloane
8 Jul 50 to 11 Jul 50

Colonel John G. Hill
12 Jul 50 to 4 Sep 50

Colonel Charles C. Sloane
5 Sep 50 to 6 Dec 50

Colonel Edwin J. Messinger
7 Dec 50 to 30 Apr 51

Lt Col Olinto M. Barsanti
1 May 51 to 11 Jul 51

Colonel John M. Lynch
12 Jul 51 to Present

23rd Infantry
Colonel Paul L. Freeman
8 Jul 50 to 14 Feb 51

Colonel John H. Chiles
15 Feb 51 to 23 June 51

Lt Col Frank Meszar
26 Jun 51 to 6 Jul 51

Colonel Frank Y. Adams
7 Jul 51 to Present

38th Infantry
Colonel George B. Peploe
8 Jul 50 to 28 Jan 51

Colonel J. C. Coughlin
29 Jan 51 to 26 Jun 51

Colonel Frank T. Mildren
27 Jun 51 to Present

Staff Officers

Engineer
Lt Col Joe A. McEachern
8 Jul 50 to 21 Oct 50

Lt Col Alarich L. Zacherele
3 Nov 50 to 30 Nov 50

Captain Lawrence B. Farnum
1 Dec 50 to 10 Dec 50

Lt Col Edmond H. Leavey Jr
11 Dec 50 to 7 Oct 51

Lt Col Robert W. Love
8 Oct 51 to Present

Ordnance
Lt Col Jack L. Grubb
8 Jul 50 to 21 Mar 51

Lt Col Henry Kirkpatrick
22 Mar 51 to 23 Jul 51

Lt Col Gervase R. Barnhill
24 Jul 51 to Present

Quartermaster
Lt Col Arnold C. Gilliam
8 Jul 50 to 26 Jun 51

Lt Col Irvin I. Luthi
27 Jun 51 to 10 Jul 51

Lt Col Homer P. Harris
11 Jul 51 to Present

Signal
Lt Col Elmer F. Berendt
8 Jul 50 to 20 Feb 51

Lt Col Theodore A. Brunner
21 Feb 51 to 25 Apr 51

Lt Col Robert C. Masenga
26 Apr 51 to 19 Oct 51

Major Claude E. Perlewitz
20 Oct 51 to Present

Surgeon
Lt Col Max Naimark
8 Jul 50 to 16 Jul 50

Lt Col Donald E. Carle
17 Jul 50 to 1 Jan 51

Lt Col Wilbur D. Dice
2 Jan 51 to 6 July 51

Lt Col Lloyd R. Stropes
7 Jul 51 to Present

Artillery and Separate Battalion Commanders

15th FA Battalion
Lt Col J. W. Keith Jr
Lt Col C. H. Wohlfeil
Lt Col J. R. McGuire

503d FA Battalion
Col Joseph Buys
Maj Geossrey Lovell
Maj Cecil B. White
Lt Col H. B. Bond
Lt Col Rovold Meeker
Lt Col H. E. Oshyes

37th FA Battalion
Lt Col W. H. Richardson
Lt Col J. R. Hector
Lt Col L. S. Boatwright

82d AAA Battalion
Lt Col Walter Killilae
Lt Col H. F. Osthues
Lt Col R. H. Johnston
Maj H. A. Gaddis

38th FA Battalion
Lt Col R. J. O'Donnell
Lt Col O. B. Lawrence
Lt Col M. W. Flora

72d Tank Battalion
Lt Col Clark Webber
Lt Col E. L. Brubaker
Lt Col C. S. Hannum
Lt Col J. W. Jarvis
Lt Col J. O. Woods

Medical Battalion
Lt Col W. D. Dice
Lt Col Robert Birnstein
Maj J. N. McNair

MAJOR UNITS

OF THE

2D INFANTRY DIVISION

9th Infantry Regiment

23d Infantry Regiment w/attached French Volunteer Forces in Korea (Bn)

38th Infantry Regiment w/attached Netherlands Volunteer Battalion

15th Field Artillery Battalion

37th Field Artillery Battalion

38th Field Artillery Battalion

503d Field Artillery Battalion

82d AAA Battalion

72d Tank Battalion

2d Engineer (C) Battalion

2d Medical Battalion

2d Reconnaissance Company

2d Quartermaster Company

2d Signal Company

702d Ordnance Company

2d Military Police Company

2d Replacement Company

2d Division Headquarters and Headquarters Company

Headquarters and Headquarters Battery, 2d Division Artillery

2d Counter Intelligence Corps Detachment

This is the story of a great fighting Division and the part it played in one of the most miserable wars in history.

For those who know all or part of this story first-hand it may serve as a reminder of a dirty experience which had few equals in the past and, God willing, none in the future. For those who know of Korea only through the press and radio, it is but a glimpse of the actions behind the bitter hardship and fleeting moments of triumph which characterized the war which was once called a "police action."

The story begins on 17 July 1950. A lumbering naval transport, the **USNS M. M. Patrick**, was steaming west out of Seattle, hull-down, bound for Pusan, Korea. The Second Infantry Division was going to war again.

The heavily laden transport was the vanguard of a fleet of ships. In little more than a month from 17 July, the entire Indianhead Division would have reached its destination. Aboard the first ship were the advance elements, men and equipment of the 9th Regimental Combat Team (RCT), the 2d Reconnaissance Company and the 2d Quartermaster Company.

The following day the **USNS General C. G. Morton** set sail in the wake of the Patrick. Down in the holds, in the troop quarters and on the decks were the supplies and soldiers of the 3d Bn, 9th RCT; 15th FA Bn; and additional elements of the Reconnaissance and Quartermaster companies.

Other ships followed daily—the **California Victory**, the **Sultan, Funston, Freeman, Darby, Towle, Mormacson, Arcadia, New World, Linfield, Elko, Greely, Stewart, Robinhead, Mitchell, Joplin, Rutgers, Wake Forest** and finally, the **Collins.**

It wasn't easy, getting this great Division to sea. But superhuman effort, cooperation from every service, arm and agency made it possible. Just ten days before the Patrick set sail for the Far East, the Second Infantry Division had been following the ways of all Army divisions during the days of peace—training, maneuvers and routine military duties. And then from Washington came word to the Commanding General, Major General Laurence B. Keiser—"The Second Infantry Division had been alerted for movement in the near future to the Far East Command."

At 1000 hours, 9 July, the Division and the world were notified of the urgent alert.

The happenings that took place between that time and 20 August when the entire Division had arrived in Korea will not soon be forgotten by those who took part.

Many officers and men were on leave when the alert was received. Others were at school or enroute to new assignments. A number of men were due for discharge in the near future; some had received orders but had not yet cleared Ft. Lewis, home of the Division.

Telegrams poured out of Ft. Lewis by the hundreds—"Your leave cancelled. Report this station immediately. Unit alerted for early overseas shipment." Wires were sent to the various service schools recalling all Second Division officers and men. Answering messages flocked in—"Two officers, 13 enlisted men your command attending courses this station. Will depart and arrive your station soonest."

A call for replacements went out. Five thousand men were needed to bring the Division up to strength. The availability of shipping became of utmost importance. Speed was essential.

At the request of General Keiser, key officers of the division who had received transfer orders prior to the alert were retained, the orders cancelled.

Telephone wires hummed between Ft. Lewis, Sixth Army Headquarters in San Francisco and Washington. Shortages in men and equipment were compiled and requisitions went out.

Interpreters were required. Equipment was in need of repair and replacement. Tanks and ammunition were called in from the Yakima firing ranges. Packing and crating were requested from the engineers. Doctors were needed to bring the medical units up to strength. Teams of instructors to teach Second Division personnel the operation of the new 3.5 inch rocket launcher were flown from Ft. Benning. Loading plans were drawn up. Shipping was diverted from scheduled runs, priority was to apply to the Infantry Regiment Combat Teams.

Army depots throughout the nation opened their doors to the Second Infantry so that shortages could be filled.

On 10 July, Colonel Charles C. Sloane Jr, commanding officer of the 9th Infantry Regiment, initiated formation of the 9th Regimental Combat Team which was to be the first to leave. On 12 July, with Colonel Sloane retaining command of the Regiment, Colonel John G. Hill assumed command of the RCT.

It was neccessary to transfer men whose enlistments were due to expire and so the order went out sending them to the 4th RCT and the 6006th Army Service Unit at Ft. Lewis. Replacements diverted from the pipeline to the Far East began to arrive but their numbers were not nearly sufficient.

The answers to the calls for help began to come in as the days progressed. With newly arrived equipment more than 1,000 signal items were rehabilitated and twenty percent of the division signal equipment was replaced. Each of the three regimental combat teams was equipped with a thirty day supply of expendable signal items.

The 2d Signal Company sent wire, radio and photo teams to accompany each of the RCTs.

The Division medical units checked shot records for Division personnel and administered smallpox, typhoid, tetnus, cholera and typhus injections. In addition, the Division Surgeon's office inspected each ship to be used and stocked it with serum for anyone who might have missed his shots.

Transportation personnel loaded eleven cargo and ten personnel ships in nineteen days. It was a tremendous task. Tonnage, space requirements and number of personnel had to be calculated. Ships had to be ordered, loading plans made. A shortage of longshoremen slowed the loading at first but was soon overcome. Busses had to be chartered to move men from Division to dockside.

Division Finance processed 31,500 allotment applications that month. Seventeen thousand, five hundred advance payments were made to help officers and men settle financial obligations. More than 14,000 pay records were sent to higher offices after the alert was received.

The 2d Military Police Company, after being brought to wartime strength, organized control platoons to accompany each of the RCT's. Garrison prisoners were released. Training for wartime duties was undertaken and continued until the last moment before departure.

Division Special Services sent out requests for magazines, games, cards, writing paper and other recreational material to be used aboard ship.

The Staff Judge Advocate cleared 335 courts martial cases from the books by 25 July. The division stockade population was reduced from 275 to 115. The SJA also gave legal assistance to 5,000 replacements who arrived at the division during the preparation for movement.

And as each element of the division technical and special services prepared for movement, the infantrymen, artillerymen, tankers, recon troops and engineers were training, processing and packing, getting set for movement and inevitable combat.

In Korea, the hastily committed 24th, 25th, and 1st Cavalry Divisions together with ROK Army units were being hard-pressed and driven back. Help was needed badly.

On 17 July, the advance guard of powerful help was at sea. It was the Second Infantry Division, born of war in France in 1917. It had accumulated nine battle stars in two World Wars. In the first war the entire division had been decorated with the Croix de Guerre by the French government. In World War II it was twice cited by the Belgian government. More than 6,000 of its members, past and present, had won individual awards. The men who sailed from their homeland to Korea on 17 July 1950 and the men who were to follow them were to add new glories to the history of the "Second to None" Division.

*   *   *   *

Even as the first ships carrying the Second Division steamed from Tacoma and Seattle, an advance party under the assistant division commander, Brigadier General Joseph S. Bradley, was planning to fly to Tokyo. Plans were to be made to stage the Division in Japan; for at the time the advance party winged away from McCord Field it was still believed that a staging period would be required. This sentiment was reflected in the thinking of many of the officers as evidenced by a statement in the official history of the Division—"Contrary to the belief of the officers, most enlisted men were convinced that the Division would be committed as soon as it arrived in the Far East."

The advance party arrived in Tokyo on 25 July and set up temporary headquarters. The members toured camp sites the division units were to occupy. On the following day equipment requirements were presented to General Headquarters. Then, on 27 July, their plans were changed. A message from the Commander in Chief, Far East Command, was directed to all elements of the division—"Desire entire Second Infantry Division be routed direct Pusan, Korea. Upon arrival assigned Eighth United States Army in Korea."

The journal of the Advance Party had this entry on 28 July: "Plans for Second Division (-9th RCT) to stage at Yokohama area cancelled. Entire Second Division to 'go in' at Pusan, Korea."

A plane bearing the advance party sighted the shores of Korea at 1015 on 29 July but bad weather forced it to return to Japan. Another trip was begun later in the morning. At 1320, 29 July 50, the first members of the 2d Infantry Division set foot on Korea soil. The spot was an airport 17 miles Northwest of Pusan.

Less than 48 hours away, the **USNS Patrick** plowed steadily forward toward Pusan, leading a great column of ships, the last of which had not yet left Tacoma.

*   *   *   *

As the advance party was arriving at Pusan, the last few ships were being readied for loading back in Washington. On that day, 29 July, the **SS Rutger** put to sea with equipment of the 72d Tank Battalion, 2d Engineer Battalion (—), 2d Signal Company (—) and elements of 2d MP Company. Aboard the **SS Joplin** went cargo of the 38th RCT and 72d Tank Battalion. Only four troop ships remained, the **Greeley, Stewart, Collins** and **Mitchell.**

Replacements, who had begun flowing into the Division, were scheduled to be placed on the last ship. Their arrival brought the Division up to almost 100% of its authorized strength. The status of equipment and supplies was improved to such a point that with the exception of a few nationally unavailable items the Division was almost 100% strength in all ordnance items.

BATTLE INDOCTRINATION

The first elements of the Indianhead Division arrived at Pusan on 31 July 1950. Three ships, the **Patrick**, **Sultan** and **Towle**, docked that first day and immediately began unloading their men and cargo. And as they unloaded, the North Korean army pushed relentlessly southward against the slowly withdrawing UN forces. Eleven enemy divisions had been identified on the line of contact. The disposition of the invading forces formed a disconnected line from Chinju through Kochang, Hwanggon, and Yongju, to Yongdok with the greatest concentration of divisions in the Central part of the line. The enemy action of major significance was the wide envelopment in the south and southwest.

The first troops of the 2d Division to land in Pusan were shuttled as soon as possible northward to the little village of Kyongsan. It was typical of thousands of such hamlets which the men of the Division were to encounter in the coming months as they drove up, down and across the Korean peninsula.

In two days, Kyongsan was headquarters for not only the lead elements of the 9th RCT but the 2d Division command post.

Back at Pusan, one platoon of the 2d QM under Major Webster and Captains Cunningham and Tennant prepared to stage the rest of the Division as it arrived.

4 August—the **Mormacsun, Funston** and **Darby** arrive in Pusan. Aboard are elements and equipment of the 23rd Inf, Div Arty Hd, 37th FA Bn, "B" Btry, 82d AA, and "B" Co, 2d Engrs.

5 August—The **USNS H. B. Freeman** arrives in Pusan with the 1st and 2d Bns, 23d Inf, elements of the 2d Med Bn, 2d MP's, and 2d Sig Co. And on that same date, the 1st Bn, 9th Inf was alerted for action in the zone of the 24th Division. Early the next morning it moved out. With it went the Heavy Mortar Company and "A" Btry, 15th FA Bn.

"A" Battery of the 15th Field became the first 2d Division unit to fire on the enemy when it shoved out its initial rounds on 6 August. The following day during the early morning hours it was attacked by enemy ground forces who had infiltrated between the front lines and the battery position. Standing their ground, the artillerymen repelled attack after attack and finally dispersed the North Koreans. Daylight revealed 15 enemy dead scattered on the fringes of the outfit's perimeter. For their action the members of the battery were officially commended by the 24th Division's Artillery Commander, Brigadier General H. J. D. Meyers.

On 8 August, the 2d Bn and Hdq of the 9th RCT moved into the lines near Yongsan in the vicinity of the 34th RCT near the Naktong River. Upon arrival, the First Battalion which had moved up earlier, reverted to the control of the 9th RCT and a Tactical Air Control Party (TACP) was attached. An attack was scheduled for 1500 that afternoon.

The mission of this force was to resume an attack which had been initiated previously by elements of the 24th Division. An enemy force of between 10,000 and 15,000 had to be driven back across the Naktong River.

With Colonel John G. Hill and his executive officer, Lieutenant Colonel Joseph O. Gerot, on a hill overlooking the line of departure, the 9th RCT (-3rd Bn) moved out under the covering fire of "A" and "B" Batteries of the 15th FA Bn. The First Battalion ran into heavy small arms and mortar fire but the Second Battalion advanced unopposed, moving 1,000 yards. As night came on, both battalions buttoned up but at first light they moved out again. It was in this attack that Lieutenant Colonel Fred L. Harrison, Second Battalion commander, was wounded, the first battalion commander of the Division to suffer wounds in Korea. With the evacuation of Colonel Harison, Major Joseph Walker assumed command.

"Award of the Distinguished Service Cross to Private First Class Lawrence H. BATER Infantry, a member of Headquarters Company, 9th Infantry, for action against the enemy in the vicinity of Yongsan on 11 August 1950. Private BATER was a member of a motor patrol which was suddenly ambushed by a strong and determined enemy force. From well concealed positions, the hostile troops directed intense and accurate fire on the patrol, forcing it to withdraw. Private BATER, completely disregarding his personal safety, voluntarily remained behind to cover the withdrawal of the patrol. Under withering enemy fire from three sides, he steadfastly remained in place, fearlessly engaging the enemy with his rifle. Until killed by the intense enemy fire, he defiantly resisted the fanatically charging enemy, inflicting heavy casualities on them with his deadly accurate fire. His heroic and selfless action resulted in the successful withdrawal of his comrades. Three days later, when his remains were recovered, he was found in the position he had held, the area around him littered with enemy dead."

For the first time, the terrific heat and high humidity of Korea began taking its toll. Canteens were soon emptied and a lip-cracking thurst engulfed the men. Water became a critical item. The oppressive sun beat down on the attacking battalions and their exhausted men. Drinking water finally had to be sent forward with the ammunition.

The Second Battalion met heavy resistance on the second day. It stopped and pulled back while artillery fire was called on the resisting enemy. The attack was resumed at 1700 hours. After fighting until dark in face of heavy enemy fire, the force again buttoned up for the night. Early the next morning the North Koreans counter-attacked. The valiant 9th clung to its positions in face of machine gun, artillery and mortar fire which landed throughout the regimental area wounding the regimental surgeon.

The first attacks were beaten off but enemy reinforcements were pouring across the river and Russian-made tanks were being readied on barges for a crossing. Again and again the enemy attacked, taking a heavy toll which was increased by the terrific heat. On 15 August, four T-34's entered the zone of action. A bazooka team from 'H" Company destroyed one, becoming the first unit of the 2d Division to knock-out an enemy tank. The other three retreated to enemy lines.

"Award of the Distinguished Service Cross to Corporal Robert C. Carroll, Infantry, a member of Company H, 9th Infantry, for action against the enemy in the vicinity of Yongsan on 15 August 1950. At approximately 0300 hours on 15 August 1950, four enemy tanks penetrated the defense perimeter of the 2d Battalion and succeeded in disrupting communications and destroying several company supply points. Obtaining a 3.5 inch rocket launcher Corporal CARROLL crawled to within 50 yards of the lead tank, fired at the tank and succeeded in immobilizing it. The three remaining tanks immediately withdraw. Armed with a hand grenade, Corporal CARROLL charged the disabled tank which was still firing its guns. Un-

able to locate an opening through which to drop his grenade, he removed an axe and sledge strapped outside the vehicle and used them to force open the turret hatch cover. As the hatch cover flew open, an enemy tanker stood up in the hatch, firing a sub-machine gun. In the face of this sudden and unexpected attack, Corporal CARROLL was forced off the tank and the enemy tanker again fastened the hatch cover. Procuring a five gallon can of gasoline from a nearby abandoned vehicle, Corporal CARROLL mounted the tank a second time and poured the gasoline around the turret and on the deck of the tank. Then, after climbing down to the ground, he made a rag torch which he threw on the tank, igniting the gasoline. The enemy tankers remained in the tank, firing all guns, until they were burned to death."

The heaviest enemy attacks against the outnumbered force came on 16 August. Bitter hand to hand fighting developed and continued throughout the day. Friendly air was called in and succeeded in blunting but not stopping the North Korean attack. It became apparent that the troops on hand were not enough to do the job.

In the late afternoon of 16 August, elements of the 1st Provisional Marine Brigade arrived and the next day the entire force consisting of the newly arrived Marines, and the 9th RCT (-3rd Bn) launched a new attack. This failed to succeed although "F" Company chalked up another T-34. But on 18 August the attack was again resumed and the enemy was forced back, withdrawing across the Naktong River.

The following day, the 9th RCT was relieved of its responsibility and began withdrawing to an asesmbly area near Yongsan. But while the First and Second Battalions had been fighting, the Third Battalion had also been engaged.

On 10 August, a special Task Force Bradley, commanded by the Assistant Division Commander, was assembled with the mission of protecting the vital airbase at Pohangdong on the east coast. It was composed of the 3rd Bn, 9th RCT; "C" Btry, 15th FA Bn; Tank Company, 9th RCT; "A" Co, 2d Engrs; "A" Btry, 82d AAA; and Headquarters, 9th RCT (rear). The task force moved out tactically in column formation and advanced to a point three miles north of Kyongju. There a destroyed bridge delayed the tanks bringing up the rear and as a result they were separated from the rest of the column. Unable to close the distance after crossing the river the tanks with "K" Company on the decks were proceeding alone. At 0100 hours. 11 August, while still twelve miles from Pohangdong, the tank-infantry force was ambushed. Upon learning of the fight, the TF commander directed "I" Company to return to the ambush area and render aid. But while moving back, "I" Company was also cut-off. And as the two trapped units were fighting their way free, the Task Force moved into the important airbase and set-up defenses against attack. After hours of bitter battle, the two units which had been ambushed managed to fight their way north to the airbase. "K" Company, however, had suffered heavy casualties in the action and was forced to withdraw to the town of Kyongju where the survivors were reassigned to other units of the 9th RCT. Task Force Bradley remained at the airbase until 20 August when it was dissolved. The Third Battalion with "C" Battery, 15 FA Bn, remained in the Pohang area, however, until mid-September.

This baptisim of fire of the 2d Infantry Division became a preview of what the future had in store. And the praise showered down on these advance elements of the division was also a preview of the future. Letters complimenting the 9th RCT for its action with the 24th Division and the Marines came pouring in. From the 5th Marine Regiment came a typical comment, this one passed on to Colonel Hill by a Marine major—" "F" Company, 9th Infantry, is the best Infantry Company I have seen and worked with. I would like to have a company like that with me at any time."

But while Task Force Bradley consolidated its positions at Pohangdong and the remander of the 9th RCT withdrew to Yongsan after defeating the enemy it had found, other elements of the Division were unloading and moving Northwest out of Pusan. The 23rd RCT had closed into Wondong on 6 August. Then, on 10 August, it departed for Kyongsan minus its Third Battalion which moved to a position southwest of Taegu to operate with elements of the 1st Cavalry Division.

On 12 August, the 23rd RCT (—) commanded by Colonel Paul L. Freeman moved to Miryang where it came under operational control of the 24th Division. On 16 August it moved again, this time to Kyongju where it was still under the 24th Division. It made another move on the 18th to Kyongsan and on the 19th it went into defensive positions north of Taegu. On 20 August, the Third Battalion rejoined the 23d RCT but the Second Battalion assumed the mision previously asigned the Third—operation with the 1st Cavalry.

Such rapid and frequent moves and changes in control were the practice in the early days of the campaign. Defending forces were spread so thin that constant shifts were necessary to maintain maximum strength as pressure became apparent in various sectors.

The 38th RCT arrived in Pusan on 19 August and on 20 August the last tactical elements of the 2d Infantry Division had arrived in Korea. The 38th RCT was already closing toward Miryang on the 20th and the regimental commander, Colonel George B. Peploe, was making arrangements with the 21st Infantry, 24th Division, for relief of the 21st on the Naktong. The 37th FA Battalion had already been in action near Kyongju as had the 15th and 503d FA Battalions in the area of the 9th RCT. The advance elements of Division Forward had closed into an area four miles northeast of Miryang before nightfall, 20 August.

A critical situation that was to become an all too familiar pattern in those early days developed on 22 August. The Second Battalion of the 23rd RCT, comamnded by Lieutenant Colonel James W. Edwards, was in defensive positions about ten miles north of Taegu protecting the 8th and 37th FA Bns when an enemy force of at least regimental size struck against its positions. For three hours the savage attacks were beaten off. 'I' Company of the Third Battalion was sent in as a reinforcement and the strengthened force beat off another attack just before dark. However, even though the attacks were repulsed the North Koreans succeeded in placing artillery, mortar and small arms fire on the MSR for a five mile distance. The nights of 23 and 24 August were spent in repelling repeated enemy attacks. The morning of 25 August the Second Battalion counter-attacked the enemy and was successful in gaining the high ground overlooking the MSR and the artillery positions. At the same time, the Third Battalion cleared the ground bordering the highway.

When the action was completed with slight casualties, it was determined that the entire North Korean regiment had been wiped out in the fighting. Lieutenant General Walton H. Walker, Eighth Army Commander, personally congratulated the regiment on its success.

As the 23rd RCT was cleaning its sector of the enemy, the Second Division received orders from Eighth Army to relieve the 24th Division on the Naktong. For the first time since World War II, the Indianhead Division was to operate as a unit against an enemy. At the time of the relief, the 23rd RCT (-1st Bn) was attached to the 24th Division but it reverted to 2d Division control on 27 August. The Third Battalion of the 23d RCT had been sent to the 1st Cavalry

Division sector.

When, on 24th August, the 2d Division assumed responsibility for the zone of the 24th Division along the Naktong River, it was composed of the following units; 2d Division Headquarters, 38th Inf, 15th FA Bn, 82d AAA Bn, 72d Tk Bn; 2d Signal Company; 2d Div Arty Hdq; 1st Bn, 23d Inf (reinf.); 38th FA Bn; 2d Engr (c) Bn; 2d MP Co; 2d Med Bn; 9th Inf (3rd Bn at Pohangdong); 503d FA Bn; 702d Ord Co; 2d Recon Co, and attached temporarily were the 19th RCT and the 11th FA Bn.

The division front extended along the Naktong River line from where it joined the Nam River in the south to the town of Hyonpung in the north. It was 35 miles in length. Battalions maintained fronts three times wider than those recomemnded for regiments by establishing strongpoints on commanding terrain with combat patrols traversing the area between. Outposts kept visual contact between neighboring units. Such was the thin line the division occupied.

Across the Naktong, building up for a mass attack, were elements of four North Korean rifle divisions with supporting artillery and armor. The day of battle for the Indianhead Division was drawing near.

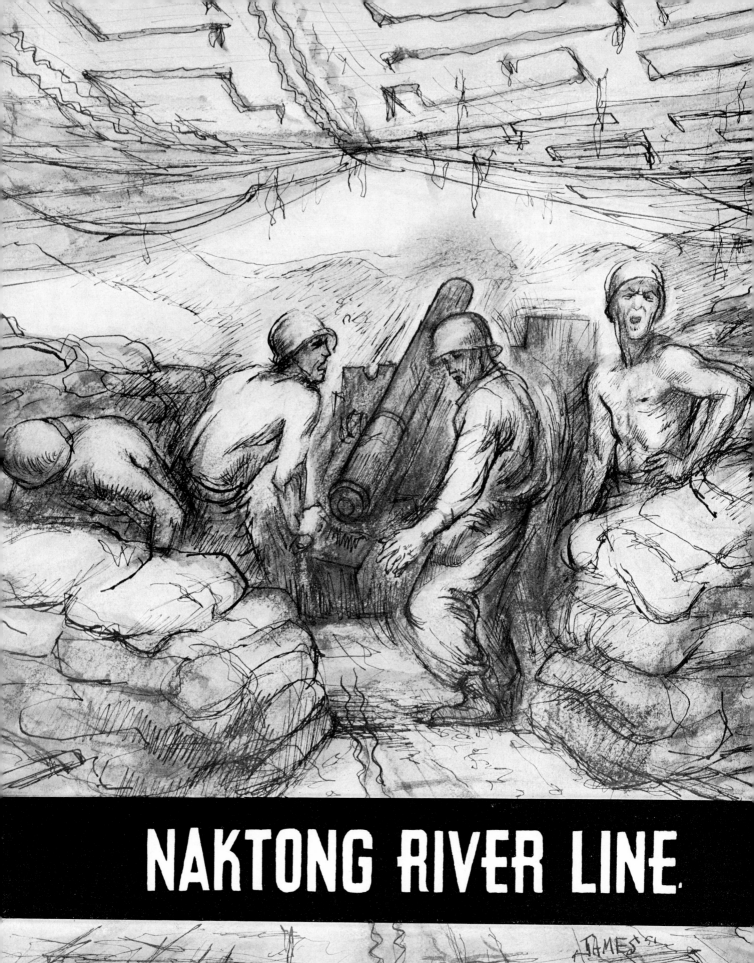

NAKTONG RIVER LINE.

TERRAIN SKETCH

The NAKTONG River defense line was a defensive line set up on the south and east banks of the NAKTONG River. The NAKTONG River varied in width from fifty yards to two hundred yards and depth from waist deep to twelve to fifteen feet deep. The NAKTONG River was not a fast flowing river and it was possible to make log rafts and pole across the river with little difficulty. In the vicinity of HILL 409, the enemy constructed two underwater sand bag fords which were almost impossible to destroy. The defensive positions were located along the near bank of the river on terrain features which averaged slightly over two hundred meters in height. The highest terrain feature on the near bank of the river was HILL 409 and was in enemy hands. Paralleling the defensive positions was the HYONPUNG-CHANGYONG-YONGSAN-MIRYANG road. This was a dirt surface, dry weather road and not originally constructed to carry the loads required at this time. There were only two roads leading from this main road to the river itself. The roads were one way only and because of a great amount of rainfall were often impassable to all traffic. Throughout the sector other roads and trails had been hacked out of the side of the hills, but the first rainfall made them impassable.

Generally, in the center of the division sector, just west of CHANGYONG, was a large lake surrounded by swamp land and rice paddies. There was no definite system of compartments or corridors, but more of a maze of both. As a whole, the sector was one of relatively low rolling hills overlooking the slow moving, relatively narrow, shallow river. The existing road net was barely adequate, but additional one way dry weather roads were easily constructed.

Refugees! A moving sea of humanity poured southeast through Korea in advance of the invading North Korean armies. Nothing like it had been seen since the early days of World War II when the German blitzkrieg rolled across the Lowlands and France. In Korea they streamed down the roads and over mountain trails. Hordes of white clothed, steadily plodding peasants saturated the area of the Second Division as it sought to beat off increasing numbers of enemy patrols and brace itself for an expected attack. And intermingled among the displaced farmers and their families were agents of the communist army. Their mission was to hinder the desperate UN forces in any way possible—sabotoge and roadblock, spy and harrass, you name it, they did it.

Although the problem of controlling the refugees fell to every unit, front and rear, the real burden was upon the shoulders of the Provost Marshal, the 2d CIC Detachment and the South Korean Police. A directive was put out warning the refugees to stay clear of battle areas. Unit commanders were told to shoot any who failed to heed the order prohibiting movement at night. Screening stations were established with MP's searching as many of the refugees as possible. Mine detectors were utilized to expose weapons hidden in the packs of agents mingling with the crowds of displaced persons. Assembly points at 15 mile intervals were set-up where the Koreans were given food and permited to rest. Every effort was being made to clear them from the Division zone, moving them by groups accompanied by South Korean police. Susan-ni, a town on the Naktong River at the Southeastern tip of the Division zone was the point to which the Koreans were guided. From there they were evacuated from the Division area of responsibility.

A special force had to be organized, finally, to assume a major portion of the responsibility for the refugee problem. Major Jack T. Young, an American officer of Chinese descent with an extensive knowledge of the ways of Oriental people was put in command. The force, known as the 2d Division Security Force, was also used as a raider unit. Major Young also assumed operational control of the South Korean Police and this force subsequently proved invaluable in securing information about the enemy as well as bringing some order out of chaos created by the refugees.

Meanwhile, the enemy continued his buildup and increased the number of patrols he sent into the Division area for reconnaissance and to harrass the rear.

Members of the Division Band were used as guards to ride the supply trains from Pusan to the forward areas and protect them from ambush.

On 27 August, the enemy was observed building sandbag bridges across the Naktong and preparing rafts and wooden barges. Mortar and artillery fire were were called in on these craft but proved ineffective. In the zone of the 38th Infantry, an unusual operation took place which did prove effective in destroying many of these river-crossing craft. Lieutenant Clifford Philipsen and three enlisted men from "K" Company volunteered to destroy the rafts across from their area. After extensive planning, the four prepared several partially filled drums with gasoline and pushed them across the river. Under cover of a curtain of automatic weapons fire, they saturated the rafts with the gasoline and set them afire. Although under constant and heavy enemy automatic weapons and small arms fire, all the men returned safely to the friendly shore. The entire volunteer group later received the Silver Star for the action.

The Third Battalion, 23rd Infantry, relieved elements of the 1st Cavalry on 28 August and was attached to the 38th Infantry. The following day, the First Battalion of the 23rd reverted to control of its parent unit and relieved the Third Battalion of the 38th which went into regimental reserve.

In the meantime, the enemy funneled particularly large troop concentrations into the area opposite the 9th RCT. Although daily raiding parties were sent across the river to disrupt this buildup it was realized that this type of effort was not enough, so a raid in force was planned. Since the bulk of the raiding party was composed of 9th Infantry units, the code name given the operation was "Manchu." (The 9th was nicknamed the "Manchu" regiment during its participation in subduing the Boxer rebellion in China at the turn of the century.)

On 31 August, the force was engaged in preparation for the raid. The units involved were 'E' Company of the 9th reinforced with additional 57 mm recoilless rifles, 60 mm mortars, and demolition teams. Supporting fire was to come from the 15th FA Bn (—), a battery of the 38th FA Bn, "A" and "B" Companies of the 72d Tank Battalion, and "D" Battery of the 82d AAA. "D" Company of the 2d Engineers was to orient all the troops participating and to build the bridge over which the Manchu force was to cross the river.

As darkness fell on the 31st, the tanks moved into position. The Heavy Weapons support group began to move to the foot of a hill from which it was to suuport the river crossing.

Suddenly, at 2100, enemy artillery, which had been falling intermittently throughout the day, began to incerase. At the same time, the 23rd Infantry reported large groups of North Koreans gathering on the river banks, carrying torches. Friendly artillery was called and the groups dispersed but the 38th RCT reported heavy artillery fire was being received on its right flank. Great numbers of enemy were observed wading the river in the 9th RCT sector but suddently the enemy artillery slackened and the front became quiet. Then at 2300, the artillery again opened up and heavy mortar fire fell into all line elements of the Division.

At 2330, the enemy launched a heavy attack along the entire front. The Manchu Force whose mission was called off but which was still on its jump off point was surrounded and help was unobtainable for the Naktong River line had exploded. Extending from the right flank of the Division where it joined the 1st Cavalry to the left flank along the river, the enemy poured in savage barrages of artillery and mortar while waves of troops swam and waded across the waters.

"Award of the Distinguished Service Cross to First Lieutenant Edward Schmitt, Infantry, Company Commander of Company H, 9th Infantry for action against the enemy in the vicinity of the Naktong-Gang River near Yongsan, during the period 31 August to 3 September 1950. On the night of 31 August the entire front of the 9th Infantry Regiment was heavily attacked by two divisions of the enemy who penetrated the lines of the regiment and surrounded some of its units. Lieutenant SCHMITT assumed command of a group of about 70 men consisting largely of members of "H" and "D" Companies. Fully realizing the critical position of the group, he took charge immediately and organized a perimeter defense. On the morning of 1 September the enemy began the first of many fanatical attacks against the position. All day and all night the attacks continued. One attack after another was repulsed. Lieutenant SCHMITT moved from man to man on the perimeter displaying great courage and inspiring leadership. He explained to his men the importance of holding the position, thereby delaying the enemy's advance and allowing the regiment time to regroup and counter-attack. Under his dominant leadership men rose to great heights of bravery and daring. Some left the perimeter to gather weapons and

ammunition from enemy dead and to attack and destroy enemy machine guns. On 2 September Lieutenant SCHMITT gained radio contact with his battalion and requested an air drop of water and ammunition. His men were suffering greatly from lack of water and some of them were delirious. Nevertheless, under Lieutenant SCHMITT's leadership they continued to fight off the enemy's continued fanatical attacks and pile up enemy dead in hundreds on the hillside. He was wounded as he supervised the recovery of the air drop, but continued his duties although very weak from thirst, hunger and loss of blood. Lieutenant SCHMITT transmitted his last message on the 3rd of September, informing his commanders of the group's situation and stating that he and his men would fight on no matter what happened. Late on the day of the 3rd of September his radio sustained a direct hit and was destroyed. Still later on the same day, he was mortally wounded as he continued to move among his wounded and dying men". The remnants of his force subsequently made good their escape.

September was to be a month of desperate struggle and overwhelming victory for the United Nations forces. And for the 2d Division, the first dawn of September found every man fighting with his back almost to the sea. The massive communist assault which began in the fading moments of August rolled against the thinly held defense line. The northern sector of the Division front, manned by the 38th RCT with Colonel George B. Peploe in command was the least heavily hit. The "Rock of the Marne" Regiment lived up to its name when it halted the waves of attackers who broke and curled backward. But to the south, the situation was not going as well. The 23rd RCT, Colonel Paul L. Freeman comamnding, holding the central sector was depleted by the absence of the Third Battalion which was attached to the 1st Cavalry Division. The 9th RCT, Colonel John G. Hill in command, was responsible for the southern sector or left flank of the Division and was also minus its Third Battalion which was still guarding the vital Pohangdong airstrip. And it was in the zone defended by these two under strength regiments that the enemy concentrated his effort. Against each he hurled a reinforced division with full artillery and armor support. Identified along the entire 2d Division front were elements of the 2d, 4th, 9th and 10th North Korean Rifle Divisions and the 14th and 16th Mechanized Divisions.

The terrific assault was marked by infiltration

of enemy units behind our lines. Widely scattered defending companies were cut-off. Command posts were struck and supporting artillery and mortar positions found themselves under attack as the communists by-passed strong points and hit in the rear. By daylight the enemy had established a strong bridgehead on the east side of the Naktong and already he was bringing armor and supplies across.

As the attack progressed the entire Division found itself seriously threatened. By noon on 1 September, the First and Second Battalions of the 9th RCT and the Second Battalion of the 23rd were only fifty per cent effective. The First Battalion of the 23rd, also suffering from crippling casualties, had become cut-off from the rest of the friendly units in the vicinity of Hill 209, north of a small lake. Air-dropped supplies kept the valiant group in action but its critical position made it imperative that a relief force be sent.

Subsequently, the Third Battalion of the 38th was ordered into the 23rd sector. But as it moved south along the MSR it encountered an enemy force one-half mile from the regimental CP, threatening Division Artillery Headquarters. The battalion commander ordered an immediate

attack but was wounded in the first skirmish. Colonel Peploe, 38th regimental commander, took over the attack and proceeded to direct the battalion in clearing the enemy penetration. Completing this, the battalion launched an attack west towards Hill 209 to rescue the stil embattled First attalion of the 23rd.

On 2 September, the Third Battalion of the 38th accompanied by a platoon from the regimental Tank Company under command of Captain Hinton, succeeded in breaking through to the surrounded First Battalion of the 23rd and then proceeded to secure Hill 209.

The rescued battalion returned to its regimental sector but only 600 of the original eleven hundred members were present. The New York Times later wrote of the battle as "The Last Stand of the Six Hundred."

The savage battle raged throughout the day and night of 1-2 September and by 2400 hours on the 1st, the entire Division reserve had been committed including the 2nd Engineer Combat Battalion which saw its first action about 0400 hours on 1 September. Time and time again the engineers were to prove as good at combat as they were in engineering activities.

"Award of the Distinguished Service Cross to First Lieutenant Lee E. Beahler, Jr., Corps of Engineers, Commanding Officer, Company D, 2d Engineer Combat Battalion, 2d Infantry Division, for action against the enemy in the vicinity of Yongsan on 2 September 1950. When an enemy force supported by artillery and armor continued an attack which had already overrun three infantry battalions, the 2d Engineer Battalion was rushed into the line to hold the vital communications center of Yongsan which was the key to the pass leading back to Miryang on the Pusan-Taegu lifeline. With other elements of the battalion fighting as infantry south of the town, Company D was given a "stand or die" mission overlooking Yongsan itself. Deployed without supporting artillery or mortars, the unit beat off two enemy attacks, but at a cost of twelve dead and eighteen wounded including all of the company officers excepting Lieutenant BEAHLER. Assuming command of the battered and shaken unit, Lieutenant BEAHLER, rushed from man to man directing the fire of their small arms, automatic weapons and rocket launchers in such a matter as to regain fire superiority. When the enemy returned to the attack for a third time and actually penetrated into the town with tanks, Lieutenant BEAHLER, fearlessly exposing himself to the heavy fire being directed at

*him, manuevered his men to more advantageous
positions from which they soon destroyed one
of the enemy tanks with a rocket fired at close
range. Ranging up and down his line, this
Engineer Officer inspired his men to pour a devastating fire upon the advancing North Koreans until the attack was broken up and the
enemy driven back. By his superb leadership
and aggressive actions throughout the entire day
the town was saved and the threat to the whole
position was elimnated."*

"Task Force Strom" under Major V. E. Strom,
Division Special Service Officer, and composed of
the Division Band and clerks from Division rear
was dug-in on 1 September on two mountain
passes on the MSR where it remained for the
next seven days.   Roadblocks were set-up by the
infiltrating enemy all along the Yongsan-Changyong road.   The 8th Army Commander personally visited the division sector and ordered a
"stand or die" defense.   And the Division stood.
But the situation was precarious.   Reinforcements were sorely needed, for high casualties had
severely depleted the understrength regiments
and the swiftness of the enemy advance had disorganized many units.   Throughout 2 September the bloody defense continued but in spite of
heroic efforts, the enemy succeeded in blunting
the lines, throwing in more troops and increas-

ing his murderous barrage of mortar, artillery
and tank fire. Sometimes under cover of a white
flag the communist forces would advance to the
beleaguared positions only to open fire as they
closed-in.

As the day wore on, it became necessary to
reorganize the entire division in order to maintain control.   Two task forces were formed.
One, under the command of the Division Artillery Commander, Brigadier General Loyal M.
Haynes, was responsible for the northern sector
of the Division Zone.   It consisted of the remaining elements of the 38th and 23rd Infantry
(-3rd Bn), "C" Company of the 72d Tank Battalion, and supporting artillery.   The second
task force was commanded by Brigadier General
Joseph S. Bradley, assistant division commander,
and consisted of elements of the 9th Infantry
(-3rd Bn), 72d Tank Battalion (—), 2d Engineer
Combat Battalion, and supporting artillery.
Task Force Bradley was responsible for the
southern sector of the Division Zone.   The 2d
Recon Co was to continue to screen the left
flank.

While this reorganization was being planned,
another enemy tank-infantry team entered Yongsan.   An assault force composed of troops from
the 9th Infantry, 2d Engineers and "A" Company of the 72d Tank Battalion attacked this

penetrating force and drove it out. Another event occured in Yongsan on 2 September. Sgt E P Parker and Cpl J C Howard, 2d MP Co, were instructed to quit their posts if the enemy entered Yongsan. When the North Koreans did enter the city the two MP's remained until the last vehicle went out then joined up with the infantry to help hold a nearby hill overlooking the town until a counter-attack begun. They advanced with the infantry and upon entering towns and clearing enemy in vicinity of their posts returned to their job.

"Award of the Distinguished Service Cross to Brigadier General Joseph S. Bradley, United States Army, Assistant Division Commander, 2d Infantry Division, for action against the enemy in the vicinity of Yongsan on 1 September 1950. On 1 September 1950, a few hours after the enemy had broken through the lines of the 9th and 23rd Infantry Regiments... General BRADLEY was ordered by the Commanding General, 2nd Infantry Division, to take command of the scattered units south of the breakthrough and to defend the town of Yongsan and the pass leading back to Miryang at all costs. Hastily gathering disorganized elements of the 1st and 2nd Battalions, 9th Infantry, General BRADLEY reorganized them together with the 2nd Engineer Combat Battalion and elements of the 72d Tank Battalion, and under continous and intense hostile fire for three days and nights, beat off repeated enemy attacks. On 2 September, with enemy tanks in the town of Yongsan, General BRADLEY personally took charge of the disorganized Engineer Battalion and placed D Company in position to beat back and destroy the communists in the town. On the next day, a force of eight hundred enemy infantry with tanks and self-propelled guns threatened to come in from the south and overrun the Command Post of the 9th Infantry and the nearby artillery positions from the rear. General BRADLEY again went forward under heavy fire and directed a task force consisting of tanks and engineers against this threat, and with two batteries of 155mm howitzers firing at extreme muzzle elevation, so short was the range, succeeded in driving back the enemy force with heavy casualties. Throughout the period of this desperate, last-ditch defense in which even elements of the Division Band and clerks from the Rear Echelon were put into the line, General BRADLEY was always in front, encouraging individual riflemen to stand fast in spite of enemy penetration to their flanks and rear. On

the 4th and 5th of September, with the enemy stopped but still capable of exploiting their success, General BRADLEY rallied his decimated force to make a coordinated counter-attack with the 1st Provisional Marine Brigade, and again leading the forward elements, successfully restored the position. By his extraordinary heroism and outstanding example of valor, General BRADLEY was an inspiration to the entire command and was directly responsible for stopping the enemy attack."

The 1st Marine Brigade was attached to the 2d Division on 2 September to give new impetus to the weary defenders. Immediately plans for a counterattack were made.

The 9th Infantry (—), "A" Company of the 72d Tank Battalion and "D" Battery of the 82d AAA jumped off on an attack at 0830, 3 September. After securing intermediate objectives designated by Division, this force was passed through by the 1st Marine Brigade. The enemy drive was finally stopped by this savage counterattack and forced back from 1,500 to 2,000 yards.

In the meantime, friendly air was ranging the skies on both sides of the Naktong. Enemy assembly points, supply dumps, troop concentrations, artillery positions and tanks rolling to the front were attacked repeatedly. Bombs, napalm, rockets and machine gun fire rained down on the attackers, seriously hindering their efforts to press the attack and giving the defending troops the measure of support which helped them stem the assault.

As 4 September dawned, the ravaged battlefront was still aflame but the enemy offensive had been blunted. The attack the previous day by Task Force Bradley and the 1st Marine Brigade had played a vital role in stemming the tide although it was costly in casualties. For the first time since the enemy offensive had begun, the North Koreans were forced to employ defensive tactics. Air reported that mines were being laid and defensive positions constructed.

"Award of the Distinguished Service Cross to Corporal Clovis R. Taylor, Infantry, a member of Company H, 9th Infantry, for action against the enemy in the vicinity of Yongsan during the period 31 August to 7 September 1950. On the night of 31 August the enemy launched an all out attack in overwhelming numbers aginst the thinly held lines of the 9th Infantry Regiment and was attempting to make a complete breakthrough and take Miryang, the gateway to Pusan. Corporal TAYLOR was a member of a small group of men from Companies H and D, 9th Infantry who, during the initial phase of the enemy attack, were surrounded and cut off

by the enemy. This group formed a small perimeter defense in an attempt to hold this ground and to slow down the general advance of the enemy. The perimeter was constantly subjected to intense enemy small arms, automatic weapons, mortar and artillery fire and the enemy made continuous fanatical attacks against their position in an attempt to dislodge them. On 1 September Corporal TAYLOR was in the midst of every fire fight and continually encouraged all those present by his actions and utter contempt for the enemy. He was wounded during one of the attacks but refused medical aid as medical supplies were low and there were others more seriously wounded who needed medical attention. On 2 September Corporal TAYLOR observed a long column of enemy climbing Hill 209 carrying large mortars with them which could be used against the men in the perimeter if set up on Hill 209. Expecting them to stop for rest before they reached the top of the hill he had his machine gun section hold their fire. True to his expectations the enemy column did stop for rest and he directed the fire of his machine gun section so effectively that sixty-seven of the enemy were killed and the mortars destroyed. On 3 September during a particularly vicious enemy attack Corporal TAYLOR, with utter disregard for his own personal safety, stood in a fully exposed position and alone killed twenty-five enemy with his rifle. On 4 September it was decided to abandon the perimeter and to leave in small groups and attempt to reach friendly lines. Corporal TAYLOR led six men through enemy territory, engaging in numerous firefights with the enemy, and finally arrived safely with all but two of them.

On 4 September, Capt W. L. Armstrong and Lt W. A. Baugh flew the first "Horsefly" operation in an L17 by leading Air Force fighters in close support of ground troops.

Prisoners who were being captured in increasing numbers revealed a lack of food throughout the communist force. Morale among the North Koreans was low and going lower as a result of the savage defense put up by the 2d Division and the Marines. The terrific artillery and air effort of the friendly forces had taken a high toll of the attackers.

But even with the improved position, the status of the friendly defending forces was far from good. A critical ammunition shortage existed for 57 mm recoiless rifles, 105 mm howitzers, for 60 mm, 81 mm and 4.2 inch mortars, and for 3.5 inch rockets. But in spite of this the two task forces, Haynes and Bradley, continued to

attack. The Marines jumped off again at 0800 on the 4th with the other forces following suit at 0830.

A new threat developed in the rear of the attacking forces on 4 September. A group of approximately 300 infiltraters had entrenched themselves on Hill 285 located 800 yards north of the 38th Regimental Command Post. About 200 of these North Korean troops launched an attack on the CP on the 4th. Forming the defensive perimeter were personnel from Headquarters Company, a section of "A" Battery, 82d AAA and a platoon of tanks. The defenders repulsed the attack but the threat posed by the enemy group remaining on the hill had to be eliminated.

Consequently, "G" Company was released from its duties of guarding the Division Artillery Headquarters and ordered to clear the hill. The resulting action was one of the most desperate small unit actions up to this time. Twice the attackers were driven from the crest of the hill but on the third attempt it was captured. One hundred and fifty enemy dead were counted on the overrun position and 150 more were observed fleeing to the north in confusion.

Such attacks were numerous throughout the Division zone for large numbers of enemy troops had succeeded in slipping into the rear of friendly positions.

As the day lengthened, more reports came into the Division Command Post which indicated that perhaps the turning point had been reached. The enemy had been unable to follow-up his initial successes. His troops, well organized for the assault, had failed to carry-through. Leadership in the NK forces was poor on the attack and appeared unable to cope successfully with changing situations. And, finally, the attackers appeared to have underestimated the holding power of the 2d Division.

On the 5th of September the fury of the battle appeared to support the growing belief that the enemy was temporarily beaten off. Mine fields and additional defensive structures were encountered more frequently as the friendly troops advanced. All enemy attacks for the day were contained.

On 5 September, a counter-attack was ordered to drive the enemy back across the Naktong. The task organization for the attack consisted of the 9th Inf (-3d Bn); 3rd Bn, 23rd Inf; "A" Co, 72d Tk Bn; "D" Btry, 82d AAA Bn; and the 2d Engr (C). Bn. Task Force Haynes consisting of the 23rd Inf (—), 38th Inf, and "C" Co, 72d Tk Bn formed the second element of the organization. The 2d Reconnaissance Company was to continue screening the Division left flank.

The fire support for the two forces was to be furnished by the 15th, 37th, 38th and 503rd Field Artillery Battalions, 82 AAA Battalion (—), and the 72d Tank Battalion (—).

Both forces moved out as scheduled and encountered stiff resistance. Task Force Haynes repulsed a frenzied counter-attack by more than 3,000 enemy troops then continued to move forward.

"Award of the Distinguished Service Cross to Private Dale J. Crow, Infantry, a member of Company G, 35th Infantry, for action against the enemy in the vicinity of Sibi-ri on 6 September. On this date, while participating in an attack against a strongly defended enemy position on Hill 285, he was seriously wounded. While his wound was being dressed by a comrade, an enemy grenade fell nearby. Without hesitation and with no concern for his own life, Private CROW threw his body over that of his comrade thereby receiving the full blast of the grenade, which took his life."

While the action on the front mounted in intensity, slowly driving the enemy back to the Naktong River which he had crossed on the night of 31 August, the refugee problem grew steadily worse. In Chongdo alone, more than

27,000 refugees had gathered. In the area of Task Force Haynes the refugees were particularly heavy. Major Young, commanding the

South Korean Police, together with Military Police units assumed responsibility for clearing the sector. A refugee raider unit was ordered to sweep the road from Changyong to Chongdo as soon as it could be formed.

Intelligence reports received during the first week of September began to indicate a new effort by the enemy to penetrate the 2d Division lines. Increased probing attacks, mostly at night, were encountered and it was believed the improved enemy defenses resisting desperate friendly attacks were screening a new buildup.

"Award of the Distinguished Service Cross to Private First Class Richard L. Fleischmann, Army Medical Service, a member of Medical Company, 23d Infantry, for action against the enemy in the vicinity of Changyong, on 6 September 1950. On the afternoon of 6 September, Private FLEISCHMANN was assigned as aid man to the machine-gun platoon of Company H, 23rd Infantry Regiment. One section of the platoon came under extremely heavy machine-gun and mortar fire and the section leader was wounded. In spite of concentrated enemy fire on the immediate area, Private FLEISCHMANN ran forward to the gun position, removed the section leader to safety, and rendered medical treatment. A few moments later, the gunner of this weapon was also wounded, and once again Private FLEISCHMANN ran into point-blank machine-gun fire and removed this wounded man to safety. Although wounded on the second trip to the machine-gun position, he then took over the machine gun and held off the enemy so that the remainder of the section could reorganize and move to a better position. He remained in position firing the machine gun until he was killed.

These signs pointing to a new communist offensive increased. On 8 September enemy artillery registered on the approaches to Yongsan and Changyong and on the MSR running between the two towns. An enemy battalion attacked a 38th Infantry outpost but was beaten off. Infiltration continued as a total of 17,600 refugees were screened in less than five days at the Susan-ni screening point established in the southeastern tip of the Division zone. However, G-2 predicted the expected enemy assault would not jump-off before the battered North Korean forces had had an opportunity to regroup, resupply and reorganize. In the meantime, plans for destroying all the communists east of the Naktong progressed.

South Korean soldiers, the first of 4,500, were incorporated into the Division during the first week of September to fill the depleted ranks.

The ammunition supply was improved although a shortage of 155 mm howitzer ammunition now existed.

By 10 September, the need for further reinforcement of 2d Division combat forces became critical. Losses suffered by the Division since the initial attack by the North Koreans had not been made-up, even with the addition of the ROK's. Consequently, 200 ROK's from the 9th RCT were shifted to the 23rd RCT, the most depleted of the combt tems. In addition, four company grade officers from the Division Headquarters staff were sent with the ROK's and a levy was placed on all service units and Headquarters Company. Ten percent of the enlisted personnel of these units with an appropriate number of officers were tagged for duty with the infantry regiments.

While the demands for replacement officers and men were being placed on the service units, the enemy buildup increased. A total of 26,700 enemy troops with supporting armor and artillery were known to be opposite the 2d Division sector. Artillery units were observed moving forward—a sure sign of renewed offensive. Supplies and reinforcements were grouping in strategic spots. The situation of that day was described in the Division Command report as "Improved but precarious."

Task Force Duncan, an unusual organization consisting of Headquarters Company of the 9th Infantry, three tanks from the 72d Tank Battalion, and "B" Battery of the 82d AAA Bn, initiated patrols on the Yongsan-Changyong road the second week of September to clear it of infiltrating guerillas. And, as T. F. Duncan rolled along, an even more unusual force was engaged in clearing enemy patrols from behind our lines. Labeled 'Sani Flush," this unit was composed of two squads of riflemen, six military policemen, ten South Korean policemen, and 81 mm mortar section and an M19 personnel carrier. But in spite of the unusual organization it was effective. An enemy patrol of one officer and 16 enlisted men was captured while engaged in reconnoitering the Changyong area in preparation for a North Korean attack.

In the Ammunition Supply Point servicing the Division on 10 September there was a zero balance of 105 and 155 mm howitzer ammunition and even though this was eased somewhat the next day Division Artillery was limited to 25 rounds per gun per day.

The enemy buildup began to concentrate on 12 September in two areas. The first was in the north in the vicinity of Hill 409 and the second in the south near Changyong and Hill 201. But an even more significant event occurred the same day. A courier from Eighth Army arrived at 2d Division Headquarters bringing with him the operation order which directed the Division to attack on 16 September. It was to be an attack which would turn the tables of the war. Made in the face of overwhelming odds from the midst of what appeared to be almost certain defeat the 2d Division and the entire Eighth Army began preparing for an assault on which they pinned their hopes for victory. The depleated ranks of a battered but spirited United Nations force were to astound the world.

The next few days were frantic ones. On one hand the Division gathered its strength for an attack. On the other it warded off increasingly sharp enemy patrols while keeping an eye peeled for another red assault it knew was in the making.

The main effort of the Eusak attack was to be along the Taegu-Kumchon-Taejon-Suwon axis. The 2d Division was to drive directly west from its present position. The 38th RCT was to cross the Naktong in the center and hold the bridgehead. The 9th RCT was to take Hill 201 and then support the attack of the 23rd RCT. The 2d Engineer Combat Battalion was to assemble in Yongsan as division reserve. The 3rd Battalion, 9th Infantry and the Tank Company, 9th Infantry were returned from Pohangdong and ordered to act as Eusak reserve. The Ivanhoe Security Force under Major Young was to secure Changyong and clear all the enemy east of the town. Every unit of the Division was readied for the assault upon which hung the fate of the UN troops in Korea.

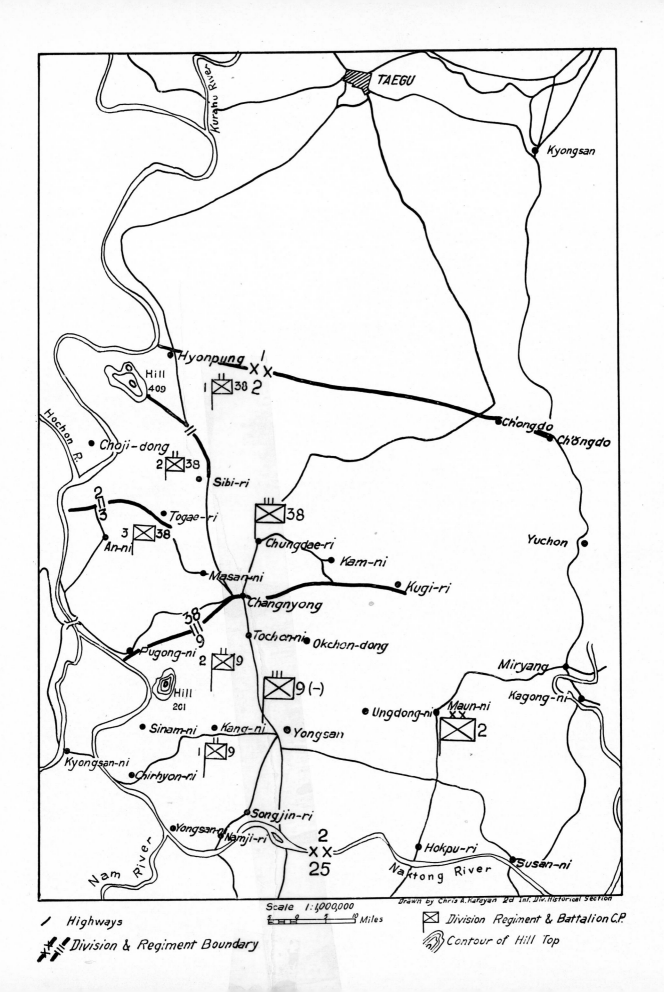

TAEGU

Kyongsan

Kurahu River

Hyonpung

Hill
409

Choji-dong

Hochon R.

Sibi-ri

Togae-ri

An-ni

Chungdae-ri

Kam-ni

Kugi-ri

Masan-ni

Changnyong

Yuchon

Ch'ongdo
Ch'ongdo

Tochan-ni   Okchon-dong

Pugong-ni

Hill
201

Sinam-ni   Kang-ni   Yongsan

Miryang

Kagong-ni

Maun-ni

Ungdong-ni

Kyongsan-ni

Chirhyon-ri

Songjin-ri

Yongsan-ni

Nam River

Namji-ri

Naktong River

Hokpu-ri

Susan-ni

Scale 1:1,000,000

Drawn by Chris A. Karayan 2d Inf. Div. Historical Section

Miles

Highways

Division & Regiment Boundary

Division Regiment & Battalion C.P.

Contour of Hill Top

Doing a little "cramming" on shipboard before the final examination in Korea.

Tacoma piers were busy places as the 2d Division loaded for sea.

Mortars were the specialty of Corporals Earnest B. Harkey and Earnest J. Dockery in late August of 1950.

Mines along the roads near the Naktong River caused lots of trouble. Just ask the Engineers.

There weren't any keys to the city of Chonju when these men of the 72d Tank Battalion and the 38th Infantry rolled into town in September of 1950.

Sometimes you didn't need a BC scope to see what you were shooting at down on the Naktong.

Corporals John Emerson, Emory Bainey and Harold Carter take time out for chow as Corporal Paul Abernathy serves along the Naktong.

Korean Telephone Exchange, 23rd Infantry Branch, doing business as usual.

These replacements never underwent the pleasures of a pipeline. They just happened to be on the Korean end and found themselves in the 2d Division.

An old soldier and real trouper was Al Jolson, shown here at Miryang in September, 1950.

Only one winner when a jeep hits a mine. This is the loser.

This weapon found itself a long way from home and in unfamiliar hands in September, 1950.

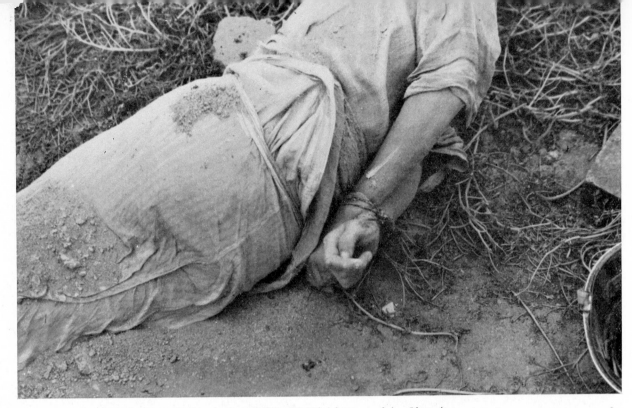

A murdered South Korean found by a 2d Division patrol in Chongju.

These tanks didn't have to pay a toll charge as they roared North from the Naktong River.

It wasn't quite like they told him it was going to be. Pfc. M. L. Brown, Sgt. E. B. Collinsworth and Pfc. E. L. Brown look on from the rear.

The heart-warming clatter of the 82d Ack Ack's quad fifties gives support to the 38th Infantry.

This was all too familiar a scene to the men of the 9th at the bottom of Hill 201 on the Naktong.

These were plentiful in the early days but soon became hard to find.

Only the men in the 9th Infantry in September, 1950, will remember this kind of country. No need to say it's NOT north of Yanggu but down on the Naktong.

Thanks to the Air Force, a T-34 and two North Korean trucks enjoy an extended ten-minute break.

More than preventative maintainance will be re-required to put these T-34's back in operation.

It's Al Jolson once again in a repeat performance which he gave without hesitation when and where he could.

Sfc. Floyd E. Nortan makes like a cavalryman with a liberated steed.

The Hyopchon Visitors Bureau operating at full blast for some liberators who were left behind in the rush.

Master Sergeant George L. Rice donates a bandolier to a 2d Division replacement with a real reason for being in Korea.

South Koreans recover bodies of friends and relatives murdered by the communists at Chonju.

Men of the 2d Quartermaster unload supplies at the Miryang railhead in the early days.

One hill where you didn't need an oxygen mask but where you did find it handy to have a rifle—Hill 201 on the Naktong.

Services in the field always found a ready audience.

There's only one way to get a wounded man out of a spot like this—carry him or help him help himself.

Getting ready to jump-off from "the" perimeter in mid-September, 1950.

BREAKTHROUGH

A strong communist probing attack against both flanks of the Second Division was repulsed on 15 September. The 38th RCT was struck on the right by a full enemy battalion whose attack against the First Battalion was supported by tanks. An enemy company hit at the 9th RCT. Throughout the division zone heavy mortar and artillery fire was received. But the communists gained little ground. This was not their main attack.

H-hour for the 2d Division offensive was set for 0700 on 16 September. The division received word it was to have air priority from 0635 until the jump-of time. If any change in these plans were made, the division was assured it would be notified prior to 0400.

At 2040, the night before D-day, word was received that the 1st Marine Division had made a successful amphibious landing at Inchon, the port city for the Korean Capital of Seoul. Accompanied by the 7th U.S. Division and ROK troops, the Marines had begun an "end run" on the invading communist troops. A second front had been opened. When word of this success swept through the ranks of the division, morale soared sky high. Here, at last, was proof that the UN forces were to taste victory. Hopes for a successful attack in the morning mounted hourly as the importance of the Marine landing was realized.

Attack plans for the division were struck a sharp blow at 0630 on D-day. It was then the division was notified that its air priority had been cancelled. The commitment that such notification would be issued prior to 0400, if the priority had to be called off, apparently could not be kept. The word was flashed to division artillery to begin laying down a preliminary barrage, as mortars began to cough out their precious ammunition. An urgent request was sent to higher headquarters for increased artillery ammunition allowances for the attack, even with air support, had been planned with dangerously limited artillery ammunition supplies. The need for increased allowances became urgent. It was too late to change plans for the attack.

At 0700, the first major offensive of the Korean War from the Pusan Perimeter began. Men who had been tasting defeat and suffering heavy losses for weeks moved out, hopeful but wondering if they could suceed. Knowledge that it was a "shoestring" offensive was widespread. Everyone knew how much depended on victory.

The North Korean forces put up fierce resistance to the attacking troops. Holding key terrain features on both flanks of the division, they poured artillery, mortar and machine gun fire on the lower ground. The attacking troops were hindered by slimy roads made seas of mud by recent rains. "A" and "B" Companies of the 2d Engineers were released from division reserve to work on the road in the sectors of the 23d and 38th RCT's. It had to be done so that ammunition and ration trucks could be passed through. Initially the losses suffered by the division were heavy. More South Korean soldiers were channeled to the fighting units although they were not nearly as effective as American troops.

The 9th RCT met savage resistance in its effort to take hill 201. The enemy was dug in two-battalion strength and laying down a murderous curtain of fire from within well-fortified bunkers.

The 23d RCT on the right of the 9th was more successful and succeded in seizing the commanding terrain although it, too, came under heavy fire from the enemy lodged on hill 201.

"Award of the Distinguished Service Cross to First Lieutenant Stephen E. Gray, Infantry, a member of Company L, 23rd Infantry, for action against the enemy in the vicinity of Changyong on 16 September 1590. As one of the leading elements in the 3rd Battalion, Lieutenant GRAY led the 3rd Platoon of Company L in an attack on enemy defensive positions along the Naktong River. His platoon immediately came under extremely heavy and accurate enemy mortar, machine-gun, and small-arms fire. Under direct fire from an enemy machine gun, Lieutenant GRAY led his platoon forward in a charge on the first objective. He destroyed one enemy machine gun and assisted in eliminating a group of sixty enemy soldiers who had the advantage of entrenched positions. Reorganizing his platoon, he prepared to continue the attack toward the second objective which was better defended than the first. In spite of this fact, Lieutenant GRAY, shouting to his platoon to move forward, courageously led the attack. At times prior to the second assault, he directed supporting mortar fire to within twenty-five yards of his own position. Although the binoculars hanging around his neck were hit by shell fragments, he did not hesitate in the face of this intense enemy fire, and the ferocity and daring of his assault along with his platoon routed the enemy from their positions. Upon receiving a third objective, Lieutenant GRAY organized a tank-infantry attack, and again personally led the assault on the objective. The third assault completely de-

moralized enemy and drove them from their main line of resistance. Lieutenant GRAY's daring and inspiring leadership on this occasion was a major factor in the success of Company L's attempt to reach the Naktong River. His actions accounted for an estimated one hundred enemy dead and wounded, the elimination of three mortars, two fortified machine-gun positions, and one enemy field piece."

To the north, the 38th RCT was able to secure the southern portion of the commanding terrain in its sector including Hill 209 which it took by 0930. It then continued the attack to the west against stiff resistance and captured a small village 2,000 yards east of the Naktong.

The battle continued to rage furiously throughout the first night. On 17 September the first signs of a break appeared. In the central sector of the 23rd RCT the enemy was forced across the Naktong and he abandoned large quantities of arms and ammunition as he pulled out. The division artillery poured barrage after barrage onto these retreating troops as they exposed themselves, inflicting terrific casualties. Before the day was out it was believed that the North Korean 2d Rifle Division had ceased to exist as an organized unit.

But to the south the going continued rough. Hill 201 in the 9th sector remained in enemy hands in spite of all that could be done to dislodge or render them ineffective. This position posed a threat to the division flank for the enemy also retained his bridgehead across the river in this sector as well as in the north.

But plans for the attack continued. The 2d Engineer Combat Battalion sent men forward to reconnoiter for a bridge site in the 23d sector. At dark, "K" and "L" Companies of the 9th RCT had fought their way to within 200 yards of the crest of 201 and were digging in prior to attacking anew in the morning.

Back in Miryang, nerve-center of the division, the men who had been wounded in previous days were given a treat that none will ever forget. Al Jolson, known and admired by everyone, was giving personal appearance shows for the men in the hospitals. As usual, he was among the first of the "big-name" entertainers to come to the war zone. Little did the men who enjoyed his antics realize that in a few short months he would be dead. Certainly his tremendous effort on their behalf that day belied his ill-health.

Back on the front, by 1400 hours of the 18th, elements of the 38th RCT had completed the first crossing of the Naktong becoming the first UN troops to cross the river from the perimeter.

Each battalion of the regiment had succeeded in placing four platoons in a bridgehead 2,000 yards deep on the western bank. However a bridge was badly needed over which the equipment so necessary to hold the ground could be transported. By 1700 hours the bridge site had been selected and every foot of bridge in the division was being brought forward.

The 9th RCT to the south was still bitterly locked in the struggle for Hill 201. The enemy, supported by every kind of ground weapon, continued to cling to the crest while he shoved reinforcements up over the rear approaches. To the south of the 9th RCT, the 2d Reconnaisance Company, which was screening the division's left flank, reported that enemy mine fields were slowing its progress toward Agok but that it was inflicting heavy casualties on the enemy.

At midnight of the second day of the attack, "F" Company of the 23rd RCT reported it had fought its way behind Hill 201 and had succeeded in cutting the MSR over which the enemy had poured supplies and reinforcements. With this help, Hill 201 finally fell to the 9th RCT on 19 September. But the enemy was still far from routed. Probing attacks were reported by the First, Second and Third Battalions of the 38th which clung to the all-important bridgehead across the Naktong. And between the First Battalion of the 38th and the regimental supply trains the infiltrating enemy had succeeded in setting up a roadblock although this was soon reduced.

General Walton H. Walker visited the division sector on the 19th and was strong in his praise for the successful crossing of the river which, he said, not only inflicted heavy casualties on the enemy but forced him to displace his Command Post.

The friendly situation improved greatly on the 20th, the fourth day of the offensive. By 0800 hours the 23rd RCT in the center was able to place three companies across the river and by 1200 hours the 9th in the south had reached the river and was scouting for a bridgesite. The enemy resistance east of the Naktong had all but ceased, the last of it beaten off by the 9th RCT assisted by the Second Battalion of the 23rd and the 2d Reconnaisance Company. However a critical shortage of bridging existed throughout the Army area and this shortage seriously hampered units of the division in their efforts to transport their men and equipment to the western banks of the Naktong from which they could follow up their initial successes. However, the engineers were able to complete the bridge in the 38th sector and supplies and equipment began to blow across.

While the bridging equipment was being procured, plans were made for continuing the attack. At 2400 hours on 20 September, the task organization for the offensive west of the Naktong was drawn up.

The 9th RCT under Colonel Charles C. Sloane consisted of the 9th Infantry (—); "B" Company, 72 Tank Battalion; "D" Battery, 82d AAA; the 15th FA Battalion, and a platoon from the 2d Reconnaisance Company.

The 23d RCT, commanded by Colonel Paul W. Freeman, was made up of the 23d Infantry; "C" Company, 72 Tank Battalion; "B" Battery, 82d AAA; and the 37th FA Battalion.

Colonel George B. Peploe commanded the 38th RCT consisting of the 38th Infantry; "A" Company, 72d Tank Battalion; "C" Battery, 82d AAA; and the 38th FA Battalion (—).

The 2d Battalion of the 9th Infantry and the Tank Company of the 9th Infantry were to remain in EUSAK reserve.

With the new task organization revealed, the attack plan was published with H-Hour set for 1200 on the 21st. The 9th RCT (—) had the mission of establishing a bridgehead, protecting the Division's left blank and preparing to attack on order. The 38th RCT had a triple role. The First Battalion, which was taken under Division control when it became evident that its mission would separate it by a great distance from its regiment, was to patrol south and east of Hill 409 and the village of Hyongpong, both of which were still in enemy hands. The Third Battalion was to guard the bridgehead while the Second Battalion was to spearhead the first attack to the west down the Chogye-Hyopchon road.

The 23d RCT was to attack from its bridgehead with one Battalion Combat Team reinforced with tanks. Its objective was Sinboni from which it was to launch an attack from the South toward Hyopchon in conjunction with the northerly attack by the Second Battalion of the 38th.

The remainder of the 2d Reconnaisance Company was to stand-by to move through the 9th and 23rd RCT's so it could screen the division advance south of Hyopchon.

The morning of the 21st was spent in preparation for the attack. At 1200 hours the attacking units moved out. The enemy met fire with fire on the entire front. The 9th RCT in the south had particularly bad luck. Using ten amphibious trucks it managed to ferry two platoons across the river under cover of fire from tanks, artillery, anti-aircraft guns, and air strikes. However, the enemy put up stiff resistance and succeeded in damaging nine of the ten river-crossing vehicles. As a result, the two platoons already across were recalled, withdrawing under cover of a heavy smoke screen laid down by the 9th's 4.2 mortars.

The battalion combat team advancing from the 23rd RCT bridgehead in the center of the front moved forward but the advance was slow. To the north in the sector of the 38th RCT, the advance was likewise slow. One of the tanks in the 38th attacking force was destroyed by a mine. Two others were disabled by fire from enemy anti-tank guns.

"Award of the Distinguished Service Cross to Corporal Robert Cooper, Infantry, a member of Company L, 23rd Infantry, for action against the enemy in the vicinity of Changyong on 21 September 1950. His platoon was holding a position on Hill 409 when it was attacked by greatly superior number. He remained in position with his machine gun for a period of 4 hours under constant artillery and mortar fire. Finally, despite an enemy banzai charge up the

PFC BROWN

hill, he left the comparative safety of his fox hole and moved his weapon over an open route to an exposed position far down the hill in order to occupy a more favorable firing position. When his machine gun was destroyed and he was wounded by enemy grenades, he continued to fight off the enemy with his pistol until his ammunition was exhausted. He then took his assistant's rifle and, ordering his helpers to the rear, held off his foes with rifle fire until he was killed by the enemy."

All along the front the 2d Engineers worked desperately to support the advance. The MSR's were in need of constant upkeep against the damaging effects of heavy traffic and downpours of rain. Mine-sweeper teams attempted to clear the route of advance. And while one team worked to complete the pontoon bridge, another operated a 50-ton ferry carrying tanks, equipment and supplies across the river.

The second day of the offensive saw a great improvement in the operation. The First and Third Battalions of the 38th were freed from guarding their bridgehead to join the Second Battalion in its attack to Chogye and Hyopchon. The 9th RCT (—) took over the duties of the two relieved battalions protecting the bridge and its approaches and also screening south of Hill 409 and in the vicinity of Hyonpung.

Throughout the afternoon the enemy continued to offer heavy resistance using tanks and artillery to the maximum. However, by 1800, "K" and "L" Companies of the 23rd had captured Sinbon-ni and "G" Company of the 38th and attached tanks of the 38th secured Chogye. The Third Battalion aided in this attack, having reverted to regimental control. Immediately, "I" Company of the 38th and a platoon from "A" Company, 72d Tank Battalion, thrust out the road northwest from Chogye, burning enemy hiding places and flushing his delaying forces.

By the morning of 23 September it became apparent that the enemy covering force had been penetrated and subsequent intelligence revealed that the North Korean 4th and 10 Rifle Divisions were the only effective remaining units. They appeared to be withdrawing north and west of Hyopchon. The Air Force exerted its maximum effort in striking at the withdrawing communist troops and vehicles.

On the 24th, while the Division Advance Command Post moved to Tugong-ni, the 9th attempted to force its way into Hyonpung, the only remaining strongpoint in the old bridgehead area. However, stubborn resistance prevented the entry. Meanwhile, an armor-tipped column composed of the Second and Third Battalions of the 23d RCT moved rapidly northwest 15,000 yards and entered Hyopchon at 1030.

The 38th, attacking west from Chogye, beat down stiff resistance and crossed its Second Battalion over the Hwang-gang River just north of Hyopchon to cut-off a force estimated at two enemy battalions which had been flushed from the south by the First Battalion of the 38th and the 23rd Infantry. In a pincers movement the forces cut into the enemy and completed its destruction with the help of exceptionally good air support.

Subsequently, the 38th moved on into Hyopchon and completed the double envelopment which placed that vital road junction town in 2d Division control.

The following day, 25 September, an advance party from Division Headquarters arrived in the newly captured town to make arrangements for billeting the Division CP.

The situation broke even better for the Division on the 26th. The 65th RCT from Puerto Rico arrived, was assigned to the Division and ordered to take over responsibility for all the area formerly held east of the Naktong. In doing so, it relieved the Second Battalion of the 9th RCT and initiated a patrol along the north-south MSR from Changyong to Yongsan to the river crossing in the former 9th RCT sector. By 2400 hours, the 9th RCT was moving up to rejoin the rapidly advancing elements of the division, screening the left flank in the process.

Advances as great as 30,000 yards were being reported by the 38th RCT with the enemy unable to establish a defense in face of the onrushing troops. The 23rd RCT followed up the route of advance, mopping up by-passed North Koreans. And in the skies, the Air Force ranged well ahead of the lead advancing elements, striking the fleeing enemy.

Late in the afternoon of the 26th, the 23d RCT passed through the 38th and secured the town of Anui. The 38th remained in battered Kochang, establishing outposts on the high ground to the north. The Division CP moved up again, this time to the vicinity of Kochang.

The enemy continued to offer resistance in the South where an attempt by the 9th RCT (—) to take Samga was repulsed. Here the communists had dug-in about one and a half miles from the city, utilizing extensive mine fields which hindered efforts to advance.

The night of the 26th, the enemy unleashed a mortar barrage on the positions of the 23d RCT in Anui.

The following day, 27 September, the 65th

RCT patrolling the old Pusan perimeter succeeded in forcing the enemy from Hill 409 and the town of Hyonpung thus eliminating the last organized resistance east of the Naktong. With the town secured, the 65th moved forward toward Anui to join the other elements of the Division including the Division CP which already had its advance party in the town.

A humorous incident occured in Anui during the early morning hours of 27 September. It was an indication of how rapidly the situation was changing. Headquarters Battery, 37th Field Artillery Battalion, was in a rendezvous position in column in Anui. The rear vehicle in its column was a captured North Korean truck. Two North Korean officers drove to the tail of the column in a Russian jeep, parked and promptly went to sleep thinking their own unit still held the town and oblivious to the presence of the Americans. The sentry awakened them and it was found both were drunk as hoot owls and had been up to the next town north having a big time for themselves while their outfit was being pushed out of Anui by the Indianhead Division.

To the south, while its First and Second Battalions patrolled the roads radiating from the MSR, the 9th RCT sent its Third Battalion in

another attack against Samga. On the 28th, Samga was secured and the 9th sent patrols to the south where a link-up was made with patrols working north from the 25th Division sector.

The 23rd, also patrolling from Anui, reported further contact with 25th Division patrols along the Anui-Hanyang Road.

The leading elements of the 38th RCT left Kochang at 0400 hours, 27 September, passed through the 23rd at Anui and by brushing aside road blocks and by-passing the bulk of the enemy forces broke out onto the western plains of Korea and captured Chonju after traveling some 77 miles in ten hours. The complete RCT closed in Chonju in twelve hours but was completely out of gas. Plans were immediately made for further advance to the north on foot if necessary.

"Award of the Distinguished Service Cross to Colonel George B. Peploe, Infantry, Commanding Officer, 38th Infantry Regiment, for action against the enemy in the vicinity of Sadung, during the period 16 September to 27 September 1950. During this period, when two battalions of his Regiment formed the spearhead of the 2nd Infantry Division's advance toward the Naktong River, Colonel Peploe placed himself with the point of the advance guard and personally directed the assaults against ridges, defiles and passes where the enemy had massed his artillery and heavy weapons for an offensive of his own and was putting up a most stubborn resistance. Unmindful of the intense artillery, mortar and heavy weapons fire, he personally directed the operations of his two battalions and closely coordinated their advance in order to assure a maximum of offensive power. In one instance he led the advance guard and enveloped the enemy flanks. This maneuver enabled the command to continue the offensive with a minimum of losses and drove the enemy across the Naktong River. Two days later, Colonel PEPLOE was again well in front of his troops directing the crossing of the Naktong at a point near Sadung. Colonel PEPLOE proceeded to the river's edge and, with utter disregard for the hostile artillery fire which was falling in the area, personally directed the crossing of patrols to the far side of the river. Keeping the defeated enemy off balance, Colonel PEPLOE pursued them to Hyopchon and then to Kochang, a vital enemy communications center in South Central Korea. Regrouping his Regiment, he renewed the attack on 27 September and broke out the western coastal plain to capture the key city of Chonju with thousands of prisoners and tons of supplies and

equipment. In this pursuit, his Regiment fought forward seventy-seven miles in ten hours."

The remaining few days of September were used by the division in extensive patrolling, mop-up operations and consolidation of the ground so recently won. It had been an eventful month and, while the final days found the regiments in relatively stable positions, the drive to the north was to continue with unabated speed in the near future.

The speed of the advance to the areas occupied by the Division at the end of September had severely taxed the supply trains. Practically every item needed to support the troops had to be trucked more than 200 miles from Miryang to Nonsan. The road was unimproved, snaking over the mountains and subject to the constant pounding of the supply trucks. In many stretches it was one-way. A trip from one end to the other took 48 hours. The units operating under the G-4 supervision—702d Ordnance Company, 2d Quartermaster Company and 2d Engineer Combat Battalion—did a magnificent job in operating the rail and truck heads, building bridges and maintaining their vehicles under the most adverse conditions.

Because the extensive area through which the Division had fought necessitated spreading the supporting units far and wide, the small liaison planes and helicopters were called upon to fly round-the-clock schedules on observation missions, evacuation of wounded, and liaison work. Frequent air-drops to isolated units were also delegated to the L-5's.

On 1 October, EUSAK announced that all organized resistance had ceased in South Korea.

Thus, two months to the day after the communists had launched their all-out attack on the weary defenders of the Pusan perimeter, the invaders had been either killed or driven back behind the parallel which was once the boundary between North and South Korea.

The Division CP moved forward again on 1 October, this time to Chonju, the town previously secured by the 38th Infantry after its spectacular 77 mile advance in 10 hours. Four days later the 65th RCT was relieved from its attachment to the Division while the combat units continued patrolling by air and ground.

On 8 October, for the first time since the 2d Division had begun operations in Korea, the total of replacements and returnees exceeded the losses to the Division.

The Division received notice on 10 October it was to receive a breather period. All units of the Indianhead Division were alerted to move into reserve in the area between Suwon and Yongdongpo. In four days the assembly was complete. Long-delayed activities were finally begun. Personnel and weapons were inspected, shortages were revealed and filled, training programs were initiated with emphasis placed on increasing the efficiency of the many South Korean soldiers now in the Division. There were critiques of small-unit actions. Tactical training was begun and supply discipline measures were instituted. In short, for the first time since its alert in early July, the Second Division had an opportunity to 'sit-down' and take stock of itself and its situation. Needless to say, there was much to be done.

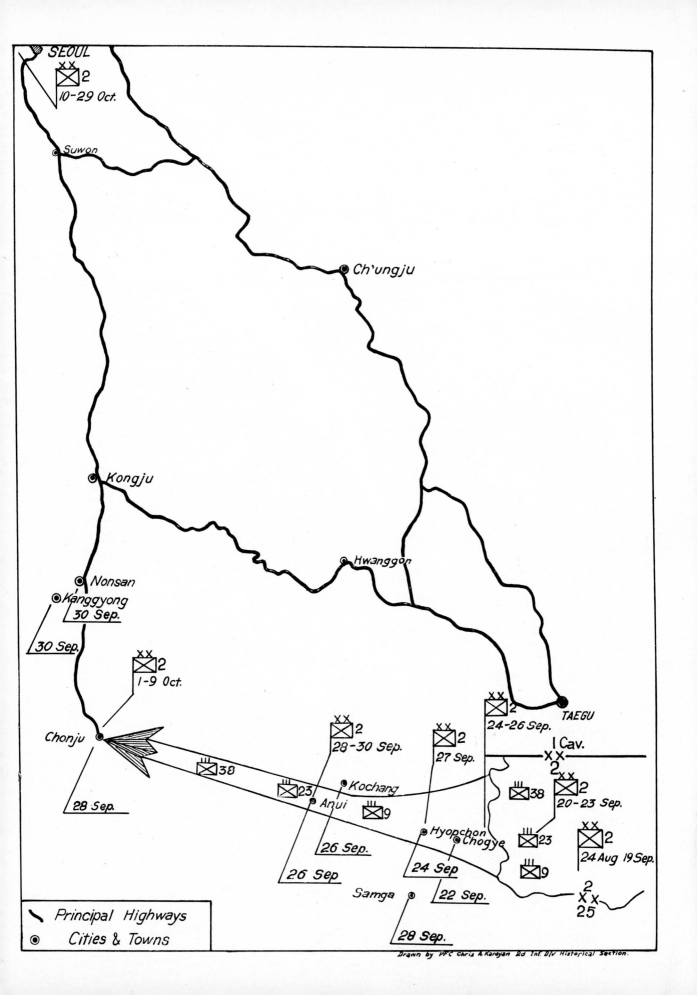

SEOUL
2
10-29 Oct.

Suwon

Ch'ungju

Kongju

Hwanggon

Nonsan
Kanggyong
30 Sep.

30 Sep.

2
1-9 Oct.

Chonju

2
28-30 Sep.

2
27 Sep.

2
24-26 Sep.

TAEGU

I Cav.
2

38

23

2
20-23 Sep.

Kochang

28 Sep.

9

Anui

Hyopchon
Chogye

23

2
24 Aug 19 Sep.

26 Sep.

26 Sep.

9

24 Sep.

Samga

22 Sep.

2
25

28 Sep.

Principal Highways
Cities & Towns

Drawn by PFC Chris A. Karayan 2d Inf. Div. Historical Section.

BUSY INTERLUDE

There is little opportunity in wartime for any combat outfit to rest, no matter how great the need. This was particularly true in the early stages of the Korean War when every unit was doing the work of two while not having the personnel or equipment which would enable it, under normal circumstances, to carry out routine duties. And so it was that on 16 October, two days after closing into its assembly area, the Second Infantry Division received another mission. The "Second to None" was to be the first to enter the North Korean capital of Pyongyang. To do the job, Task Force Indianhead was born.

The key note of the Task Force was speed. The order which spawned it was published on 16 October. The following day at 1000 hours the elements which composed it were assembled at Chuoe-Myon where the 2d Reconnaisance Company was bivouaced.

Lt. Col. Ralph L. Foster, G-2 of the Second Division, commanded "Indianhead." From the 38th Infantry there was "K" Company with seven officers. From the 72d Tank Battalion came five M-26 tanks, one M-4 tank, a half track and seven 2½ ton trucks. The 2d Reconnaissance Company had sent two M-24 light tanks and a half track. The 2d Engineer Combat Battalion added a demolition squad of one officer and 14 enlisted men. The medics were represented by one doctor and two aid-men. A section from the 82d AAA included one M-16 and one M-19. The 2d Military Police Company was represented; there were CIC agents and interpreters. The entire group was motorized and carried with it basic loads of ammunition and fuel to complete the force.

Task Force Indianhead departed from its assembly area late in the afternoon of 17 October. Separated into three serials it moved rapidly north and by 1830 hours of the next day two of the serials were in Sariwon and the other in Sinmak. On the 19th, the lead elements rolled into the former capital of North Korea. The honor of being the first American soldier to enter the city went to Sergeant M. V. Parker of the 2d Military Police Company.

Throughout its trip the Task Force had encountered no trouble but on the banks of the Taedong River, which flows through Pyongyang, the first hitch in the plans to take the entire city developed whenever it was found that there was no river crossing suitable for the heavy motorized equipment. However, the attached signal group began sending messages back to Division Headquarters on the findings of the Task Force up to that point. The next morning a small group from the force crossed the river in assault boats. Later, the jeeps crossed over on a railroad bridge and the tanks found a suitable crossing at a point further up the river. By nightfall, the force was in possession of the entire city including two communist radio stations.

The members of the force met no opposition and were able to concentrate on the collection and recording of material found in the capital. By the 25th of October, with all of its activities completed, the task force was dissolved and the units returned to their parent organizations.

In the meantime, the 9th RCT had been reconstituted and was assigned to I Corps effective on 17 October. On the 18th it moved to Singye and was ordered to move forward and secure the airfields in the vicinity of Pyongyang and to patrol all roads in the vicinity.

On 20 October, the 23rd RCT was also reconstituted and ordered to move-out the next day to the vicinity of Haeju to relieve elements of the 24th Division. And so the elements of the 2d Division became scattered once more. On the 25th of October the 9th RCT and Task Force Indianhead returned to the Division and, in turn, the Division went into I Corps reserve with responsibility for area between Seoul and Pyongyang. In addition, it initiated the famous "Red Ball" express and soon had over 300 trucks hauling every imaginable type of supply and equipment over the Seoul-Pyongyang highway.

During the same period the 187th Airborne Regimental Combat Team was attached to the Division and ordered to secure the airfields east of Pyongyang. The 9th RCT occupied Pyongyang itself and patrolled the roads. The 23rd RCT remained in Haeju and patrolled to the north while the 38th RCT, division artillery and the 72d Tank Battalion remained in the Seoul area. The 2d Engineers had moved north to Sariwon where they worked up and down the MSR maintaining the roads.

As October drew to a close, an intelligence report from Eusak revealed that the I and II ROK Corps operating in the north were meeting opposition from elements of the Chinese Communist Forces. On 31 October, the Division periodic intelligence report revealed that 316,000 Chinese troops were massed at the Manchurian border. This constituted a force of 44 divisions organized into 12 armies. The intentions of this massive army were not yet known but the 2d Division, on instructions from higher headquarters, proceeded with plans for continuing its forward displacement.

* * * *

As the month of November began—a month which was to be one of the blackest in the history of the Indianhead Division—reports from the front occupied by the I and II ROK Corps became increasingly alarming. In some sectors the South Korean troops were undertaking withdrawals which endangered the right flank of the Eighth Army so on 1 November EUSAK ordered the 2d Division to move immediately to the vicinity of Sunchon. When the order was received, the Division was scattered from Pyongyang to south of Seoul. More than 300 of its trucks were engaged in transporting supplies on the "Red Ball" express. As a result, the move was difficult to undertake and it was necessary to shuttle trucks back and forth, bringing up a unit at a time. Nevertheless, the First Battalion of the 9th Infantry arrived at Sunchon late in the afternoon of 1 November and was ordered to establish blocking positions far to the northeast in the vicinity of Tokchon, an important road net center. Then, at 1800 hours, an order was received attaching the 2d Division to I Corps and the remainder of the 9th Infantry, which was already rolling into Sunchon, was given the new mission of patrolling northward toward Kunu-ri. The Division's misison was security of the rear areas, and blocking to the east. The 1st Cavalry Division and the II ROK Corps behind whose fronts the Division was deploying were then under heavy pressure from North Korean and CCF Forces.

The 2d Reconnaissance Company, which was to play an important role in the coming days, was ordered to Pyongyang in preparation for further moves northward. The remainder of the Division was then moving toward Sunchon.

On 2 November, air observers reported large numbers of enemy troops moving toward Tokchon and from the Tokchon area the First Battalion of the 9th reported its "A" and "B" Companies under heavy small arms fire. Because the terrain at Tokchon was not suitable for defense by only one battalion, the First Battalion was ordered to positions south of Kunu-ri moving by way of Suchon.

The Second Battalion of the 9th was already in blocking positions on the Taedong River at Samso-ri, almost midway between Kunu-ri and Sunchon. And a patrol from "K" Company had succeeded in contacting elements of a 1st Cavalry Division patrol at Kunu-ri.

The Division was ordered to occupy, organize and defend in depth at all costs the I Corps area north and east of Anju, protecting the Corps right flank.

The following day, 3 November, the 38th RCT arrived in the Samso-ri area. The First and Second Battalions of the 9th had then established a strong defensive perimeter in the Kunu-ri vicinity with the Third Battalion of the 9th on its way north to join them.

To protect the Division's area from enemy groups which might filter down from the north, the 2d Reconnaissance Company with "L" Company of the 23d Infantry attached set-up a road block at Pukchang-ni which was north east of Sunchon and almost two thirds of the distance to Tokchon. The following day this force was augumented by the arrival of the Reconnaissance Platoon from the 72d Tank Battalion. And on that same day, 4 November, while on a screening patrol, the 2d Recon engaged a force of 200 enemy, killed 20 and dispersed the remainder. It then went on to set-up another road block slightly south of Pukchang-ni.

While the 2d Recon with its attached elements was conducting sweeping patrols to the north east, the 9th and 38th Infantry Regiments were establishing positions to the rear of the 7th ROK Division roughly along the Chongchon River line. Lateral contact was made on the left with elements of the 5th RCT and on the right with the ROK's.

A prisoner of war picked up on 4 November reported 50,000 Chinese Communist Force (CCF) troops had crossed the Yalu into Korea.

On 5 November, the 2d Division was shifted from the I to the IX Corps with the 9th RCT being attached to the 1st Cavalry Division. Intelligence reports now listed eight North Korean Division plus large, unidentified combat units of the CCF concentrating opposite the IX Corps front on a line between Tokchong and Yongwon.

Upon transfer of the Division to IX Corps, the 38th RCT was reconstituted with the 38th Infantry, 38th FA Bn, "C" Company of the 2d Engineers, and 'C' Battery of the 82 AAA. It was immediately sent to the Pukchang-ni area, held by the 2d Recon, where it set-up positions. The First Battalion went further east and established blocking positions at Yongdong-ni. Thus, the 38th RCT controlled two towns south of Tokchon. These, with Tokchon, formed a triangle in which advance elements of large enemy forces were known to be assembling. The 2d Reconnaissance Company found ample evidence of their presence when its position was fired on by mortar and small arms in the Tokchon vicinity late in the afternoon of 5 November.

The following day was quiet. On the main front the enemy continued small scale attacks against the II ROK Corps. Elements of all three regiments of the 112th CCF Division had been identified there. The 8th ROK Division, attacking north from the blocking positions of the 38th, was unable to take Tokchon.

By the 7th of November, the 38th RCT had established its three battalions along the base line of the triangle formed by Tokchon, Puckchangni and Yongdongni. Its mission was to block to the north and east, conduct aggressive patrols and contact and maintain liaison with the ROK's. The 23d Infantry had a similar mission and was patrolling south east of Sunchon along the road to Yongdok. One patrol, upon reaching that town, discovered 16 railroad cars with fuel and ammunition. Searching further it uncovered several mines which contained munitions and machine tools for making Russian-type weapons. The supplies and material not needed by ROK units were destroyed. Another patrol from the 23d Infantry attempted to contact elements of the X U. S. Corps, which had landed on the east coast, but was unsuccessful although it went several miles east of Yangdok.

Meanwhile, the North Korean forces were jabbing at the positions of the 23d and 38th and all patrols reported contact. An "E" Company patrol from the 38th was ambushed at Taum-ni on 8 November and only 5 of the 18 members escaped. An armored patrol was sent into the area and recovered 9 wounded and 4 dead. All had been stripped, beaten, bayonnetted and left to die.

Award of the Distinguished Service Cross to Second Lieutenant R. M. Rhotenberry, Infantry, a member of Company H, 38th Infantry, for action against the enemy in the vicinity of Yongdong-ni between 6 and 7 November 1950. On the night of 6 and 7 November 1950, a machine-gun section of Company H, commanded by Lieutenant RHOTENBERRY, was attached to Company G of the regiment to furnish supporting fire in holding positions on high ground where the company was deployed. When a concealed enemy machine gun opened fire on the left flank of the company with such accuracy that several machine gunners and nearby riflemen were wounded, his men became demoralized, abandoned their weapons and ran for cover. Displaying outstanding courage, Lieutenant RHOTENBERRY moved through the hail of enemy fire, rounded up his men and returned them to their positions. Observing an abandoned light machine gun lying close

by, he moved the gun and ammunition to a point from which he could direct intense fire on the enemy positions. The heavy volume of fire delivered by him, together with the fire of his section, silenced the hostile fire and forced the enemy to withdraw. Shifting his fire to the opposite flank which was heavily engaged, he assisted in repulsing the attack on the right flank of the company. After the initial attack was repulsed and while the lead platoon was being reorganized, a heavy concentration of mortar fire struck the position, killing the infantry platoon leader and causing several other casualties. Lieutenant RHOTENBERRY unhesitatingly assumed command of the platoon and, organizing both the platoon and machine-

gun section, personally directed them in renewed action, forcing the enemy to retreat with heavy losses.

On the same day the I&R platoon from the 38th ran through an ambush without casualties. The Third Battalion of the 38th, following the platoon wiped the enemy out. And in the sector of the 23d Infantry, a patrol discovered a freight train stalled in a tunnel which yielded a rich prize—four T-34 tanks, two box cars of ammunition and two tank cars half full of gasoline.

The following days were taken up with patrolling by all units, patrols which swept wide and deep into suspected enemy buildup areas. Little was found. Some enemy fire was received, an occasional small fire fight took place, but no large enemy groups were found despite repeated and insistant civilian reports of roving bands of North Koreans and Chinese.

A 38th Infantry contact patrol journeying far to the east on 10 November failed to meet a similar patrol from X Corps but a liaison plane reported spotting the X Corps units. At the same time, the 38th began assembling in Puk-changni to be available to aid the ROK's in case of a major attack which was anticipated.

East of Pukchangni, the Reconnaissance Platoon of the 72d Tank Battalion, operating as an attached force to the 2d Reconnaissance Company, made what is believed to be the first fire contact with a CCF unit made by a unit of the 2d Division. Conducting a sweeping patrol, the friendly force encountered a reinforced enemy platoon apparently screening a larger body of troops. A fire fight flared briefly before the enemy broke contact after suffering an estimated 20 casualties. Two prisoners were taken by the Recon Platoon and one turned out to be a CCF commissioned officer whose excellent equipment, arms and supply indicated much to the P.W. interrogation officer.

Cold weather set-in in earnest about 10 November and it found many troops without winter clothing. That which had been issued went to front-line troops but there was not nearly enough to go around. The result was cold, misery, frostbite and very severe hardship.

The 9th RCT, attached to the 1st Cavalry Division, was ordered to capture the city of Pugwon and the high ground west of the Chong-chon River on 11 November. It moved out the following day and moved into the toughest battle in had faced since its fight for Hill 201 down on the Naktong River. The fighting raged for three days with Pugwon falling late on the 14th with the 9th then crossing the river and attacking north and west where it established contact with other friendly elements attacking north.

Days passed with more and more patrolling and less and less contact. Some civilians reported the enemy was withdrawing. But one ominous fact stood out in those uncertain days—the ROK's were still unable to take the city of Tokchon although reports that it had been captured only to be lost again filtered down down through the ranks. And Tokchon was a vital key to control of the road network behind the front lines.

A disturbing report came from the 2d Reconnaissance Company on 16 November—a band of 200 enemy, possibly Chinese, had been contacted southeast of Songchon, a town well to the rear of the Division CP at Sunchon. And from the 9th Infantry, over in the I Corps sector, came a report that they were being heavily opposed by elements of the CCF.

The 2d Reconnaissance Company was the only Division unit in IX Corps to contact the enemy on 17 November. It killed two, captured one and dispersed ten in a running fight. The ROK's were again reported fighting in the streets of Tokchon in another attempt to take the town.

Plans for the attack which would end the war were put into motion on 18 November. The Division command post moved forward to a point one mile north east of Kunuri. As the move took place, motor and foot patrols reported little enemy contact. But the next day the 23d reported its patrols had made contact in the vicinity of Songchon and Kapyong-ni far to the south.

More and more reports of enemy units in the rear snow-balled into Division on the 20th of November. An entire North Korean Division was reported asesmbling in Hoechang. And well south and east an unorganized enemy group of over 12,000 was reported. A prisoner reported that 1,000 CCF troops were in Hoechang; the ROK's reported contact with three Chinese regiments south of Yongwon on the Division's right. And on the same day a patrol from "K" Company of the 23d was ambushed, losing two trucks, three jeeps, one M-16, two 81 mm mortars and two 75 mm recoilless rifles.

But, on orders, the Division continued preparation for attack. The 9th RCT reverted to the Division on 21 November and once again the Indianhead Division had all its units under its control.

The operations order for the coming offensive was issued 20 November. The organization and attack plans were as follows:

9th RCT composed of the 9th Infantry Regiment; D" Battery, 82d AAA; "C" Company, 2d Cml Mtr Bn; and 'A" Company, 2d Engineers to attack in zone.

38th RCT composed of the 38th Infantry Regiment; 38th FA Bn; "A" Battery, 503d FA Bn; Ammo Sec, Srv Btry, 503d FA Bn; "C" Battery, 82d AAA; "C" Company, 2d Engineers; and the 2d Cml Mtr Bn (—) to relieve elements of the II ROK Corps in the 2d Division zone, attack in zone and protect the right flank.

Supporting the 9th RCT was the 15th FA Bn whose fires were reinforced by those of the 37th FA Bn while the 503d FA Bn (—) was in general support. One platoon of the 82d AAA (—) was assigned for protection of the Army ASP in Kunu-ri and two sections of "B" Battery were providing air and ground support for the head-quarters of IX Corps, 2d Division and 2d Division Artillery.

Division reserve consisted of the 2d Reconnaissance Company, 72d Tank Battalion, and the 23rd Infantry (—) which was located in the vicinity to the north of Kunuri. "A" Company, 23rd Infantry was assigned to the IX Corps as command post guard.

On 22 November, the 23rd RCT was disbanded with its units returning to their parent organizations. The 9th RCT completed its return from IX Corps and prepared to jump-off on the scheduled attack. All other units of the Division were closed into their new positions.

KUNURI

TERRAIN SKETCH

KUNU-RI is a communication center which is astride the north-south SUNCHON-HUICHON-KANGGYE road and rail axis. It is also located on the lateral east-west road which runs from SINANJU on the west coast and HUNGNAM on the east coast. These two roads are gravel surface, all weather roads and generally two way with the exception of various mountain passes and defiles. KUNU-RI is located on the east bank of the CHONG-CHON River which parallels the KUNU-RI -HUICHON Road. It is also located at the northern end of the TAEDONG River Valley and on the western slopes of the northern TABACK Mountains Range, generally known as the "Spine of KOREA". This area is dotted with an abundance of low grade coal mines and the range itself is very precipitous and averages over one thousand meters in heigth. One mountain, known as PIROBONG, reaches to a heighth of one thousand nine hundred nine meters. The area to the west of KUNU-RI is a relatively low mountain range lying between the KURYONG River and the CHONGCHON River, which averages approximately four hundred to five hundred meters in height. During the winter months it was possible to drive lightly loaded vehicles across the ice which covers the rivers in this area. The rivers are slow and fordible for both men and equipment in various spots. One other lateral road leads from KUJANGDONG, approximately fifteen miles north of KUNU-RI to TOKCHON. The area is entirely devoid of passible roads or trails. The valleys are generally short with very steep walls rising on either side. South of KUNU-RI and parallel to each side of the KUNU-RI-SUNCHON Road, is a ridge line in the shape of a horseshoe, with the closed portion of the ridge crossing the road approximately twenty miles south of KUNU-RI. It was from these ridges and heights that the attacking enemy placed his withering fire on elements of the Division moving south on the icy roads from KUNU-RI.

The drive to the North began on 23 November. Gains of several miles were made initially against light opposition. On the second day of the offensive, the 9th and 38th Regiments with attached units moved ahead with good lateral contact. The 23rd remained in reserve near Kunu-ri. On the right, the II ROK Corps had also jumped off as had the 25th US Division on the left across on the west bank of the Chongchon River.

During the daylight hours of 24 November, air observers reported large masses of enemy troops assembling forward of the Division front. Prisoners of war were interrogated and reported large Chinese troop units were massing near Uhyon-dong, a town five miles east of the right flank of the 38th RCT and directly north of the ROK II Corps. Our offensive ground forward.

The night of 24-25 November was quiet.

At noon on the 25th, the Division line, which was moving slowly forward against increasingly heavy resistance, extended generally east and west. The 9th Infantry held the left flank with the Third Battalion on the west bank of the Chongchon River. The 38th Infantry was on the right flank and the 23d was moving up behind the lead regiments as reserve.

At 1255, a reported concentration of enemy tanks, troops and anti-aircraft weapons forward of the friendly lines was hit by air and then pounded with the eight-inch howitzers of corps artillery.

As darkness fell on 25 November, the temperature rocketed down into the minus 20's. It was a bitter cold night, pitch black.

Out of the darkness in the final hours of 25 November the Chinese struck. A new war had begun.

The fury of the attack dispelled the hopes among men and officers alike of Christmas at home and an end to battle. Blotting out every other thought was the terrible ordeal which unfolded so quickly, an ordeal of sleepless, frigid nights, confusion, unbelievable slaughter and near disaster. A new chapter in the book of human misery had begun.

Three Chinese regiments made the initial attack against the 2d Division. Two of them struck at the center and right (east) flank of the Division, hitting the 38th Infantry and part of the 23rd. The third CCF regiment slammed against the 9th Infantry on the left (west) flank causing heavy casualties.

The attack in the 9th Infantry sector subsided at daylight on the 26th but the pressure continued against the 38th and the II ROK Corps

on the right of the 38th. To make-up for the heavy losses in the 9th, the First and Second Battalions of the 23d Infantry went into positions on the 9th's right flank and the 2d Engineer Combat Battalion was attached as infantry to the 9th to bolster the Division's left flank along the west bank of Chongchon River. This resulted in the disposition of units from west to east as follows: 9th Infantry, two battalions of the 23d Infantry, and the 38th Infantry. This line, running east-west, was about four miles north of Kujang-dong. The 38th Infantry positions were particularly vulnerable due to the lack of a north-south road leading into the sector. The only exit routes available to the 38th Infantry ran southeast through Tokchon, or laterally across the division front to Kujang-dong and then south through Kunu-ri. By early morning on the 26th, the ROK's had withdrawn almost to Pukchang-ni, completely exposing the right flank of the 2d Division and the 38th Infantry. Remnants of the 3rd ROK Regiment closed westward and joined the 38th.

Tokchon fell during mid-morning and it became imperative that the 2d Division line be held north of Kujang-dong if the 38th Infantry was to have a route for the withdrawal which now appeared to be a strong possibility.

Just before Tokchon was captured, the liaison team from Division Artillery, which had been attached to the ROK's holding the town, was surrounded. Planes were sent out from the Division immediately and landing on a makeshift strip within the crumbling perimeter lifted out every member of the team from under the very noses of the attacking forces. By 1800 hours, the Chinese were in the center of the city.

Late in the afternoon of 26 November, the enemy resumed his attacks against the 9th Infantry with particular pressure against the Third Battalion to which "A" and "B" Companies of the 2d Engineers were attached as infantry. The Third Battalion had, at this time, sent a small force of tanks and infantry westward to give help to the Second Battalion of the 24th Infantry which had been surounded for three days. Unable to get help from its own hard-pressed Division, it had appealed to the 9th for aid. The relief force was successful in breaking the encirclement and together with the remnants of the 24th's Battalion withdrew to the 9th Infantry sector. The Second Battalion of the 24th fought with the 9th for two days before returning to its parent unit.

The pressure against the 9th increased steadily and all battalions were forced into limited withdrawals. At 2200 hours, the Chinese overran the command posts of the First and Third Battalions and the Engineer Battalion forcing them to withdraw east of the Chongchon. At 2300 hours, the Chinese shifted the weight of their attack to the Second Battalion and utilizing 3.5 inch rockets and recoiless rifles he forced the Second to withdraw south of the Chongchon with heavy losses in personnel and equipment. Many of the men waded the frigid water to escape the onslaught, their clothes turning to ice as they staggered up on the opposite bank.

Award of the Distinguished Service Cross to Corporal James L. Brown, Infantry, a member of Company E, 9th Infantry, for action against the enemy in the vicinity of Sinjang on 26 November 1950. On the morning of 26 November 1950 remnants of the 1st and 2nd Battalions of the 9th Infantry Regiment were surrounded by the enemy and had been repelling fierce enemy attacks for several hours. Due to heavy fighting many casualties were received; however the wounded men could not be evacuated because of an enemy roadblock along the main supply route one mile south of Company E's positions. Corporal BROWN was personally selected by his company commander to take charge of the casualties of the two besieged battalions, break through the enemy roadblock, and get the wounded men to safety. The roadblock was established in a culvert which crossed under train tracks on the left of the road and continued along a river on the right. Scattered around the culvert were approximately fifteen or twenty of the enemy. Corporal BROWN immediately estimated the situation and directed the walking wounded to lay down a base of fire on the culvert. He then took two men with him and advanced down the railroad tracks pushing a small railroad hand car in front of him. Corporal BROWN began engaging each enemy position as he ran down the tracks, exposing himself many times to enemy grenades and rifle fire, but destroying each position as he went along. When he was close enough, he engaged the main body of the enemy in the culvert, using grenades and rifle fire, and even using his rifle butt and boots when he ran out of ammunition. By destroying this roadblock he made it possible to evacuate the wounded and secured a route for the withdrawal of his company and other units.

A special task force commanded by Lt. Gene Takihashi was encircled late on the 26th while protecting the three 9th Infantry command posts and the river crossing. The next morning Captain Crawford commanding "D" Company, 2d Engineers, led elements of his Company in an attack to recapture the equipment left in the CP positions. He was successful in this mission and also made it possible for Lt Takihashi to break through to the east bank of the river.

The First and Second Battalions of the 23rd, which were on the right flank of the 9th, were struck by the Chinese early at night on 26 November. At 2115, a group of 300 Chinese overran the regimental command post, forcing the two battalions to displace southward 300 yards. The small units fought bitterly until their ammunition was gone or their positions completely overrun.

The 38th Infantry was, in the meantime, beating off wave after wave of the attackers from the north, east and south. Finally, under intense enemy pressure, further aggravated by the collapsed ROK defense on the right flank, limited withdrawals were begun.

Award of the Distinguished Service Cross to Corporal Robert K. Imrie, Infantry, a member of Company F, 38th Infantry, for action against the enemy in the vicinity of Yong Bong Dong, on 27 November 1950. On 27 November 1950, the platoon of which Corporal IMRIE was a member was ordered to retake a hill which the enemy had seized during the operations of the previous night. On approaching the crest of the hill, the platoon was subjected to intense machine-gun crossfire and the advance halted. Corporal IMRIE, aware of the possible annihilation of the entire platoon by the deadly machine gun fire, singlehandedly charged the machine gun position on the right flank, completely disregarding his personal safety, and continually fired his automatic weapon until he had neutralized the position. After neutralizing the right flank machine-gun, he was hit by a burst of fire from the machine gun on the left flank and mortally wounded. His gallant and intrepid actions had diverted the enemy machine gun fire from his platoon, thereby saving his comrades from annihilation and enabling them to eliminate the one remaining machine gun position and secure the objective.

On 27 November, Division Operations Order 11 was issued ordering defense of the highground northwest, northeast and southeast of Kujang-dong. To become effective at 0600 on 28 November, it ordered the 9th Infantry into Division reserve with the 72d Tank Battalion (—). The line was to be taken over on the left by the 23d Infantry with the following attached units; "A" and "B" Companies, 72d Tank Battalion; "B" Company, 2d Engineer Combat Battalion; 2d Chemical Mortar Battalion and "B"

Battery, 82d AAA. The 38th Infantry was to continue holding the right flank of the Division front with the attached 3d ROK Regiment; "C" Company, 2d Engineer Combat Battalion; and "C" Battery, 82d AAA. Supporting the 23d was the 15th FA Bn while the 38th FA Bn supported the 38th. In general support of the Division were the 37th, 503d and 17th FA Bns with the attached 82d AAA (—).

Before the operation order became effective, however, all units of the Division were to undergo severe combat. Five Chinese divisions were now being hurled at the 2d. The II ROK Corps was a nonentity on the right of the 38th and the enemy had infiltrated behind the positions of the 38th, making them untenable. It was necessary to pull the entire right flank back to the southwest. At 2300 hours on 27 November, the 38th assumed control of the 3d ROK Regiment and the ROK's were used to extend the endangered flank.

The early minutes of 28 November brought with them a furious attack against the battered First and Second Battalions of the 9th Infantry. By 0115 the First Battalion was forced with withdraw, utilizing transportation of the 23d Regiment. The Second and Third Battalions held their positions but the Third Battalion was overrun. Communication with the line companies was maintained only through the artillery forward observers. "I" Company and "A" and "B" Companies of the 2d Engineers were locked in a desperate slugging match while attempts were being made to tie in with elements of the 23d Infantry moving up on the right of the reeling 9th.

The 23d Infantry, meanwhile, had succeeded in regaining the ground it had lost the night previously when its command post had been overrun. But at 0615 on 28 November, its First Battalion was under Chinese attack with the enemy streaming down the MSR from the north.

Award of the Distinguished Service Cross to Lieutenant Colonel Claire E. Hutchin, Jr, Infantry, Commanding Officer, 1st Battalion, 23d Infantry, for action against the enemy in the vicinity of Kujang-dong during the period 25 through 30 November 1950. During this period, the 1st Battalion was engaged in a series of defensive actions, counterattacks and withdrawals being conducted against superior enemy forces by the 23d Infantry Regiment. On the morning of 28 November, Company C was forced from its positions by a numerically superior enemy unit, with a resultant loss of equipment and weapons and the company was completely disorganized. Learning that all the company officers and a majority of the senior noncommissioned officer were either killed or wounded in this engagement, Colonel HUTCHIN quickly went to the unit's position, reorganized the remnents of the company and personally led the remaining men in a counter-attack to regain the positions. In the face of extremely heavy enemy small-arms fire, Colonel HUTCHIN personally directed and led this operation, succeeded in recovering the greater part of the lost equipment, and relieved groups of men of Company C who been surrounded when the positions were overrun. That afternoon, when the 1st Battalion was designated as rear guard for the 2d Division's withdrawal from Kujang-dong. Colonel HUTCHIN personally took command of the rear guard element, consisting of one rifle company and a company of tanks. The pursuing enemy force, estimated at two battalions, pressed hard on the rear of the division's column, which was forced to move slowly due to traffic congestion. Each time the column was forced to halt, the enemy would attack the rear guard from both flanks, using small arms, automatic weapons and grenades. During one of these attacks, Colonel HUTCHIN was painfully wounded in the face by flying shrapnel, but remained in control, brilliantly directing the defensive actions of the rear guard with outstanding success. His aggressive leadership and sound decisions during this action were unquestionably a decisive factor in the ultimately successful wtihdrawal of the 2d Division.

The 38th Infantry also came under increased attack early on the morning of 28 November. At 0105 hours, a large enemy force had passed through the disorganized ROK's to the north and was attacking the 38th front line positions. All communications were gone with the ROK's. No sooner had the attack begun than the regimental command post and the command post of the Second Battalion were attacked and in both instances the enemy was beaten off. The Regimental CP moved a short distance to the west for the night as enemy mortar fire had begun to fall on the area. At 2300, the CP again came under small arms fire and again moved to the west where it set-up with the CP of the Second Battalion. It was known that the First Battalion had been under constant attack since midnight and at 0400 it was learned the attack was continuing with all companies low on ammunition. "C" Company of the 2d Engineers and "L" of the 38th had been forced to withdraw.

At daylight, the CP again came under small arms fire and displaced for the third time in 12 hours. The situation was rapidly becoming critical.

At 0440, a platoon of tanks from the 38th Regimental Tank Company and a ROK Company had gone forward to break through to the battered First Battalion which was being overwhelmed. The rescue mission was successful after the force had cleared a roadblock in the original location of the regimental CP. Communications were thus reestablished with the First Battalion.

At 0615 hours, the enemy was flowing through the abandoned ROK positions on the right of the 38th and threatening the firing positions of

"A" Battery of the 503d FA Battalion. By 1025, the situation was even worse. "A" Company of the 2d Engineers and "L" of the 38th had been overrun. The fate of "B", "C", "F" and "G" Companies was unknown. All communications with Division headquarters were gone.

By noon, it was obvious the Division could never carry through with the plan to defend in the arc north of Kujang-dong. At 1300 hours, Operations Order 12 was issued. It called for a defense along a new Main Line of Resistance in an attempt to stop the onrushing hordes of Chinese. The new order permitted a gradual withdrawal of the torn front line into an arc around Kunu-ri. The 23d Infantry with the Second Battalion of the 9th and the 72d Tank Battalion were to cover the withdrawal, holding the vital road junction of Kujang-dong. The 9th Infantry (−) was to withdraw as quickly as possible and take up defensive positions at Wonni between Kujang-dong and Kunuri. The battered 38th was to withdraw west and then south to take up positions northeast of Kunuri.

The 38th fought its way to Kujang-dong despite heavy pressure to the north and east. There, while the 23d and attached units held off the tide of onrushing enemy, the 38th turned south. This operation placed the entire traffic load on the Kujang-dong-Kunuri road and vehicles were literally bumper to bumper. Advance Chinese elements took the tail of the column under fire and only a skillful rear-guard action by the First Battalion of the 23d prevented the enemy from inflicting severe damage to all thet units. By 0030 hours, 29 November, "A" and "B" Companies of the 23d were deploying for the fifth time in the rear-guard operation while the entire First Battalion was under intense artillery and mortar fire.

The withdrawal from north of Kujang-dong was a costly success but setting up the new defensive positions presented a brand-new situation. The 9th Infantry took up positions on the left flank of the Division defensive arc with its left elements on the bank of the Chongchon just north of Kunu-ri. The 23d, with the enemy sniping at its heels, moved south and tied in on the right of the 9th. The 38th found the enemy already in possession of its positions upon arrival and was forced to take up positions short of the assigned line. The Turkish Brigade, which had come under Division control the previous day and had been badly battered in an heroic stand east of the 38th positions, attempted to tie-in on the right of the 38th. The 3d ROK regiment under the command of the 38th was employed on the left flank of the 38th in an effort to tie-in with the 23d. This disposition formed a shaky, leaky arc northeast of Kunu-ri with the remnants of the Turks on the extreme right flank. It was now early on 29 November.

The units manning this line—9th, 23d, 3d ROK's, 38th and the Turks—bore little resemblance to their previous organizations. Terrific losses in manpower and equipment had been suffered. Confusion existed throughout the ranks but the troops, aware of their precarious situation, lacked no courage and did everything humanly possible to carry out their orders. The

situation permitted no breather. As the haggard remains of the units moved exhausted into their new positions they found the enemy already upon them. The frozen ground would have prevented digging-in even had there been time. There was little cover, no concealment.

During the early morning hours of 29 November, the Division command post moved to a new location six miles south of Kunu-ri.

Throughout the morning every unit of the Division was under heavy attack by the numerically superior enemy. At about 1000 hours, the 2d Reconnaissance Company reported an enemy roadblock had been set-up approximately ten miles south of Kunuri on the Kunuri-Sunchon road, the lifeline of the Division and the only escape route in the Division zone. First estimates placed the strength of the enemy at a reinforced company. At 1240 hours, after the Reconnaissance Company had failed to reduce the block, "C" Company of the 38th Infantry reinforced by tanks from "C" Company of the 72d Tank Battalion were enroute to assist the 2d Recon. At 1350 hours, a battery of 155 howitzers from the 503d Field Artillery was directed to support the attack on the roadblock.

The 38th sent its trains south by way of Anju and they arrived in Sunchon intact.

The situation with the regiments grew worse as the afternoon lengthened. There were many wounded needing immediate treatment, ammunition was low, supplies scarce, and the combat units were suffering such heavy casualties that their effectiveness decreased with every hour.

Back at the roadblock, frantic efforts to push back the enemy failed. At 1630 hours, Major General Keiser relayed a message for help to IX Corps—"Serious roadblock to South. Estimate enemy battalion or more. Air strikes, artillery and infantry company attacks have failed. Road jammed with vehicles prevents movement North or South. Request immediate assistance from the south to relieve situation. Please notify action taken as all infantry elements definitely engaged."

Ten minutes later at 1640 hours, the commanding officer of the 38th Infantry reported his right battalion under attack by the Chinese from the north, northeast, east and south with the Turks unable to hold on his right. At 1655, the 23d Infantry relayed a message to Division headquarters indicating the entire 38th Infantry under attack from the north and northeast and the 3d ROK also under attack. The Turks were giving ground to the east and south. A few minutes passed and the situation in the 38th sector became critical. The Third Battalion was surounded and attempts were being made to establish a defense on the high ground east of the 38th CP.

The Turks reported at 1700 hours that their elements which had been withdrawing down the road were under attack and their escape route to Kunuri was blocked.

The roadblock in the south was still "in" and the enemy force grew stronger. The 23rd and 38th Regiments holding below Kunuri were ordered to pull back. The 23rd was to pull back first except for one company which was to guard the bridge over the Kaechon River which flowed just south of Kunu-ri and over which the 38th was required to move.

The Third Battalion of the 23rd barely escaped annihilation as a burning ammunition truck blocked its escape and forced the remnants to move out by foot, leaving the vehicles behind.

The 23rd completed its withdrawal by 0130 hours except for the company guarding the bridge. However, the remnants of the Second and Third Battalions of the 38th had not reached the 38th perimeter held by the First Battalion and the 3rd ROK Regiment so Colonel Peploe, the regimental commander, waited until 0430 when all that was left of the two battalions had reached safety and the withdrawal was completed.

Neither of the two regiments would have been able to make their moves had it not been for the exceptionally fine artillery support on all likely positions and routes the enemy could be using.

The 3rd ROK Regiment was reported not in position after the two regiments had withdrawn. As it was the only organized force of any strength left in the 38th Regiment, its absence caused great consternation for it was to occupy positions south of the Kaechon on the right of the 23rd and as dawn broke there were no friendly troops on the 23rd's right flank. Immediately the remnants of the Second and Third Battalions of the 38th were assembled and prepared to occupy positions on the 23rd's right.

South of the mounting confusion, all efforts to break the roadblock met with failure. A crisis faced the 2d Division for annihilation was certain if it stayed in Kunu-ri and the only escape route in its sector was blocked. A request went out to IX Corps for permission to take the Division out of the trap by way of the Kunuri—Anju—Sinanju Road, still open and offering an escape through the I Corps sector. IX Corps stated it would have to clear the request through

I Corps.

In the meantime, the shocked and tattered remnants of the 9th Infantry, less the First Battalion, were thrown against the roadblock. The Second and Third Battalions were down to ap-

In the meantime, the shocked and tattered throughout the night together with the 2d Recon, elements of the 72d Tank Battalion and the remains of the 2d Engineers.

During the night of 29-30 November an attack on the 2d Division command post was repulsed.

"Award of the Distinguished Service Cross to First Lieutenant Chew-Mon Lee, Infantry, a member of Company H, 9th Infantry, for action against the enemy in the vicinity of Kunu-ri on 30 November 1950. On 30 November 195fl, Company H was defensively deployed near Kunu-ri when a numerically superior enemy force succeeded in completely surrounding the company and subjecting it to intense small-arms, machine-gun and automatic-weapons fire. During the initial phase of this action the company suffered heavy casualties and the company commander was killed. Lieutenant LEE, a platoon leader, immediately assumed command of the company and, with complete disregard for the intense enemy fire, deployed the company in a tight defensive perimeter. Realizing that the loss of the company commander had tended to panic the men, Lieutenant LEE moved from one position to another, encouraging his men and steadying those who were confused and bewildered by the heavy casualties suffered and the intensity of the enemy attack. When accurate sniper fire from a hill about 150 yards distant began harassing his men, Lieutenant LEE and a small group of volunteers attacked the hill and cleared it of enemy opposition. After establishing a small outpost on the hill, he dispatched a messenger through the enemy lines in an attempt to obtain reinforcements. Under his capable leadership the men repulsed several fanatical enemy attack until a friendly tank force broke through to their position. As it became apparent that the tank crews could not identify the friendly forces, Lieutenant LEE attracted the attention of the lead tank crew, then mounted on top of the tank and, headless of the enemy fire, directed return fire on the hostile positions with such accuracy that all enemy reasistance was eliminated."

The situation was desperate by daylight of the 30th with the pressure increasing on all sides. Conflicting reports filtered in regarding the Kunuri-Sinanju road as a possible route of withdrawal.

A final decision was necessary and the commanding general ordered the Division, less the 23d RCT which was directed to cover the withdrawal, to be ready to move south to Sunchon. The 38th was ordered to go out on trucks or whatever vehicles were remaining.

The haggard remains of the entire Division, except the 23d RCT, were fighting near the area of the Division command post or already attacking the roadblock by noon on 30 November, awaiting orders to move out.

Reports from the south indicated the enemy had entrenched at léast a regimental combat team astride the route the Division was to travel. From the north, the 23rd RCT (23d Inf; "A" Co, 72d Tk Bn; 15th FA Bn) reported beating off attack after attack of Chinese.

By 1300, heavy sniper fire began to fall into the Division assembly area. At 1330, with the only alternatives being to fight out of the trap or make a vain, last-man stand, the Division was ordered to move out and run the roadblock.

The 2d Engineer Combat Batalion supported by "A" Battery, 503d FA Battalion was fighting on the high ground southwest and south of the assembly area while the units moved onto the road. The lead vehicles had moved less than a mile when heavy enemy fire was received from both sides of the road. It was the start of the most agonizing withdrawal the 2d Infantry Division had ever undergone.

The column creeped along as dusk approached. From every side poured mortar, small arms and automatic weapons fire. Men riding in the few remaining trucks fired their rifles into the hills swarming with Chinese. Countless times burning and disabled vehicles stopped the column until they could be pushed off to the side. The bitter sub-zero cold took its toll of the wounded and the well alike. Tanks, interspersed through the column, knocked out enemy strong points along the flaming, twisting, jam-packed road. Every truck and every jeep crawled with men who had no other means of transportation. The ridges paralleling the road were completely in enemy control and from every angle the Chinese poured fire into the slowly crawling line of vehicles and humanity.

Exploding ammunition trucks effectively blocked the road in several places, forcing the column to halt where the Chinese had set-up machine gun crossfires. The lead elements emerged from the trap after 8,000 meters of heavy fighting but the rear vehicles, bumper to bumper, were subject to continuous fire.

Night and the darkness brought the Chinese close-in with bayonets, small arms and hand grenades. Hand to hand fighting broke out all along the road. The field artillery units were firing point blank off the road into the swarming Reds and every man who could fire a weapon did so until his ammunition was exhausted. The dead toppled off the trucks, the wounded hung on or were held on. The number of vehicles pushed off to the side of the road grew larger. The truck loads of wounded endured additional wounds from the close-in fighting. Hundreds who had no transport and who were able to walk, took to the hills in attempts to evade the enemy and make their way to safety. Some were successful, many were not.

Award of the Distinguished Service Cross to Lieutenant Colonel James H. Skeldon, Infantry, Commanding Officer, 2nd Battalion, 38th Infantry, for action aganist the enemy in the vicinity of Sunchon and Kaechon on 29 and 30 November 1950. The 2nd Battalion was under heavy enemy attack and the allied units on the right and left flank had withdrawn. After committing his reserve company and exploiting all available means to stem the enemy attack, Colonel SKELDON ordered the withdrawal of his companies west to the next ridge. Displaying the highest degree of leadership and with complete disregard for personal safety, he personally controlled this operation from the most advantageous positions, although continuously exposed to enemy small-arms and mortar fire. Not satisfied that all his men and equipment had been removed, Colonel SKELDON recrossed a large open area which was being swept by heavy enemy fire and returned to his old command post where he made a personal reconnaissance of the area. He then moved to a nearby battalion command post and assisted another battalion commander in the withdrawal of his troops and tanks. During this move he was painfully wounded in the left shoulder, but refused evacuation. Colonel SKELDON soon discovered that elements of the 38th Infantry and allied troops had been surrounded, also that the road was jammed with vehicles and most of the troops and drivers were located in a ditch along the road. Taking command of the situation, and under the cover of approaching darkness, he ordered the men to high ground along the south side of the road, where he supervised their deployment to assure maximum effectiveness of their fire power. Later upon regimental order he personally led these men from their encirclement to the regimental perimeter. On 30 November the battalion was ordered to at-

tack and clear a strong enemy roadblock which had halted movement of the 2d Division and other allied units. He personally led this attack and continued to expose himself to intense enemy fire so that he could best control his battalion which was encountering stiff and determined resistance. When the 2nd Battalion was ordered to break through the roadblock and link up with allied units near Sunchon, Colonel SKELDON successfully spearheaded a motorized column that fought through the roadblock under intense enemy fire, thus opening the road for succeeding elements of the division.

While the nightmare of the withdrawal through the roadblock was taking place, the 23d Infantry with the attached tankers from "A" Company of the 72d and artillerymen from the 15th Field were standing alone to stem the tide of Chinese and keep them from overtaking the withdrawing Division. Gradually the units of the RCT assembled into a large bowl to the south of Kunu-ri, fighting the enemy on three sides. With the Air Force bombing, rocketing and strafing the ridges and the artillery firing its last ammo at the highest possible rate of fire, it was possible for the 23d to maintain its effectiveness and control. One time the enemy succeeded in penetrating between the disengaging infantry and the assembly area but was beaten off as the tanks moved onto the high ground and across the bottom of the bowl and poured a curtain of fire into the enemy as he attempted to expand his penetration.

The rear-guard units still had the prospect of running the roadblock ahead of them for they, too, were to use the Kunuri-Sunchon exit route. However, as the time approached for the force to move out, a plane circled the assembling vehicles and dropped a message authorizing the use of the Kunuri-Sinanju road and ordering immediate departure.

With remarkable orderliness and precision the columns of trucks were channeled onto the road with the RCT commander, Col. Paul L. Freeman, personally directing the flow of units. The tanks were ordered to bring up the rear and as they ground their way up the banks and onto the road bringing up the tail of the column, the Chinese could be seen appearing over the ridges on the opposite side of the area.

The 23d RCT had relatively easy going as it withdrew down the coastal route for the enemy had not yet cut the road. But on both sides, the Air Force kept a protective watch, bombing the ridgelines and firing the forests to provide light and cover for the rear guard.

* * * *

No story of the withdrawal from Kunuri will ever be complete. Records of many of the units were either lost or not kept at all. Many of the men who could tell the story have not returned. There were countless instances of individual and unit heroism which will forever go unrecognized but without which many thousands more lives would been lost. No one single unit should be singled out for to do so would be an injustice to the others but special mention must be made of the elements of the 2d Engineer Combat Batalion and "A" Battery, 503d who held the hills near the Division CP while other units moved out. Not a man escaped from the northernmost of the two hills. The men of "A" Battery fired their massive 155 guns point blank at the onrushing enemy until they were completely overwhelmed. They stayed to the death so that others might escape.

No account of the withdrawal could ever tell of the suffering endured by the heroic men of the Division. The wounded suffered ten fold. Only those who were there can know of the cold, the hunger, the unutterable misery and heartsickness of defeat.

The losses in men were tragic; the losses in equipment disastrous. More than 5,000 casualties were suffered by the Division in November with 95 per cent of that total inflicted in the last five days of the month. Equipment losses ran from the 95 per cent suffered by the 2d Engineers to lesser rates by other units. Artillery units were particularly hard hit with entire battalions losing all their field pieces and the big majority of their vehicles.

The 2d Division had met the full impact of an overwhelming Chinese force. Although it was battered and forced to fight its way out of a trap it successfully slowed an attack which threatened to destroy the entire Eighth Army. If it had not made the magnificant stand which it did, the lives of tens of thousands of other troops would have been in jeopardy. Even in defeat, the "Indianhead" Division proved to be a rock which held fast, giving other units an opportunity for survival.

Gradually the battered ranks of the 2d Division moved southward, out of contact with the enemy and destined for a period of rest, reorganization and resupply. It's basic organization was intact, and from the remnants of the riddled columns was to emerge an outfit which would make the CCF pay twentyfold for its victory; a Division which was destined to be described as "the most perfect fighting organization in the world", "Second to None".

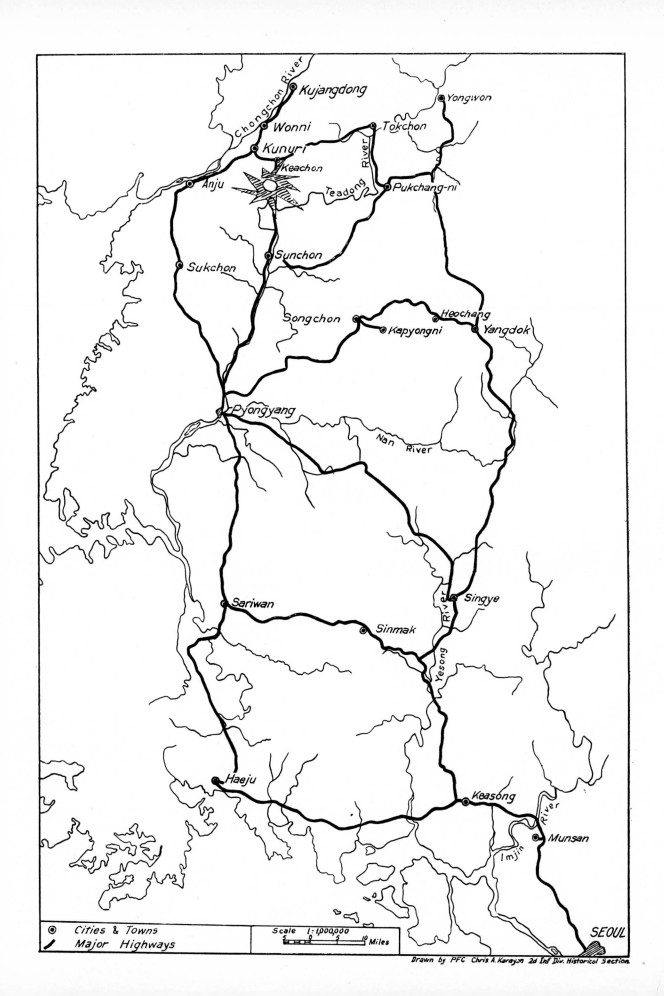

Kujangdong

Yongwon

Chongchon River

Wonni

Tokchon

Kunuri

Keachon

Teadong River

Anju

Pukchang-ni

Sunchon

Sukchon

Songchon

Kapyongni

Heochang

Yangdok

Pyongyang

Nan River

Sariwan

Singye

Sinmak

Yesong River

Haeju

Keasong

Munsan

Imjin River

SEOUL

◎ Cities & Towns
╱ Major Highways

Scale 1:1,000,000
5 0 5   10 Miles

Drawn by PFC Chris A. Karayan 2d Inf Div. Historical Section.

Chaplain Oscar M. Lifshutz conducts Jewish services for Division personnel in September, 1950.

The first official flag-raising ceremony is conducted by the 2d Division as it reaches the banks of the Han River in the Fall of 1950.

Whent the 23rd RCT's ammunition dump blew-up in January of 1951 at Mohkye-dong,
this was all that remained.

One of the few material casualties inflicted on the Division by enemy aircraft
was this 38th Infantry truck which
received a direct hit with a phosphorous
bomb in the Fall of 1950.

One of the few things which a two-and-
a-half truck can't do is talk back to a
land mine.

This tank from the 72d Tank Battalion did a quick "turn-around" when a direct hit on its muzzle break turned it in the opposite direction from which it had been going. Doing the damage was a 76mm gun firing from a 1,500 yard distance.

Proof of the effectiveness of artillery fire is this North Korean soldier who was killed when Division guns shelled a town suspected as being an enemy assembly area. It happened in the 38th Infantry sector on the Naktong.

These North Korean soldiers were killed during an action against the 2d Division south
of Sunchon in October, 1950.

Just a few of the prisoners captured by the 2d Division when it screened the area north
of Pyongyang in October, 1950.

Men from the 2d Battalion, 9th Infantry, check phone lines in North Korea in October, 1950. The weather, believe it or not, was not always like this.

With a barricade of gasoline cans facing him, Lt William F. Soul in charge of gasoline for the 2d Division in October of 1950 checks his supply while other men of the 2d Quartermaster start filling up the cans. Left to right are Sgt Mac Ovier, Pfc Bernardson, Pvt Elbert L. Couch and Lt Soul.

This man of the 9th RCT was one of four killed during a night attack by the Chinese communists on a platoon position in the Kunuri sector in November.

Some of the 5,000 prisoners captured in North Korea in October. They are shown on their way south to PW enclosures.

These North Koreans were rounded up by Task Force Indianhead and Division patrols in October are assembled prior to questioning.

Not all the red prisoners walked south. These were loaded onto flat cars headed for Seoul.

First man in the United Nations forces to cross the Naktong River from the Pusan Perimeter and stay there tells his regimental commander Colonel George B. Peploe (later Brigadier General) of the crossing. The man, Corporal Nicholas H. Snyder, crossed on a raft with two other men and he was first ashore.

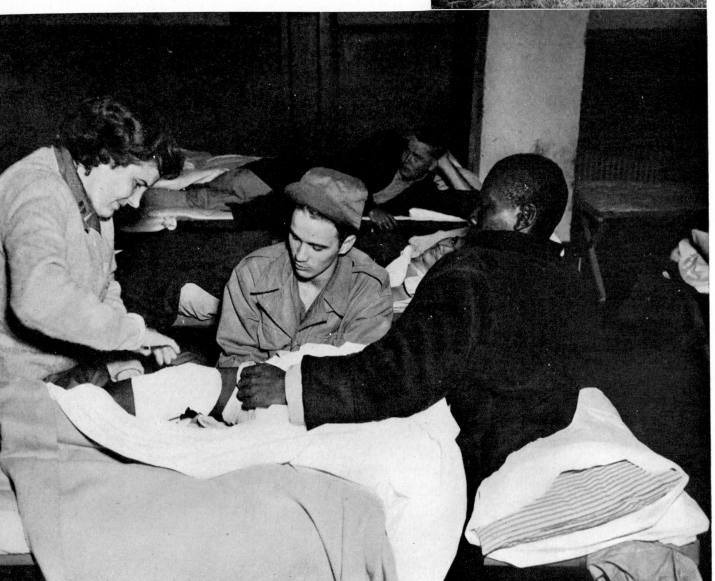

Pfc Aaron Mathews of the 9th Infantry receives treatment for his wounds from Captain Nora C. Hasselmire and aid-man Pfc Perry Jackman at the 4th Field Hospital in late October 1950.

Crossing the Kum River on the way to Seoul, these trucks of the 38th Infantry use a hasty bridge to avoid the deep spots.

In late October of 1950 the 38th Infantry chaplain was Captain John E. Gannon shown visiting with Pfc Wilbur J. Cox during a lull in the fighting near Kunuri in mid-November.

Pfc Ernest Tidwell and Pfc John Adams carry rations up onto their outpost north of Sunchon in November 1950.

One way to beat the lack of showers in the winter of 1950 was to do as WOJG Edmond C. Ellison did—cut a damaged gas drum in half and fill with hot water.

Hill 219 near Kujangdong was the scene of bitter fighting in the days following the one when this picture was taken, 25 November 1960.

Three Russian-made anti-aircraft guns captured in early October are checked by ordnance men from the 702d.

Laying wire near the Chongchon River in North Korea are Pfc Bosie Adams by the spool and Cpl Robert G. Bartusek behind the wheel.

Eggs were plentiful early in the campaign as witness these held by Pfc Daniel H. Gunn and Pfc Hebdige, both of the 2d Division.

Men of the 2d Engineers build a bridge across the Tudong
River at Sunchon in November 1950.

First Lieutenant Murray of the 702d Ordnance Company places a fuse in an enemy mortar shell to destroy 18 railroad cars of enemy ammunition captured by the 23rd RCT at Yangdok.

A 2d Division patrol uncovered this underground machine shop used by the North Koerans for manufacturing parts for their Russian-made weapons.

WONJU I-"TWIN TUNNELS"

TERRAIN SKETCH

The Korean City of WONJU is a typical communication center for a mountainous country. It lies almost in the east-west geographical center of Korea and in the south end of a valley basin which is approximately eight miles in width. The city itself is comparable to a wheel, it being the hub and the roads being the spokes. Five important roads pass through this city. The WONJU-HOENGSONG road and the WONJU-SAEMAL road run north and northeast respectively, thus forming the avenues of approach from the north. These avenues were dominated by large hill masses to the north and by steep, rocky mountains directly east which ranged in elevation from five hundred ninety seven to one thousand two hundred eighty meters. Small trees, brush, and undergrowth covered the lower terrain features. To the southeast runs the road to CHECHON. The road to MOKKYE-DONG runs south from WONJU. The mountains to the east of WONJU, also dominated these roads. To the west lay the YOJU-WONJU corridor with its accompanying road. All five roads were primary routes, eighteen to twenty four feet wide, hard packed earth and gravel, and capable of supporting divisional loads. The engagement that followed was primarily for the control of this important hub and its network of roads. Enemy troops attacked simultaneously from HOENGSONG, to the north, and the rugged mountains to the east. Again, winter hindered the supply problems with snow, ice, and temperatures dropping to thirty degrees below zero.

The early days of December revealed the 2d Division moving southward into Eighth Army reserve. On the 1st it was assembling south of Sunchon although elements of the 23d RCT, including the 72d Tank Battalion (—) and the 15th FA Bn, which had withdrawn down the coastal road were still in the Sukchon area. On 2 December orderes were received to continue the southward movement and the tactical elements, service trains and the advance CP began moving toward Munsan-ni below the 38th parallel and south of the Imjin River.

However, the Division rear CP was still located in Pyongyang where it had been during the battle in the Kunuri area. At noon on 2 December, with the Chinese elements driving toward the former North Korean capital, the rear CP was ordered to prepare to withdraw to Seoul. By 1745 hours it was decided the move would be made by rail for although there was a critical shortage of locomotives there were no trucks to be had. The rear elements began loading in three serials.

The rail cars containing the Division rear personnel, records and equipment were moved into the main station of Pyongyang by 3 December but there the engine was detached to be used to pull a hospital train to the south. As the cars sat in the rail yards, hundreds of thousands of refugees and retreating ROK soldiers streamed through the area, bound for the safety of South Korea, so it was necessary for guards to be placed on all the cars to prevent looting.

At 0800 the next morning, the train commander announced that no locomotive was available to pull the cars laden with the personnel, equipment and records of the Division rear. However, it was decided to wait until the last moment before abandoning the cars. At 1130, on orders of the train comamnder, the postal officer began burning the money order files, letters and military currency. At 1230, the milling thousands of civilians had begun looting some of the cars of the train; it was an almost impossible task to keep them clear.

An engine was finally obtained by 1300 but officials of the transportation office ordered that it be used only to pull cars carrying personnel. Consequently it was necessary to abandon all but the most vital records. After what seemed like days, the train began to pull out at 1720 hours and as it left the station the mobs of civilians were observed looting the abandoned cars.

Advance parties from all units of the Division were sent south from Munsan on 7 December to locate bivouac areas in the vicinity of Yongdong-Po near the South Korean capital of Seoul. By nightfall, the division command post had been established in that city.

Maj. General Robert B. McClure assumed comamnd of the 2d Division on 7 December, replacing Maj. Gen. Keiser who had been evacuated for medical reasons. He immediately ordered all units to ship non-essential equipment to Japan and decreed that every unit must be ready to move on a moments notice. Although intelligence reports indicated the Chinese advance had slowed while the enemy consolidated his gains, the need for mobility had been learned.

All units of the Division were assembled in the area between Seoul and Suwon to the South by 8 December. Then began the monumental task of reorganization, re-equipping, resupply and training. The battle-weary remnants of the Inidanhead Division faced the prospect of building the Division anew.

But the tasks of war went on. As the units trained, they also conducted extensive reconnaissance to the east and south. The 9th Infantry patrolled the roads east of Seoul to Hongchon, Hoengsong, and Wonju. Further south the 23d Infantry sent reconnaissance parties east from Suwon to Wonju, Chechon and Chungju; the 38th Infantry reconnoitered north east from Seoul to Chunchon and Hongchon and the 72d Tank Battalion mapped the roads to the south. From all the patrols came sketches of the terrain and reports of its suitability for defense.

Two additions to the Division were made on 11 December when battalion-sized detachments from France and the Netherlands became part of the 2d. The Dutch were attached to the 38th and the French to the 23d Infantry.

The balance of the month of December was spent in extensive training, patrolling and reorganization as replacements were received and equipment was added to the Division to replace that which has been lost in the battle of Kunuri. Numerous defense plans were drawn up and later discarded as estimates of the enemy's plans and capabilities varied with each new report. By 15 December, the Division was declared sufficiently supplied to make it combat effective but there was much training to be done and the shortage of motor transport was still acute.

Finally, after many false starts, the Division began moving to the Chungju area in central Korea. Its mission upon arrival was to conduct aggressive patrols while protecting the right flank of the Eighth Army.

At that time there were increasingly frequent reports of heavy North Korean infiltration to the east where the ROK Army units has thus far failed to establish a solid defense line.

The 38th RCT was given the difficult mission of protecting this open east flank of the Division and 8th Army. Its battalions were occuying positions at Chechon, Tanyang and Wonju with its tanks at Andong, a distance of approximately 60 miles along the Chechon-Andong Road. There were no friendly troops between the regiment and the east coast.

And together with the activity on the east flank and to the rear of the Army front came reports that the main body of the enemy force was now in a position to launch a new attack on the UN troops. Along the front the 8th Army readied itself to meet the new onslaught.

The 2d Division, moving into the area around the central Korean town of Chungju, was beginning one of the most critical and successful periods of its history. Still short in men, equipment and training after the retreat from the North, it was slowly rounding into fighting shape once again. The addition of the French and Netherlands detachments did much to increase its battle potential. Another addition, the First Ranger Company, joined the ranks of the 2d Division on 23 December to add even more strength.

The new Division sector posed supply problems such such as had not hampered the Division since the early days of August. Corps and Army supply points were far to the rear. Every road was a sheet of ice and snow as the effects of the severe winter became evident. The shortage of trucks imposed further burdens on the services. Nevertheless, the Division gradually increased its meager stocks of supplies and equipment and the thin stream of replacements and returnees continued to arrive.

Christmas Day, the 2d Reconnaissance Company moved north of the Division assembly area to Hoengsong where it established a patrol base and commenced screening the Division's west flank. Hoengsong was located north of the vital road junction town of Wonju which intelligence reports pointed to as the next target for a major Communist offensive. It was only necessary to glance at any map to see the importance of Wonju. Five major supply routes formed a hub in Wonju and an important rail terminal on the Kyonggyong Railroad leading to Pusan was located there. Wonju also marked the center of the Eighth Army front. Any penetration there would succeed in splitting the front and blocking the main routes to the south, placing the enemy astride the United Nations's

principal artery of supply and evacuation in the central section.

The 2d Division was alerted on 29 December for a move. The area of responsibility charged to the Division was shifted to the North. One regimental combat team was ordered to defend the city of Hongchon, north of Wonju, while two others were to be prepared to counter-attack. An increase in guerrilla activity and probing attacks from the main body of enemy to the north indicated that increased action was not too far off. It came the next day.

The Third Battalion of the 23d Infantry became the first element of the 2d Division to go into battle as the Division moved forward. Moving up to secure Hongchon, the battalion encountered an enemy roadblock on the Hoengsong-Hongchon road. As it came to grips with this force, composed of North Korean army units, air observers reported large numbers of enemy troops massing in the area. Realizing that defense of Hongchon was impossible until the roadblock was eliminated, the 23d RCT pulled its support forces back to Hoengsong and attacked the roadblock anew. Comprising the RCT at that time were the 23d Infantry Regiment, the 15th FA Bn, a platoon from "B" Company of the 2d Engineers, and elements of "B" Battery of the 82d AAA.

The 38th Regiment was alerted to move to the Hoengsong area when news of the roadblock went from the 23d RCT to Division and the 9th was ordered to Wonju as Division Reserve.

The last day of December saw the Second and Third Battalions of the 23d locked in battle with an enemy blocking force north of Hoengsong while the First Battalion continued defensive preparations to the south. While the fight raged, elements of the II ROK Corps, which had been engaging the enemy, commenced a rapid withdrawal to the South, streaming through the new sector of the 2d Division. The 38th RCT (-3d Bn) closed into Hoengsong on the 31st and the 9th arrived in Wonju minus the French Battalion which was ordered to join the 23d RCT.

New Years Day dawned with the 23d still heavily engaged on the Hoengsong-Hongchon road. The First and Second Battalions of the 38th with the 38th FA Bn, a platoon of "C" Company, 2d Engineers and "C" Battery of the 82d AAA were well entrenched in Hoengsong.

Fighting in continued bitter cold weather with the temperature in the minus twenties, the 23d RCT finally eliminated the roadblock north of Hoengsong on 2 January. It immediately established blocking positions there which it maintained until 5 January. The plan to occupy Hongchon was postponed.

While the 23d was digging in, the Division received orders attaching it to X Corps and with these orders came instructions that a new defense line was to be established. It consisted of an arc north of Hongchon encompassing two main routes of approach to the south, the Chunchon-Hongchong road and the Hangye-Hongchon road. On both sides of this new defensive sector, the ROK's were withdrawing, leaving the Division once again holding a wedge upon which the enemy moved from three sides. By evening of the 2d of January, however, the Division defense was being hastily established with the 23d still blocking north of Hoengsong and the 38th dug-in in Hoengsong with all of its battalions plus the Dutch detachment. The 9th, in the south in the vicinity of Wonju, was sending out extensive patrols, one of which uncovered an enemy force of 430 dressed in GI uniforms. The patrol engaged the group then withdrew, called for an air strike, and watched as the Air Force slaughtered the enemy. After the action more than 400 enemy dead were counted by members of "G" Company and the regimental I&R platoon of the 9th Infantry.

Not all the action of 2d Division units was taking place in the critical Wonju, Hoengsong, Hogchon sector, however, for as the three RCT's braced themselves to meet the communist offensive in central Korea, the 72d Tank Battalion embarked on a mission all its own.

During the last days of December, the 72d Tank Battalion, commanded by Lt Col E. W. Brubaker, had assembled its tanks in the town of Sangju far to south where, because of the treacherous ice-coated roads, it seemed destined to remain until sufficient engineer work on the mountain passes would enable it to move forward to rejoin the Division. However, the critical tactical situation in the north demanded additional armor support. An order was flashed on 30 December to the 72d to move its tanks to Kumchon, south of Sangju, load them on flatcars and move north. The destination was not revealed even to the Battalion. The order arrived at 1130. Three hours later the entire battalion was on its way to Kumchon. By 1800 hours, orders came through attaching the battalion to IX Corps. At 1900 the first tanks were being loaded on the flatcars. Loading continued all night with the huge tanks being guided onto the decrepit cars by flashlight. At 0730 the next morning as the train pulled out it was learned the destination for the tanks was Uijongbu

where a battle already was in progress.

With the battalion wheeled vehicles going by road and the tanks by rail, the tanks on the first train arrived at Uijongbu well in advance of the wheel column. "B" Company, the first to depart from Kumchon, unloaded at noon on 1 January and rolled from the flatcars into blocking positions with the 5th RCT. After a stiff engagement with the attacking Chinese forces that night it was released from assignment to the 5th at 0600 on 2 January and reverted to its parent unit, the 72d, which arrived in the Seoul area at 1415 that afternoon.

The remainder of the tanks of "A" and "C" Companies had arrived in the Seoul area by this time and were unloaded there since Uijongbu was already in enemy hands. The following days the battalion did yoeman duty in delaying the enemy advance to the south with its line companies attached to practically every major UN force operating in the western sector of the front. By the 8th of January, after the whirl-wind trip north and being shuttled back and forth across the front to points of enemy penetration, the weary members of the battalion found themselves again in Sangju from whence they had begun their frantic trip to the north. In 15 days the tanks had covered more than 600 miles and had operated with the 24th Division, 187th Airborne RCT, 1st Cavalry Division, 27th British Brigade, 6th ROK Division and their own parent unit, the 2d Infantry Division.

*   *   *   *

While the line companies of the 72d Tank Battalion were operating with withdrawing United Nations units in the northwest below Seoul, the major forces of the 2d Division were preparing for a communist attack expected at any moment. On 3 January, with the 23d RCT still in blocking positions north of Hoengsong, ROK elements on both flanks of the Division continued their withdrawals. Guerrilla units were operating to the east and south of the Division positions and had succeeded in cutting the vital rail line from the south at Tanyang.

The 9th Infantry, patrolling northeastward from defensive positions in Wonju, was encountering small enemy groups attempting to enter the town. One group of 100 infiltrators was beaten off on 3 January by "B" and "C" Companies of the 9th after "F" had been surrounded earlier by an estimated enemy battalion and had fought its way clear in a brilliant withdrawal of over two and a half miles.

Early on the 4th of January, an estimated two

CCF regiments were identified 15 miles north of Yoju on the Division's left flank. At the time only five-hundred 2d Division and ROK troops were in that town and they requested immediate reinforcement. Col. James P. Barney, deputy assistant division comamnder, was dispatched to Yoju to form Task Force Barney to hold the town. Upon arrival he found UN units on the left withdrawing, exposing the west flank of his position. This development was reported to higher headquarters and the task force organized for defense.

Elements of the 38th RCT were dispatched from Hoengsong on what turned out to be a futile operation that same day. A large enemy force had been reported southeast of Hoengsong where the 38th was in blocking positions. Immediately, the Second and Third battalions with a regimental command group were sent out to engage and destroy the force. The Third Battalion went by truck but because of a shortage of transportation the Second Battalion marched the entire distance. Both units arrived near the reported enemy assembly area that night after dark, and though they sighted enemy personnel,

they buttoned up for the night and made plans to attack at first light on the following day, 5 January. However, they had no sooner jumped off on the attack at 0755 than orders were received from Division to disengage and return to Hoengsong. A major enemy thrust was considered iminent. Every unit of the Division would be needed, so the two battalions broke contact with the enemy and retraced their route to Hoengsong, the Third again by truck and the Second by foot.

While the Second and Third Battalions of the 38th were planning their return to Hoengsong, "C" Company of the 38th on outpost duty west of Hoengsong was coming under heavy enemy attack, the forerunner of the main enemy effort.

At approximately 0550, according to members of the company, men on a roadblock the company had established west of its main position observed approximately 200 soldiers marching along the road toward their positions. One member of the roadblock shouted, "Don't shoot, they're ROK's;" this call was carried down the line toward the company. (Apparently the members of the roadblock mistook the enemy for

TRAIN HEADING FOR THE FRONT LINES.   15EPT.

ROK's whose patrols were active in the area.) It was not until the marching soldiers came abreast of the roadblock that they were discovered to be enemy. It was too late; the enemy quickly overran the blocking positions and headed straight for the company's mortar positions. Simultaneously with this action, another group of enemy, numbering about 200, skirted the company flank and came up a draw to the rear going directly to the CP. In this maneuver, a rifle platoon was entirely cut off from the remainder of the company. The enemy rushing toward the CP went directly up to the individual soldiers in foxholes in the CP area and motioned for them to give up their arms. Three North Koreans walked into the CP proper and directed the company comamnder by arm and hand signals to turn over his weapons to them. A soldier standing behind the commander stepped to one side and with a burst from an automatic carbine killed all three.

Meanwhile, the enemy group which had penetrated to the mortar positions turned the mortars to the south and fired approximately 15 rounds. These were observed by other elements of the First Battalion who were unaware of what was happening at "C" Company forward positions, since all communication had been cut off by the attack.

By this time the company was fighting in separated groups. The isolated platoon began fighting its way back toward a Netherlands company, the nearest friendly unit. The Heavy Weapons, forming the roadblock, and the mortar crews suffered worst. Having lost their crew-served weapons, they joined the rifle platoons and fought their way to friendly positions.

By noon, the survivors of the company had made their way to friendly lines and the enemy had withdrawn. During the action "C" Company sustained only four KIA's, four WIA's and nineteen MIA's in spite of the confusion.

With the enemy threat to Wonju mounting hourly, a supply train loaded with critically needed fuel and rations pulled into Wonju, a week after it had been scheduled to arrive. It was imperative that the supplies be issued immediately and the train sent south so a maximum forced issue to all the units in the area was made. Simultaneously all heavy equipment was dispatched to the rear and Division headquarters began displacing to Chungju. All movements were hindered by the swarms of refugees who jammed the MSR's leading to the south and safety.

At 0900 hours, a Corps order was received issuing new defensive instructions to the Division. The 23d, which was still forward on the Hoengsong-Hongchon road, was to pull back to Wonju, blowing the bridges as it moved. The 38th was to hold its present positions at Hoengsong until all ROK elements to the north were clear and then it, too, was to pull back to Wonju, blowing the bridges in its sector. To the west in Yoju, where Task Force Barney awaited an enemy attack, went an order to disband the force, send the 2d Reconnaissance Company to Wonju and the remaining elements to Chongju. And the 50 ton bridge which "D" Company of the 2d Engineers had just completed at Yoju was to be blown when the Task Force was clear. The 9th Infantry was to hold blocking positions between Wonju and Hoengsong until the 23d and 38th had established their new positions in the vicinity of Wonju and then it was to move south on the Wonju-Chechon road and be prepared to attack with elements of the 7th US Division which were east of the 2d Division.

As the Division began forming into its new defensive positions large enemy forces were observed moving forward to launch their long expected offensive to wrench Wonju from the United Nations forces and open the way for a drive to Pusan.

An enemy force of more than 10,000 troops surged toward the line between Wonju and Chechon on the 6th of January. To the west the ROK's continued their withdrawal, exposing the flank of the 23d. At 1500, the 23d and 38th Regiments began movements to the best defensive ground in the area around Wonju. Supporting the defense were the 37th and 38th FA Bns emplaced south of Wonju and the 15th FA Bn at Sillim-ni, east of Wonju in the 9th Infantry Sector. The 503d, still not recovered from the battle of Kunuri, was not committed but continued to reorganize and re-equip in the vicinity of Kumchon.

Three North Korean divisions, the 6th, 10th and 27th, began hitting at Wonju from the southeast on 7 January while the 12th North Korean division simultaneously drove down the MSR from Hongchon to the north. Unidentified Chinese forces launched their assaults from the west on the stout defenses of the 23d and 38th. Intense fighting raged all day of the 7th and by midnight an enemy force had succeeded in infiltrating the lines of the 23d and entering Wonju in strength. Both the 23d and 38th made slight withdrawals on Division order, but stopped on the high ground south and east of Wonju and prepared to stand. Before leaving, however, the ammunition train which had of necessity been left in Wonju was blown. Orders to blow the railroad bridge went amiss, however, when the charge failed to explode. Realizing the extreme importance of demolishing the bridge, the platoon leader of the attached Engineer platoon braved a wall of enemy small arms fire, advanced to the bridge, doused the ties with gasoline and set fire to the structure, denying its further use to the enemy.

Without letup the battle see-sawed back and forth all night long. A new defensive line was outlined in an arc to the south encompassing Mokkey-dong on the west and Chechon on the east, to be withdrawn to only on orders. However, neither of the two hard-pressed regiments gave-up their positions immediately south of Wonju.

At 0300 hours on 8 January, orders came from X Corps that Wonju must be retaken. Four battalions were ordered to hold the defensive positions on the high ground south of the town while a minimum of one battalion was to attack and clear Wonju and secure the airstrip on the south edge. The Second Battalion of the 23d was designated as the attacking force and it jumped off against fierce resistance, fighting from house to house and making some progress in the initial stages. However, enemy reinforcements poured against both flanks of the attacking Second Battalion and it was forced to withdraw to its former positions.

To the southeast, the 9th Regiment was defending the Chechon-Wonju road from bases at Chupori and at 1500 hours on 8 January was engaged with elements of an enemy regiment attempting to cut the vital route. The encounter lasted throughout the day and at night the Second Battalion of the 9th was secure in the threatened area and buttoned up until daylight.

The following day, 9 January, with elements of the 23d, 38th, the French, Dutch and 1st Ranger Company occupying the high ground south of Wonju, another attempt by the 23d to clear Wonju met with failure as the enemy fought fiercely to hold his advantage. The entire battle was waged in weather similar to that of the November encounter in North Korea.

The 10th of January opened with air observers reporting thousands of enemy troops moving south from Wonju to attack the defenses of the 23d and 38th RCT's. From the high ground, friendly troops poured a rain of fire on the enemy who threatened the blanks and the front. Friendly artillery and air pounded the masses of advancing communists inflicting staggering ca-

sualties while the bitter weather exacted an increasingly heavy toll on attackers and defenders alike. Finally, after savage fighting during which the 1st and 2d French Companies repulsed four successive attempts by the enemy to envelop their positions, the enemy was turned back, his attack broken, friendly lines remaining intact. All the next day the two forces poured murderous barrages of fire at one another while friendly units were shuffled through knee deep snow to locate maximum strength at the most critical points. The Second Battalion of the 23rd with the 3rd French Company attached moved forward from the 2d Division defenses and struggled to wrest important positions from the enemy on the southern outskirts of Wonju from which he had been laying down bases of fire on the friendly positions. Hill 247, a low lying enemy-infested hill mass, was taken by the French only after they fixed bayonets and cut their way to the top where, they held in spite of savage counterattacks and sub-zero winds which cut through winter clothing.

By the 12th of January, the major units of the 23d and 38th were formed into one defensive ring. Beginning on the right were the First Battalion of the 38th, 1st Ranger Company, two companies of French Troops, the Second Batta-

lion of the 23d, Second Battalion of the 38th, two more French companies, a company from the Dutch Detachment, Third Battalion of the 23d, the remaining elements of the Dutch, and finally "K" Company of the 38th. The First Battalion of the 38th, Dutch and Third Battalion, 38th were under command of the 38th

Infantry. The remainder were commanded by the 23d Infantry.

The 9th RCT was still to the east and the Third Battalion (—) of the 38th was occupying defensive positions with the 9th on the Wonju-Hokyedong Road. The First Battalion of the 23d was also attached to the 9th while the 503d FA Bn was now operating with the 187th Airborne RCT to the east.

The Dutch, 1st and 2d French Companies, and the Second Battalion of the 38th blunted several enemy attacks during the night of the 12th. On the 13th, elements of the 23d beat off attempts by two enemy battalions to pierce friendly lines. UN air and artillery took a heavy toll of the attackers who finally withdrew in confusion after our firepower poured down upon them.

"Award of the Distinguished Service Cross to Private First Class Elmer E. Lewellyn, Infantry, a member of Company E, 38th Infantry, for action against the enemy in the vicinity of Oneamsong, on 13 January 1951. On 3 January 1951, Company E was defending a key terrain feature in the Wonju area when a numerically superior enemy force launched several fanatical attacks against the company positions. In the initial attack, Private LEWELLYN, a newly assigned replacement who had joined the company the preceeding day, was thrown from his foxhole by the force of an enemy concussion grenade which exploded near his position Quickly recovering from the shock of the blast, he crawled back to his position and aided in repulsing the attack by placing withering fire on the enemy. When the enemy troops rallied and launched a second attack, Private LEWELLYN, heedless of the intense enemy fire, moved from one position to another in order to gain a better field of fire and thus inflict greater casualties on the enemy. Although seriously wounded during the second enemy assault, Private LEWELLYN refused to retire for medical attention. When the enemy closed in for the third and final assault, Private LEWELLYN leaped from his foxhole and stood fully exposed to the hostile fire, yelling taunts at the enemy and shouting words of encouragement to his comrades. During the final assault, enemy troops approached to within a few yards of Private LEWELLYN's position but he steadfastly refused to fall back and killed several enemy soldiers at his position before he fell mortally wounded. Inspired by the intrepid courage and self-sacrifice of Private LEWELLYN, his comrades tenaciously held their positions, inflicted tremendous casualties on the enemy

and successfully repelled the hostile assaults."

On 14 January, with all elements of the Division locked in battle, Maj. Gen. Clark L. Ruffner, former Chief of Staff for X Corps, assumed command of the 2d Division.

Although fighting still flamed over the entire battle line, the back of the enemy attack had been broken. Staggering casualties had been inflicted on the communists in their last attempt to annihilate the defending forces. Following his abortive offensive, the enemy began to slowly withdraw large units to the north. At the same time it was necessary for the UN forces in the Wonju area to shorten and strengthen their lines. The order directing the movement was published at midnight on the 14th and called for a withdrawal to a new X Corps defensive line designated "3-3-3" which formed an arc extending from Unnam-ni on the west to Mossan-ni on the east. This line encompassed the two major routes leading south from Wonju and denied to the enemy an approach to the south.

The readjustment was initiated at 1000 hours, 15 January, and was completed by 1900 hours the following day with remarkable success. In the process, the artillery units echeloned southward enabling them to keep continuous fire cover while displacing to new positions. The entire Division was reassembled with detached battalions being returned to their parent unit.

The new line was established with the First and Third Battalions of the 23d on the left replacing elements of the 8th ROK Division, the 38th in the center and the 9th on the right. Thus the Division was established in excellent defensive positions and the withdrawal of the ROK units placed the 7th US Division on the 2d's right flank and the 24th US Division on the 2d's left flank.

Immediately the Division instituted unit instruction in preparing fields of fire, use of range cards, construction of individual implacements, and cold weather training. Extensive patrolling was ordered and the system of tactical air control was revamped to improve its efficiency. Plans were also drawn up to coordinate the control of all fire support weapons and agencies under a single command and by 9 January the FSCC—Fire Support Coordination Center—was established.

On 17 January, all regiments were sending out patrols deep into unoccupied territory to the north to find the enemy and determine his intentions. One such patrol from "E" Company of the 38th Infantry advanced by motorized transport to a point two miles south of

Wonju where a blown bridge forced it to dismount. Foot patrols were sent into Wonju itself and no enemy was found. Later the patrol withdrew to positions one mile south of the town where it buttoned up for the night. Night patrols, were sent out, but no contact with the enemy was made.

Early on the morning of 18 January, a 30-man patrol from "'B" Company of the 9th Infantry started toward the northwest to reconnoiter possible enemy routes of approach. Leaving five men with the vehicles at the dismount point, the patrol continued on foot until it reached a suspected enemy route. The patrol leader sent seven men to the south while he and the remainder of the patrol, 18 in all, advanced to the north. Warned by civilians that an enemy force was located in a village less than a mile to his front, the patrol leader continued to advance until reaching the village where he deployed his men and opened fire on the houses. An estimated 150 enemy were surprised sleeping and in the resulting action 20 enemy were killed, 9 wounded and two prisoners taken. The patrol returned to the company late that night with the PW's, having taken no casualties of its own during the entire action.

On 19 January, it was decided to send a battalion to occupy Wonju after patrols had reported the enemy had evacuated the town. The Second Battalion of the 9th Infantry was chosen for the job and moved out with attached "E" Company of the 38th, "B" Battery of the 15th FA Bn, "D" Battery of the 82d AAA and elements of the regimental tank company. In the following days, the reinforced battalion under Lt. Col. Barbaris made its base immediately south of Wonju from which it daily sent strong patrols out beyond Wonju where they engaged the enemy, inflicted heavy casualties, and forced him to withdraw. Severals stiff fights with enemy units of battalion and regimental strength resulted but by 21 January the Second Battalion had cleared the area immediately adjacent to Wonju of enemy units. However, there still existed strong communist troop units south of Wonju which had been hit repeatedly by friendly air in the preceeding days. The First Battalion of the 9th under Lt. Col. Landahl relieved the Second Battalion on 22 January and continued the job of cleaning out the remaining elements of the enemy forces. By the end of the following day, after a stiff battle by "B" Company with enemy dug-in near the air strip, the enemy withdrew to the north and northeast leaving the Wonju area and the area to the south relatively clear.

With Wonju and the surrounding area under control of the 2d Division, the 9th Infantry dispatched a series of motorized patrols to seek out and destroy the enemy. On 24 January, three of these patrols were sent to cover a sector extending north, northwest and northeast of Wonju. One of these embarked on the northern road leading to Hoengsong. Five thousand yards south of that city, North Korean rearguard elements were encountered but the patrol deployed and placed fire on the groups which then dispersed. Two thousand yards further on an enemy concentration of 3,000 troops was sighted, fired upon and dispersed to the north. After clearing the way, the patrol entered Hoengsong, reported it free of enemy and then withdrew again to its base in Wonju.

The other two patrols, all from the First Battalion of the 9th, reported no contact.

The French Battalion was released from the 23d Infantry on 24 January and assigned to the 38th when the 23d was ordered to assemble as Division reserve at Chupo-ri.

Throughout the remainder of the week, the 9th continued to send out patrols. On the 25th, the 23d Infantry in reserve initiated patrols running west from Wonju to the east bank of the Han River on the Division's left Flank.

On 26 January, a reinforced French Company went out from the Munmangni Valley to engage an enemy force of 50 reported by a previous patrol. Selecting a difficult route through the hills, the French surprised 450 enemy troops, inflicted 32 counted KIA's and came back in spite of several enemy ambushes. Said General Ruffner, "This may be the information we have been seeking for the last 10 days..."

On 27 January, patrols operating in the Hoengsong area reported the enemy was preparing defensive positions five to six miles north of the town so on the following day a task force was organized to engage the enemy in the area. The force, composed of "A" Company, 9th Infantry; elements of the Regimental Tank Company; "B" Battery, 15th FA Bn; and a section from "D" Battery, 82d AAA moved out early on the 28th. Entering Hoengsong at 1145, the assault group came under enemy small arms but returned the fire and dispersed the enemy. Continuing further north for two miles it sighted and placed heavy fire on newly constructed enemy positions in the area for several hours before withdrawing to its base in Wonju.

The 503d FA Bn, which had been on detached assignment, reverted to the Division on the 28th and began a rail move to Mokkyedong.

Patrolling continued by all elements of the

Division to search out and engage the enemy. A new SOP directed that if any patrol met an enemy force it could not disperse it was to be followed-up by a larger force capable of destroying the enemy. In this manner, the entire area from Hoengsong to Chupori was swept continually for infiltrating enemy groups.

On 28 January, a patrol from the First Battalion of the 23d Infantry returned from the "Twin Tunnels" area east of Chipyong-ni with a report of enemy sightings but no ground contact. Plans were made to send a larger force out to the same area the following day to clear the enemy.

The 38th Infantry relieved the 9th Infantry in the Wonju sector on 30 January and the 9th reverted to Division reserve at Mokkyedong. At the same time, elements of the 8th ROK Division moved into the area adjacent to the former 9th sector on the east and also assumed responsibility for a portion of the eastern flank of the former Division sector.

The planned patrol from the 23d Infantry to the "Tunnels" area moved out on the 29th from the Second Battalion. Upon nearing the area where the enemy had been sighted the previous day it was attacked and surrounded by two North Korean battalions which appeared from out of the wooded hills along the road. A call for aid was sent back to the battalion and "F" Company was dispatched, having to fight its way through to the embattled patrol before it could effect a rescue. Then on the 30th, orders went out to the Third and French Battalions of the 23d to move up to an assembly point four miles south of the "Tunnels" area to counter the developing enemy threat. Accompanying the two battalions were the "B" Battery of the 37th FA Bn and "B" Battery of the 82d AAA.

In the meantime, the Second and Netherlands Battalions of the 38th were ordered to Wonju to join the rest of the regiment which had closed into the Wonju area the previous day. The 72d Tank Battalion was alerted for employment in the 23d sector and moved up to a position east of Mokkyedong.

The 23d initiated a two-battalion offensive on the 31st with the mission of cleaning out the enemy in the "Tunnels" area. The French attacked the area on the left and the Third Battalion on the right, supported by the RCT artillery. Intermediate objectives were secured without contact and it appeared the enemy force had pulled back. At 1630, the task force pulled into a tight perimeter for the night encountering only sporadic enemy fire. Simultaneously, "E" Company of the 23d screened the force's right

flank, contacting elements of the Third Battalion at 1830 hours and returning to its base at Munmang-ni. To provide close-in support for the 37th Field Artillery, B" Company of the 23d moved up from its base at Iho-ri and established defenses around the gun positions.

The 23d's perimeter was attacked early in the morning of 1 February. Two enemy regiments came roaring down on the defensive positions at 0450 hours. Blowing their bugles and whistles, the horde threw the weight of their attack against the sector defended by the "L" Company on the east side of the road and the 3rd French Company on the west side. Furious fighting soon raged all around the perimeter. Reinforcements were requested.

"Award of the Distinguished Service Cross to Sergeant First Class Clarence G. Brown, Infantry, a member of Company L, 23d Infantry, for action against the enemy in the vicinity of Twin Tunnels on 1 February 1951. On 1 February 1951, Company L was occupying defensive positions in the Twin Tunnels area when a numerically superior enemy force launched an attack against the position, forcing two platoons to withdraw in order to establish a tighter perimeter. As the two platoons were effecting this maneuver, a second enemy group launched an attack that threatened to cut off one of the platoons from the remainder of the company. Realizing the seriousness of the situ-

ation, Sergeant BROWN immediately deployed his squad and began placing effective fire on the second enemy group. Throughout this action, he moved among his men encouraging them to hold their positions despite the intense hostile fire received from three sides. When the two platoons had completed their withdrawal and established a new defense perimeter, Sergeant BROWN ordered his squard to withdraw to the reestablished friendly line, then remained behind alone to furnish covering fire for the movement. He was killed at this position while hurling hand grenades at the advancing enemy."

The First Battalion, located at Iho-ri, was ordered to join the embattled units in the "Twin Tunnels" area and hastily moved out from its reserve positions at 0830 hours. The Division commander assured the 23d, "If necessary, the entire division will be moved up to do the job." At 0700, the enemy launched powerful attacks on all of the positions occupied by the French including Hill 453 where biter hand-to-hand fighting took place and in the Muchon valley where the enemy broke through the French Heavy Weapons Company and came within 200 yards of the road before it was repelled by a counterattack of the French Pioneer Platoon supported by two tanks. "L" Company was forced to give up slight ground about 1030 hours when severe pressure caused the lines to sag but by 1200 hours the ground was regained and the fighting continued to rage. In the French sector, the defenders were inflicting terrific casualties on the attackers in bayonet fighting.

By 1430 hours, the First Battalion was well on its way to assist the French and First Battalions. The Second Battalion went to Munmang-ni and moved into the positions vacated by the First Battalion. The 9th Infantry occupied the vacated Second Battalion posts. The 23d Tank Company began moving to the "Tunnels" area to lend its weight to the defense.

Enemy attacks succeeded in penetrating into the positions of the 37th Field Artillery during the afternoon and the invaders were placing fire on the gun positions. "B" Company of the 23d, providing close-in support for the artillery, engaged the enemy troops attempting to knock-out the artillery while the guns continued to pour out heavy volumes of fire on enemy masses attempting to rush the entire perimeter.

"Award of the Distinguished Service Cross to Second Lieutenant Albert B. V. MacDonald, Artillery, a member of Battery C, 37th Field Artillery Battalion, for action against the enemy in the vicinity of Chipyong-ni on 1 February 1950. On 1 February 195 , an enemy force

estimated at one regiment launched at attack against the 3d Battalion, 23d Infantry Regiment, and succeeded in forcing a breach in the line defended by Company I. When the artillery forward observer with Company I was killed early in the attack, Lieutenant MacDONALD volunteered to join the company as forward observer. Realizing the importance of close in artillery fire, he moved to an exposed position with the left flank platoon on Hill 333 from which he could accurately adjust artillery fire on the advancing enemy. As the intensity of the fighting increased, Lieutenant MacDONALD refused to leave his observation post but continued directing artillery fire on the enemy troops until they approached within 25 yards of his position. When the platoon fell back to the base of the hill and reorganized for a bayonet charge on the enemy, Lieutenant MacDONALD joined the riflemen in the assault. Reaching his former position, he found that his telephone and radio had been destroyed by enemy fire, however, he effectively continued to direct orders orally, calling for artillery fire to within 25 yards of his position. When the enemy launched a counter-attack and again drove the platoon from the hill, Lieutenant MacDONALD joined the riflemen in a second bayonet charge that carried them to the crest of the hill. Five times the hill changed hands and each time Lieutenant MacDONALD would remain in position directing artillery fire orders until the close proximity of the enemy rendered artillery fire useless, then fall back and rejoin the platoon to help retake the hill in hand-to-hand combat. His courageous actions and tenacity during the bitter engagement were instrumental in the final success of the platoon in driving the numerically superior enemy from the hill and securing the position."

By 1800, the pressure began to ease and at 1830 the lead elements of the First Battalion arrived having had to fight their way with the assistance of the 2d Recon Co through two enemy road blocks to reach the position.

By 1900, the first company of the Second Battalion arrived in the perimeter with the reminder of the Second Battalion anticipated by 0200 hours. "B" Battery of the 37th Field Artillery arrived with elements of the Second Battalion, adding its fire to that of the rest of its battalion.

And while the perimeter in the "Tunnels" area was being reinforced amid lessening enemy pressure, a company-sized patrol from the Third Battalion of the 38th was heavily engaged with a battalion of enemy troops northwest of Wonju.

Supported by artillery and air, the patrol was able to count 63 enemy dead before withdrawing to its base.

The following day, 2 February, all units of the 23d RCT were closed in the "Tunnels" area and were consolidating their positions following an enemy withdrawal. Patrols fanned out on all sides to maintain enemy contact and flush him from hiding places. The regimental tanks forced one large group from a village and as the enemy broke for cover, air, artillery and tank fire rained down upon him, inflicting heavy casualties. Throughout the night artillery laid down a curtain of fire around the position.

The First and Third Battalions of the 38th, meanwhile, closed in on Hoengsong at 2330 hours to assume blocking positions in the face of the threat uncovered the previous day by elements of the Third Battalion.

On 3 February, the 23d RCT began moving west from the "Tunnels" area toward the town of Chipyong-ni, key to an important road network on the Division left flank. Resistance was slight and by 2000 hours the town was secured

with only sporadic enemy fire from the vicinity of Hill 586 overlooking the Chipyong sector. In setting-up a perimeter defense for Chipyong, the RCT commander, Col. Paul L. Freeman, decided to use a ring of low-lying hills surrounding the town. Better, more easily defensible hills

were available further out but would have required more forces than were available within his comand so he chose to dig-in on the less desirable hills where his units would not be so widely dispersed.

The circular clock-like defense, when established, situated the First Battalion on the perimeter from the 12:00 o'clock position to the 1:00 o'clock position. The Third Battalion was occupying the hills from 2:00 o'clock to 5:00 o'clock, the Second Battalion from 5:00 o'clock to 7:00 o'clock, and the French from 7:00 o'clock to 11:00 o clock.

In RCT reserve was "B" Company and, subsequently, the 1st Ranger Company, both placed within the perimeter behind "A" and "C" Companies. The high hills overlooking those occupied by the regiment were registered on by the RCT artillery, 37th FA Battalion and "B" Battery, 82d AAA. The mission of the force was to (1) deny to the enemy the use of the road net controlled by Chipyong and (2) hold the left flank of the X Corps defense line until the 3rd ROK Division, which was in Corps reserve, could be brought abreast and launched into an attack to the north. Extensive patrols were planned by the RCT while in the Chipyong area.

The occupation of Chipyong by the 23d RCT was part of an over-all plan by the Division to occupy a new X Corps defense line, "QQ", which had its left boundry at Chipyong and its right boundry running east through Hoanhung-ni. This placed the 24th US Division on the 2d Division's left flank and the 187th Airborne RCT on the right, this latter unit having relieved the 8th ROK Division.

The 9th RCT was on the right of the 23rd. Its First Battalion was in defensive positions at Yanghyon-ni; the Second Battalion was securing the pass on the MSR leading to Chipyong from the southeast; the Third Battalion was patrolling the Wonju-Yoju road.

The 38th RCT was concentrating in the vicinity of Hoengsong, preparing to support the 8th ROK Division. The 8th ROK Division, in conjunction with the 5th ROK Division, was to launch an offensive mission, "Operation Roundup," aimed at a double envelopment of enemy units in the Hongchong area. The 2d Division was to give air, artillery and armor support to the 8th ROK's. Preparing for this, the First Battalion of the 38th with "L" Company attached was given the mission of providing part of this support. The Second Battalion of the 38th served as Division reserve at Wonju while the Third Battalion (—"L") was to occupy blocking positions north and east of Hoengsong. The 72d Tank Battalion was moved to Wonju to serve with the Second Battalion as Division reserve.

In order to provide maximum support to the ROK units in the forthcoming attack, orders were published by the 2d Division on 4 February, setting up support units. They were organized as follows: Support Force 21—15th FA Bn; "A" Btry, 503d FA Bn; "D" Btry, 82d AA; and 1st Bn, 38th Inf to provide close-in support to the artillery. Support Force 22—"B" Btry, 503d FA Bn; "C" Btry, 37th FA Bn; one section from "C" Btry, 82d AAA; and a Company, 23d Infantry. Support Team A—"K" Company, 9th Infantry; 3d Platoon, 9th Infantry Tank Company; and elements of the Heavy Mortar Company of the 9th Infantry. Support Team B—"L" Company, 38th Infantry and 3d Platoon, 38th Infantry Tank Company. Both Support Team A and B were under the operational control of the commanding general, 8th ROK Division.

The days prior to "Operation Roundup" found all units of the Division sending out extensive patrols which encountered small enemy groups. Frequent probing attacks were repulsed by the Division, and daily there was increasing evidence of a possible communist thrust. Adverse weather hindered all activities during the period. Freezing nights and thawing days inundated the roads and open country with mud, snow and slush, making unit supply and patrols extremely difficult and forcing the line troops to undergo extreme hardships in the field.

"Operation Roundup" jumped-off on 5 February with the 2d Division Fire Support Coordination Center (FSCC) acting as coordinator for the intense air and artillery support rendered the ROK units by the Division. Coincident with the attack, the Netherland's detachment relieved the First Battalion of the 38th in positions north and east of Hoengsong so the battalion could assume its duties as a member of Support Force 21, moving northward to keep pace with the ROK atack.

"Operating Roundup" maintained an unsteady movement north on 6 February although poor weather somewhat hindered the air cover. By 1200 hours, Support Force B had arrived in Saemal, 15 miles north east of Wonju. The Third Battalion, 38th Inf also closed later in the day into Saemal and relieved a ROK regiment for further commitment in "Operation Roundup".

On 7 February, the First Battalion of the 9th Infantry and Third Battalion of the 23d launched an attack on the village of Sogu, five miles east of Chipyong to eliminate an enemy strongpoint there and to "energize" the attack of the ROK's. Determined enemy resistance supported by an unusually large number of automatic weapons prevented capture of the town but, after fierce fighting, the two battalions secured the high ground over-looking the town on 9 February and thus succeeded in localizing the threat. It was believed that the same force which had ambushed a company-sized patrol from "C" Company of the 9th on the previous day was the one which defended Sogu.

Support Force 21, built around the First Battalion of the 38th, closed in the vicinity of Chadong at 1100, continuing its mission of supporting the ROK attack. Meanwhile, the 1st Ranger Company successfully raided an enemy force in the village of Changmal, killing an estimated 50 enemy before withdrawing.

The following days were repeat performances of the initial days of "Operation Roundup" with slight gains made in the face of extremely poor weather, rugged terrain and moderate resistance. In Sogu, elements of the 9th and 23d RCT's were still unable to disperse the enemy in spite of repeated attacks.

Support Team Baker, on 9 February, engaged an estimated 200 enemy in the vicinity of Changmal for two hours. The same day, the 1st Ranger Company was attached to the 23rd RCT and placed in reserve within the force's Chipyong perimeter. The continuing poor weather hampered supply and in Wonju large airdrops were being made to keep up the Division ammunition stocks.

Also on 9 February, the 3rd ROK Division was attached to X Corps and began assembling northwest of Hoengsong.

An unusual incident occured in the Tank Company of the 38th Infantry on 9 February. One of the tank commanders serving with Support Force Baker reported overhearing Chinese radio messages on his tank radio and they seemed to be coming from not too great a distance.

The presence of Chinese troops in the vicinity was confirmed on the following day when, with clearing weather, air observers reported large numbers of enemy troops moving south into the X Corps sector. Forward of the 23rd positions in Chipyong, the Chinese appeared to be massing in strength. Agents, returning from enemy lines, reported pre-assault concentrations of thousands of enemy troops. Every new report served to reaffirm the rapidly accepted opinion that another major CCF offensive was in the making.

And in the Chipyong perimeter itself, the entire 23rd RCT prepared for the test it knew was soon to come. Ammunition was stock-piled, medical sections readied for an influx of casualties. Because of the threat posed to the 23rd, fire priority for the 37th FA Bn, formerly given to Support Force Baker, was shifted to the 23rd and immediately the rate of fire was stepped up to inflict maximum casualties on the massing enemy troops. Increased air support, possible with the improved weather, was called onto the communist buildup across the Division front and B-26's were used to strike the enemy concentrations, one of which included 1,200 horses.

On 11 February, Support Force 21, had moved forward to Changbong-ni, half-way between Hoengsong and Hongchon on the MSR. Support Team B was a little to the west and almost the same distance north of Hoengsong. Both were continuing to give fire support to the ROK attack.

During the early part of the day there was little enemy activity. However, in view of the threatened Chinese offensive, "Operation Roundup" was halted and the 8th ROK Division was ordered to hold its present positions. All 2d Division units were instructed to concentrate on short-range, combat patrols and prepare for a new Red attack.

James '51
38th INF.

WONJU II- CHIPYONG

TERRAIN SKETCH

The village of CHIPYONG-NI lies twenty miles northwest of WONJU. It is situated in an oval shaped valley three miles wide and six miles long. Gently sloping, the surrounding hills range in elevation from four hundred to one hundred meters in height. Absence of undergrowth and timber is very noticeable. This town is a crossroad town, since the road from YOJU enters it from the south, and the road from YANGPYONG enters from the west. Roads in the vicinity are secondary routes, twelve to eighteen feet wide, graded earth topped with gravel, capable of supporting military equipment with maintenance and proper caution. To the southeast, the railroad coming from WONJU has high embankments on which defenses might easily be formed. The enemy seized the dominating hills surrounding the town and cut all routes of supply and evacuation. Because of this, the defense perimeter was drawn tightly around the town using the gentle slopes which afforded the best fields of fire.

The opening moves of the massive Chinese February offensive against the X Corps front came during the afternoon of the 11th. Powerful enemy units launched a heavy frontal assault against the positions of the halted 8th ROK Division and, simultaneously, reports of a roadblock on the MSR leading to the 10th and 16th ROK Regiments were received at the 2d Division. By evening, the enemy attack had gathered additional strength and all ROK elements were under pressure.

In the Chipyong sector, held by the 23d RCT, plans for an attack on Hill 583, scheduled for 12 February, were cancelled in view of the threat posed by the newest CCF move. The 9th Infantry, which had just secured an important hill in the vicinity of Sogu, was alerted to be ready to move to Yoju on three hours notice.

Air observers reported the enemy channeling his main assault south to Hongchon where it split, one column taking the road toward Hoengsong and another shifting westward to the approach route to Chipyong.

The Third Battalion of the 38th which supplied the major forces of Support Teams "A" and "B" reported it was cut off from the 10th ROK Regiment at 0035 hours, 12 February, by a roadblock in the vicinity of Chowon-ni. Two hours later, word filtered back to the 2d Division that four CCF Divisions were participating in the attack on the ROK's and the 8,000 casualties had already been suffered by the disintegrating South Korean forces. This collapse placed Support Force 21 and the two Support Teams in an extremely critical position, extended far to the north with the ROK lines now non-existant and nothing between them and the onrushing enemy. Immediately, all the support forces were ordered to withdraw to a vital bridge at Haktam-ni, four miles north of Hoeng-song on the MSR, and hold there until all UN units to the north and west were clear. Twenty minutes after the order was flashed from Division, the two units began a fighting withdrawal.

The withdrawing elements from the 38th Infantry were under general attack by 0300 hours, receiving fire from the hills and rice paddies lining their withdrawal route. Enemy fire was knocking out the accompanying trucks causing high casualties among the drivers. Artillery pieces with their crews were halted time after time in spite of fierce efforts by the accompanying infantry to fight clear of the enveloping attackers. Meanwhile, the Netherlands Detachment in blocking positions at Hoengsong was ordered to prepare to pass the former support forces through its positions.

The Third Battalion of the 38th reached the Haktam-ni bridge by 0920 hours on 12 February but there was no let-up in the action. Lead elements of the First Battalion had also arrived and together the two forces did their best to repulse the enemy who now surrounded the area. Heavy and accurate mortar fire fell within the hasty perimeter the defenders had established, inflicting a high number of casualties.

"Award of the Distinguished Service Cross to Major Leonard Lowry, Infantry, Commanding Officer, Company C, 38th Infantry, for action against the enemy in the vicinity of Hoengsong on 12 February 1951. Company C had the mission of covering the withdrawal of a roadbound artillery battalion along a road paralleled by enemy infested hills and ridges. After ten consecutive hours of heavy fighting, during which Major LOWRY heroically led his men in knocking out several enemy roadblocks designed to trap the battalion, the column reached the regimental assembly area and joined the 3rd Battalion. As the two battalions began assembling and reorganizing, a strong enemy force occupying positions on a ridge adjacent to the assembly area placed a heavy barrage of mortar and automatic-weapons fire on the friendly troops, inflicting numerous casualties. Quickly organizing a group of men from his company, Major LOWRY personally led them in an assault on the nearest enemy held hill and succeeded in killing the enemy occupying it. Although seriously wounded during this engagement, he continued to lead his men in assaults on the other hills in the area until the entire ridge had been cleared of hostile forces."

Back at Division, plans were being made to attempt a rescue of the embattled elements of the 38th and at first light a relief force composed of a platoon of tanks from the 38th Tank Company and the regimental security platoon had departed from Hoengsong but immediately it was pounced upon by a force of 400 Chinese and pushed back.

The remaining elements of the First and Third Battalions fighting at Haktam-ni were combined into one unit at 0950 hours with every able-bodied man shouldering a weapon as the Chinese pushed wave after wave of frantic attacks against the force. To make the situation worse, additional roadblocks were being established between the defenders at the bridge and Hoengsong to the south.

Orders for the First Battalion and remaining elements of Support Force 21 to withdraw to Hoengsong were radioed by Division shortly before 1000 hours. The same message directed the Third Battalion to hold its position until further orders were received. It was not until 1145 hours that Support Force 21 began its attempt to withdraw. Air and artillery support pressed into action by Division helped to ease the agonizingly slow withdrawal for the entire route to Hoengsong was a cauldron of enemy fire. The Third Battalion still struggling to hold the bridge positions, reported its ammunition supply almost exhausted and having suffered crippling casualties. Attempts by liaison planes to drop ammunition met with failure as the desperately needed small arms and mortar ammo drifted outside the meager perimeter into the enemy positions. At 1515 hours, the Third Battalion was ordered to withdraw toward Hoengsong, joining with the First Battalion which had been unable to batter its way through the roadblocks on its escape attempt. With the foot troops leading and the few remaining vehicles following behind, the Third Battalion soon joined up with the First and together they ground their way amid barrages of mortar, small arms and automatic weapons fire which poured down on them from the hills overlooking the road.

Another relief force was organized in Hoengsong to go to the aid of the two battalions. "G" Company from the 187th A/B RCT and a platoon of tanks from "C" Company, 72d Tank Battalion, fought their way northward where they finally made a juncture with the remnants of the former support forces late in the afternoon and the combined units fought back into Hoengsong, held by the Dutch defenders. There, the 38th Infantry regimental comamnder, Col. J. C. Coughlin, ordered them to continue southward to Wonju although it was necessary for them to break another, though smaller, roadblock before they could reach safety.

The defenders of Hoengsong, Company "G" of the 17th Regiment, 7th Division and the Netherlands Detachment, were engaged soon after the shocked and depleated ranks of the support forces had disappeared southward. During this action, the commander of the Dutch forces, Lt. Col. Marinus P. A. DenOuden, was killed. A group of soldiers was observed coming down the MSR from the North by outposts on the Dutch perimeter who immediately placed fire on the approaching troops. "Okay, okay, we're ROK's, okay, we're ROK's." the troops called out. The Dutch, thinking the soldiers could be part of the many withdrawing ROK units, lifted their fire and the group walked into the perimeter. Immediately the infiltrating soldiers, who were all Chinese, opened fire on the

Dutch comamnd post. Before they could be killed, five Dutch officers including the Commanding Officer were killed, 14 men were wounded and 8 were later reported missing.

Orders to abandon Hoengsong were received early the night of the 12th and the Dutch with the company from the 7th Division fought a delaying action to the south.

West of the zone of fierce action of the 38th Infantry, the 23d RCT girded itself for the assault it knew was coming. The 12th of February was quiet except for a highly successful raid west of Chipyong by a two-company-sized patrols from the French Battalion which entered a small village, found it heavily-occupied and blew up several large ammunition dumps. Air observers confirmed the southward movement toward Chipyong of large masses of enemy troops. Unusually heavy flare activity was observed north of the perimeter the night of the 12th and 13th.

Brigadier General George C. Stewart, assistant division commander, had arived in Wonju late in the evening of 12 February to assume comand of the defense of the city. He called an immediate meeting of all local unit commanders. There was to be no withdrawal, no evacuation. Everyone would stay. A perimeter defense was to be organized and all available artillery was to be positioned so massed fires could be placed on any approach to the city. Liaison pilots were ordered to fly observation missions throughout the daylight hours to warn of approaching enemy troops or impending attack.

By midnight, the shattered remains of the First and Third Battalions of the 38th Regiment had arrived in Wonju from their harrowing battle in the north. Support Force 21 had suffered more than 1,400 casualties including the commanding officer, Lt. Col. John W. Keith, CO, 15th FA Bn, who was reported MIA. All forward observers who had been with the 8th ROK Division as members of the Support Force 21 were missing. And, in addition to terrific personnel losses, fourteen 105 mm Howitzers and five 155 mm Howitzers had been lost in the bitter fighting north of Hoengsong.

The Wonju defense line was established on the high ground around the city during the night and early morning with the strength placed to the north. The Dutch detachment, now returned from Hoengsong, held the left end of the northern portion of the line. On the right of the Dutch were the 2d Bn, 38th Inf; 1st and 3d Bns, 38th Inf; and the 187th A/B RCT. The 17th Regiment, 7th US

Division was placed on the south. The eastern flank was held by the 18th ROK Regiment, the western by the ROK Rangers. In reserve was the 2d Bn, 187th A/B RCT and the 72d Tank Battalion.

As an added precaution in face of the mounting threat by the overwhelming enemy force, the 38th Infantry was directed to reconstitute its regimental combat team by attaching the remains of the 15th FA Bn; "C" Battery, 38th FA Bn; 503d FA Bn (-B); "B" Company, 72d Tk Bn; and "D" Battery, 82d AAA.

Throughout the daylight hours of the 13th, the Wonju area was quiet as the defenders feverishly prepared their defenses.

Westward on the Chipyong sector, the 23rd RCT reported increased enemy activity taking place north, east and west of its perimeter. Southeast of Chipyong, a strong patrol composed of "L" Company, 9th Infantry and the 2d Reconnaissance Company reported itself engaged with 1,000 Chinese on the MSR leading to Chipyong.

Increased flare activity marked the late afternoon and evening around the 23rd's perimeter on 13 February. Small arms and mortar fire began to fall into the area between 2200 and 2300 from the northwest, north and southeast. Shortly before midnight an intense mortar and artillery barrage crashed into the northern sector of the perimeter held by the First Battalion and immediately after it lifted, the long expected attack materialized. Bugles, whistles, and yells sounded out over the cold, night air; dull red and green flares burst and hung in the sky and the arcs of tracers flashed and ricocheted through the dark. By midnight, the frenzied attacks had spread with only the Third Battalion on the southwest not engaged. Mortar and artillery rained in upon the regimental command post, the artillery positions and the sector where the heavy mortars were set-up. The command post of the First Battalion was set on fire by the flying tracers.

Shortly after midnight, the fighting eased but a fresh attack was launched from out of the north and northwest at 0100 hours. The rushing, yelling enemy was repulsed but as the firing died down, troops on the perimeter could hear the click of shovels as the Chinese dug-in to stay. The force of the attack was shifted at 0215 hours when the Chinese launched a bloody frontal assault from the southwest and east, particularly against "K" Company. The perimeter held strong so with continued pressure in the south the masses of Chinese hurled themselves at the French in the north in yet another effort to pierce the circle of defenders. As the waves

of attackers struck the French Battalion, intense pressure on "C" Company of the First Battalion forced a slight withdrawal but an immediate counter-attack regained the lost ground. The entire perimeter blazed with fire as the artillery poured round after round into the determined, frenzied attacking troops and the defenders slammed all the firepower they could muster into the hordes. By 0530 hours, the pressure had eased once again except in front of the French Battalion and 'K" Company, both of whom were repulsing attack after attack.

"C" Company was hit again at 0545 hours but against the attack was beaten off. An attempt by the attackers to infiltrate in the south was unsuccecssful.

At first light of 14 February, the garrison at Chipyong learned that "L" Company of the 9th and the 2d Recon Co. in the southeast were under a three-sided attack with elements of the same force attacking Chipyong. But as the news arrived so did a renewed attempt by the Chinese to slice their way into Chipyong through "K" and "I" Companies. The ring of steel held. Elsewhere, the battered assault troops of the five Chinese Divisions surorunding Chipyong made stabs at the perimeter then fell back under withering mortar, artillery and small arms fire. And with the coming of daylight came a break in the action. The Chinese, fearing the devastating effect of observed artillery fire and air strikes broke physical contact, withdrew and contented themselves with intermittent mortar fire into the besieged garrison.

"Award of the Distinguished Service Cross to Colonel Paul L. Freeman, Jr. Infantry, Commanding Officer, 23 Infantry Regiment, for action against the enemy in the vicinity of Chipyong ni during the period 31 January and 15 February 1951. On 31 January, Colonel FREEMAN was ordered to move his regimental combat team to the vicinity of the Twin Tunnels area south of Chipyong-ni and prevent the enemy from occupying the area. Colonel FREEMAN with two battalions entered the Twin Tunnels area, without effecting contact with the enemy, in the late afternoon of 31 January. Realizing that the enemy forces were not yet emplaced, he deployed his troops in a tight perimeter for the night. At 0450 hours on 1 February, the enemy struck, pressing the attack with such fury that the regimental lines were penetrated in two places. The fighting was intense and the issue hung in the balance throughout the day; however, under the skillful leadership and personal example of Colonel FREEMAN, the task force finally succeeded in routing the enemy

at bayonet point, shattering two regiments of the 125th Chinese Communist Division. When the hostile force had been dispersed, 2,855 enemy dead were counted in front of the regimental positions. Reorganizing the combat team, Colonel FREEMAN led his command forward and occupied positions surrounding the town of Chipyong-ni, a critical point in the United Nations defense line. On the night of 13 February, the enemy struck these positions with overwhelming fury, employing five divisions in the assault. For forty-eight hours the enemy pressed the attack, striking at all sides of the friendly perimeter and placing intense mortar and artillery fire on the positions. Skillfully directing the defense and personally exposing himself to the intense hostile fire to restore breaks in the line, Colonel FREEMAN so inspired his troops that they successfully routed the numerically superior hostile force and counted over 5,000 enemy casualties surrounding their positions at the conclusion of the engagement. Although wounded in the final phase of the engagement, he reorganized the combat team and deployed it in defense of the secured area."

U. N. fighting Frenchman.   Bob Janes '51 KOREA

And as the 23d RCT was engaged in repelling the swarms of Chinese around Chipyong, the defenders of Wonju were also coming under attack by the eastward spear of the Chinese two-pronged drive for victory.

The Second Battalion of the 38th Infantry came under heavy, frontal assault at 0345 hours on 14 February in positions on the high ground north of Wonju. Throwing a powerful spearhead into the ranks, some of the leading elements of the attacking force pushed into the positions of "L" and "K" Companies and the outpost of "I" Company came in when it was overwhelmed by the Chinese assault. Artillery was called in on the break-through for the enemy could be heard digging-in on the flanks between the 38th and 187th RCT's. "F" Company of the 187th went forward after bitter fighting and plugged the gap.

The Third Battalion of the 38th, that part of it which remained after the costly withdrawal the previous day, had been put in on the west flank of the northern line. At 0655 hours, the Second Battalion of the 38th was shifted to relieve the Third Battalion which went into reserve. Filling the spot left vacant by the Second Battalion went the remains of the First Battalion.

"Award of the Distinguished Service Cross to Private Bruno R. Orig, Infantry, a member of Company G, 23d Infantry Regiment, for action against the enemy in the vicinity of Chipyong-ni on 15 February 1951. On that day, Private ORIG, while returning from a wire laying mission, observed a number of his comrades who had been wounded in a fierce enemy attack that was still in progress. With complete disregard for his own safety, he went to the aid of these men and remained in an exposed position in order to administer first aid to them. With the assistance of several comrades from the company command post he began removing the wounded to a place of safety. While returning from one of these trips, he noticed that all except one man of a machine-gun crew had been wounded. Without hesitation, he volunteered to man the weapon. Remaining in this position, Private ORIG placed such effective fire on the enemy that a withdrawing friendly platoon was able to move back without a single casualty. He continued to inflict heavy casualties on the enemy until the company positions were overrun. Later that day, when the lost ground was recaptured, Private ORIG was found dead beside his weapon and the area in front of his gun was littered with enemy dead."

The Netherlands Detachment came under heavy attack at 0710 and was forced to withdraw slightly. Elements of the Second Battalion were drawn off the line and together with "B" Company of the 72d Tank Battalion moved into the threatened sector to strengthen it and to refuse the left flank to the enemy.

As daylight broke, the liaison pilots had their planes in the air to seek out the enemy. First reports were of two Chinese Divisions moving in column south along the Som River with the obvious intention of encircling the Wonju defenders. AOP's could see parts of the column peel off toward Wonju as it marched southward. Every available artillery piece in the 2d Division and supporting corps artillery was laid upon the marching mass of men. Thunderous barrages roared across the hills as tons of shrapnel poured into the plodding troops. Thousands of shells wrecked havoc never before seen on any army as the pilots reported the river running red with the blood of the massacred troops. Still they came, marching into the rain of death, heedless of the carnage around them they crawled forward. Hour after hour the unbelievable slaughter mounted as dog-tired, exhausted artillerymen slammed an endless stream of shells into the exposed masses of Chinese who continued to press forward. The staggering losess began to tell. The once-full ranks were now thin, blasted, shocked remnants without leaders, without hope. Slowly, as though dazed, the remains of the ranks broke. Now only unorganized bands of useless bodies, they tried to escape north out of reach of the murderous guns. The cracking rain of steel followed them northward and air took up where artillery could not reach. The attack was broken, the threat to Wonju was no longer critical. The "Wonju Shoot" had cost the enemy 5,000 men. Although bitter fighting was waged that night and throughout the following day, the enemy had shifted his main effort to Chipyong. His armies had failed at Wonju after unsucecssfully beating against the lines then dying in unprecedented slaughter under the guns of massed artilelry.

While thousands of Chinese were being bloodily repulsed along the Som River west of Wonju, the 23rd RCT was busy repairing the damage wrought by the frenzied attacks of the previous night. Twenty four air drops helped restock the ammunition, ration, medical and equipment supply dumps. Every available man helped in retrieving the air-dropped supplies. Regimental medics worked steadily to relieve the suffering of the wounded and helicopters shuttled in and out of the tight perimeter throughout the day, evacuating the most seriously wounded. Others were treated and made as safe and comfortable as possible to await the opportunity for evacuation when the road blocks ringing the garrison could be broken.

At 1200 hours, the 27th British Brigade, which had earned the respect of the men of the 2d Division for their heroic delaying action after the November Chinese breakthrough in the North, was attached to the Division with the sole mission of clearing the enemy from the MSR from Iho-ri to Chipyong. This drive by the British was to be made in conjunction with a similar relief drive by the 5th Cavalry Regiment along a parallel road from the South..

The 6th ROK Division was also attached to the 2d Division on the 14th and placed on line. Thus the Division front extended from the cut-off garrison of the 23d Infantry at Chipyong on the left, through the 27th BCB, 6th ROK Division, 9th RCT and the 38th RCT holding down the right flank at Wonju.

Reports of increased enemy activity were received by the 23rd RCT late in the afternoon of the 14th. Then at 2030 hours, the Chinese unleashed a mortar barrage on "K" Company and an hour later "C" Company was receiving fire and could hear the enemy digging-in in its positions. In spite of the air-dropped ammo, there was a critical shortage of 8-round clips of M-1 ammunition with the entire supply already in the hands of the companies. Shortly after darkness had blotted out all observation, the first enemy onslaught of the night fell on the Second Battalion sector. Simultaneously the regimental command post came under a blasting barrage of mortar, artillery and small arms fire which, in an hour, had spread to cover the positions of the mortar company and the trains of the French Battalion. The fighting on the perimeter mounted in intensity with both the Second and Third Battalions engaged in fierce, close combat as the enemy sought to drive a wedge into the perimeter which he could expand and thus enable him to divide the defending forces. Bugles signaled new and stronger attacks as 120 mm mortars showered on the CP area.

A slight let-up occured about midnight as the enemy regrouped for another attempt. The artillery continued to pour round after round onto the outlying area.

"K" Company was struck at 0130 hours but repulsed two assaults as the pressure again mounted in the south and southwest. Ammunition shortages threatened to become critical and a radio message for relief went through Division to Japan where the supply services of the Japan Logistical Comamnd loaded waiting planes throughout the night so air drops could be made at first light.

The first penetration of the perimeter was made at 0230 hours when savage blows by hordes of Chinese drove in to the positions of "I" Company. An immediate counter-attack by "I" and "L" Companies slashed forward and cut the penetration out, restoring the positions in bitter hand-to-hand battle. It seemed impossible that the perimeter could continue to withstand the mounting pressure by the vastly numerically superior foe.

At 0315 hours, "G" Company reported a second peneration and all efforts to stem it had failed. It was withdrawing with heavy casualties. The RCT commander, Lt. Col. John H. Chiles who had been flown into the perimeter to replace the badly wounded Col Paul Freeman, ordered a composite force assembled to counter attack. The 1st Ranger Company, a platoon from "F" Company and the remnants of "G" Company gathered to attack while in the north "A" and "C" Companies beat-off severe attacks. Less than 140 rounds of 4.2 mortar and less than 90 rounds of 81 mm mortar now remained. Orders went out to the embattled lines to conserve ammunition as much as possible. No target was to be fired upon unless definitely seen and in a position to be hit.

"Award of the Distinguished Service Cross to Corporal Charles W. Sherwood Infantry, a member of Comapny D, 23d Infantry Regiment, for action against the enemy in the vicinity of Chipyong from 13 to 15 February 1951. When his unit was attacked by a large enemy force during the night of 13 February, Corporal SHERWOOD, although wounded by enemy small-arms fire, remained in his position and inflicted heavy casualties until his machine gun was knocked out by hostile fire. The enemy closed to within 20 yards, but he coolly held them off with his pistol until another machine gun could be brought up. A second attempt was made to overrun his position, but Corporal SHERWOOD, heedless of intense hostile fire, accounted for 26 enemy dead before this weapon also was knocked out. On the night of 15 February, a reinforced enemy group made a final attempt to overrun the positions. Corporal SHERWOOD once more manned his gun and, despite intense hostile mortar, artillery, and small-arms fire, inflicted heavy casualties on the enemy until he was mortally wounded."

The composite counter-attack force struck at the enemy penetration at 0615 hours. Hand-to-hand fighting raged fiercely as the Chinese attemped to hold their gains. The counter-attack force suffered mounting casualties and each attempt to move forward was repulsed. "B" Company, the only remaining reserve, was ordered to join in the attack against the petration at 0800

and, simultaneously, "B" Company of the 2d Engineers was notified it now constituted the reserve and to be ready for immediate commitment.

To the south, the 5th Cavalry relief force spearheaded by heavy tanks was fighting slowly forward against fanatical resistance in an attempt to reach the seriously threatened garrison in time.

The counter-attack effort of "B" Company was repulsed during the morning and the friendly elements were pinned down under murderous fire. The situation was desperate. At 1230, the relief column was 9,000 yards southwest of its goal but progress was slow against the fire from every side.

At 1400, with "B" Company still pinned down, the TACP called air strikes onto the enemy entrenched in the gap in the perimeter. Napalm splashed and seared over the grimly holding enemy troops. It was too much. Burned and screaming they withdrew and "B" Company rose up, firing into the retreating forces, then advancing and regaining the lost positions.

Amid the frantic battle, planeload after planeload of ammunition was dropped to the garrison which was holding on by its fingernails. Enemy mortar, falling into the drop zone, inflicted heavy casualties as the troops exposed themselves to regain the precious ammunition and supplies. Counter-battery fire from the RCT artillery and mortar units finally silenced the pounding enemy mortars and the collection of the airdrop continued without letup.

"B" Company had secured the lost positions by 1630 hours and jubilantly reported it could see the head of the tank column pushing forward to the relief of the perimeter. The enemy was abandoning his attack and fleeing in face of the steel bararge from the clanking armor column. With reinforcement in sight, the artillery of the garrison poured out its lethal rain on the exposed and fleeing enemy, inflicting tremendous casualties.

Ammunition stocks were practically depleted by 1700 hours and the regimental commander ordered all units to cease fire. Although the enemy attack had been broken there were new reports of large enemy troop movements from the north and northwest.

Twenty heavy tanks and a handful of infantrymen from the 5th Cavalry Regiment rolled into the perimeter at 1715. The victorious but exhausted defenders realized the immediate crisis had passed. A blessed relief from combat and a strange quiet descended on the area. It was time to take stock of the situation

and prepare to meet whatever the future held.

The planes of the Air Force ranged, to the north, wrecking additional slaughter on the enemy who could find no cover. More than 131 sorties had been flown in the Chipyong area throughout the seige.

Night came onto the perimeter as all units adjusted their lines and began the vigilant guard. Night airdrops provided critically needed ammunition. Flares broke the darkness but there was no attack. The whipped, torn ranks of the Chinese Armies dragged northward, tossing mortar and artillery toward Chipyong behind them.

The entire front was quiet. The 2d Division had again stood in the face of all that the armies of China could muster. Despite overwelming odds and sickening casualties it had held fast. The enemy had been broken.

The reinforced garrison at Chipyong dispatched limited patrols the morning of 16 February to contact the retreating enemy forces and determine his intentions. Only one contact was made, this by "C" Company which ran into fire from self-propelled artillery. Back within the perimeter, a few rounds of artillery had fallen. Otherwise the forces undertook the task of reorganization. The supply elements of the 5th Cavalry Regiment arrived at Chipyong late in the afternoon after an uneventful trip from the south. Immediately the vehicles were off-loaded and the wounded of the 23d RCT who had waited for transport were placed on the vehicles and started for Yoju where they were later placed in medical channels.

By midnight, foot elements of the Cavalry were within 3,000 yards of Chipyong, sweeping the high ground on either side of the road without contact.

Patrols radiated from the Chipyong perimeter in all directions on the 17th, all making moderate enemy contact, but returning safely. At noon, the 23d RCT was attached to IX Corps until full relief could be effected by the elements of the 1st Cavalry Division. Coincident with the attachment, both the 27th British Brigade and the 6th ROK Division were relieved from the 2d Division and the Division front was greatly narorwed, removing Chipyong from its area of responsibility.

The 9th Infantry initiated patrolling action on the 17th forward of the new Division front in conjunction with elements of the 38th RCT on the left and the 187th A/B RCT on the right.

The 23rd was released from IX Corps on 18 February and moved to Wonju while the other elements of the Division conducted patrols, reorganized, resupplied and tied up loose ends after the hectic days of combat.

The Division front was extended eastward on 19 February in preparation for a new operation designed to clear an estimated 67,000 communist troops from the mountain area east of Wonju and north of Chechon. The initial stages of "Operation Killer," as the new undertaking was known, called for the 1st Marine Division to pass through the 2d Division after which the Division (-38th Infantry) would move eastward and assemble in the vicinity of Sillimni-Chupori-Chechon. The 38th Infantry would assemble at Chechon as X Corps reserve.

Operation Order 24 was published on 20 February. The 9th Infantry with the 38th FA Bn; "C" Battery, 503d; and "C" Battery, 82d AAA, was to go to Sillimni and be prepared to attack north on order; the 23d Infantry with 37th FA Bn and "B" Battery, 82d AAA was directed to assemble at Nodong, moving by way of Chupori and Chechon and prepare to attack north on order. The French were designated as Division reserve and were to occupy Chechon together with the corps reserve, the 38th Infantry.

The moves and preparations called for in Operation Order 24 were completed by 1630 hours on 21 February.

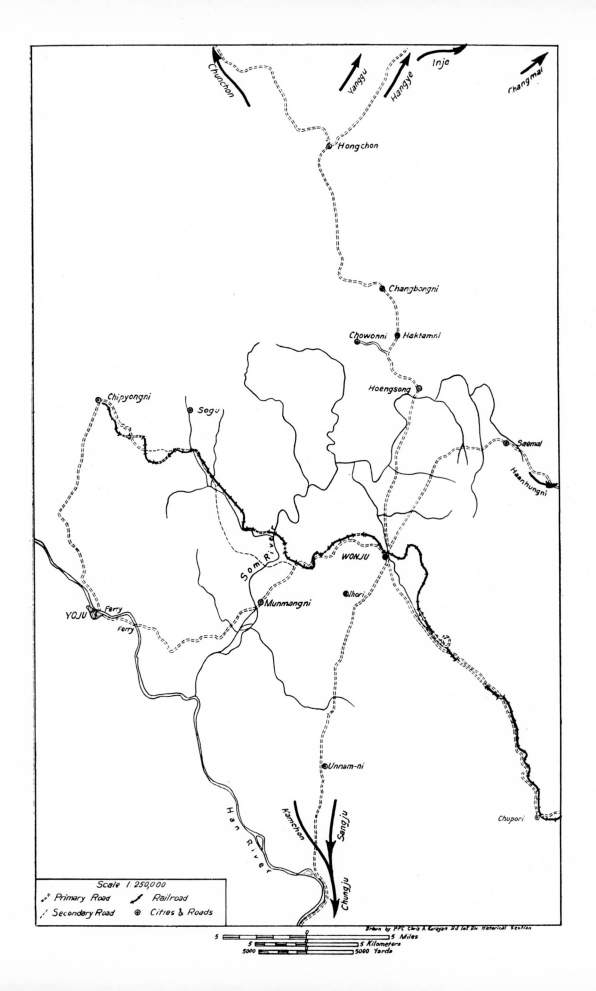

Chunchon

Yanggu   Hangye   Inje

Changmal

Hongchon

Changbongni

Chowonni   Haktamni

Hoengsong

Chipyongni   Sogu   Saemal

Haanhungni

Som River

WONJU

Munmangni   Ilhori

YOJU   Ferry

Ferry

Unnam-ni

Chupori

Han River

Kamchon   Sangju

Scale 1:250,000
Primary Road   Railroad
Secondary Road   Cities & Roads

Chungju

Drawn by PFC Chris A. Karayan 2d Inf Div. Historical Section

5   0   5 Miles
5   5 Kilometers
5000   5000 Yards

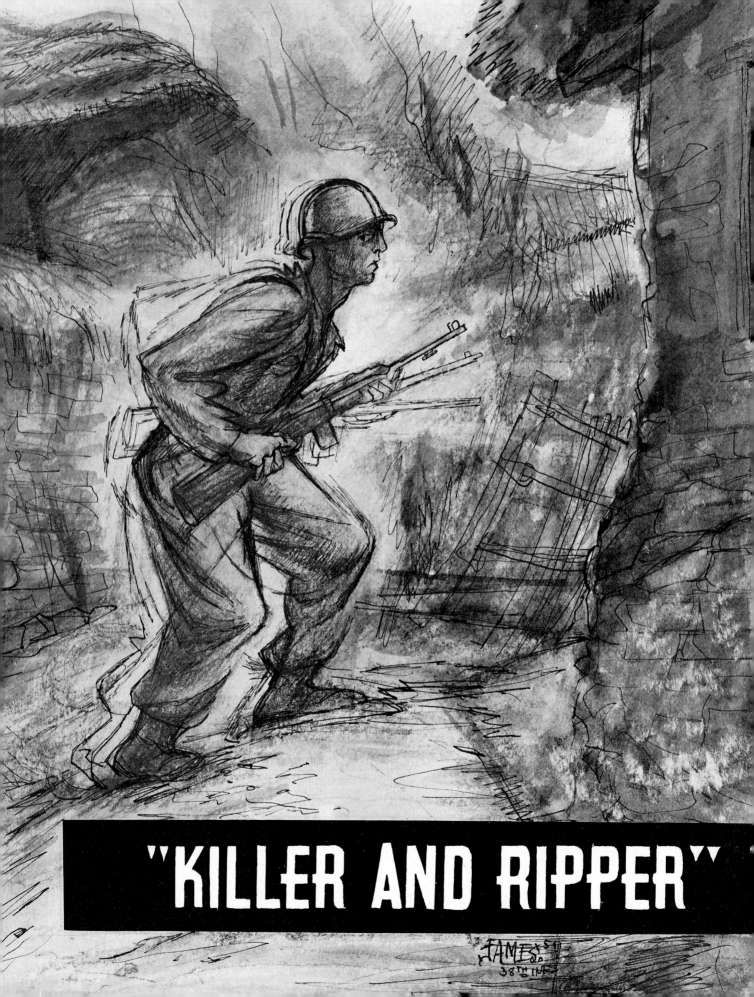

"KILLER AND RIPPER"

TERRAIN SKETCH

The area in which the operation was carried on is similar to a stone spearhead. Its point lies west of SAEMAL and the base along the SILLIM-NI east-west road. Very rocky, narrow, sharp ridgelines and spurs jutting east and west are characteristic of this sector. The area is nearly devoid of a road network. It is bounded on the north by the HAANHUNG-NI east-west road, and on the south by the SILLIM-NI east-west road. These roads are typical Korean roads, narrow, graded soil, and surfaced with gravel. All were weathered and eroded. The terrain ranged in elevation from five hundred to one thousand two hundred eighty eight meters and was characterized by several corridors running north and south between the two roads. The attack north to HAANHUNG-NI was conducted up these narrow, precipitous, ice filled streams and ravines. Undergrowth, trees, and snow gave excellent cover to the enemy positions. Supply problems were increased due to ice and hard packed snow. Track vehicles and human pack trains were the only means of supply and evacuation.

The Korean War entered a new phase with the launching of Operation Killer. The enemy had been decisively defeated by the 2d Division in his attempt to drive through the center of the United Nations line. A staggering number of casualties had been inflicted on his armies. But even with the defeat, large numbers of enemy troops still held strong positions deep in the east central mountains of Korea, some penetrating to within seven miles of the important rail terminal at Chechon. Strong elements of the 10th North Korean Division were operating as guerrilla bands as far south as Andong, posing a serious threat to the east flank of X Corps and Eighth Army.

"Operation Killer" envisaged a double envelopment of the enemy units in the Central front. The 1st Marine Division was to advance along the Wonju-Hongchon axis. The 7th Infantry Division, advancing north and west, was to link up with the 1st Marines along the Hongchon-Ogumal axis. The 2d Infantry Division together with the 3d ROK Division, in the center, was to advance north through rough, mountainous terrain between the major routes of withdrawal, exerting continuous pressure on the enemy and preventing an orderly withdrawal. The ultimate objective of the operation was the destruction of the greatest number of enemy at the smallest possible cost in men and equipment.

The sector assigned to the 2d Division presented enormous problems. The terrain was studded with mountains; it contained no reliable supply route and the few trails which did exist had been reduced to muddy quagmires by recent rains and thaw. Mud a foot deep in many places completely stopped vehicular movement. Bridges washed-out and rushing streams made crossings difficult. The cold, wet weather made any travel a miserable, sliding, slogging experience. The services were forced to wrestle with new problems created by a total lack of adequate routes of supply. Air drops were difficult and, at times, impossible to arrange.

The 2d Division jumped-off on "Operation Killer" on 22 February. The initial advance was slow, not so much due to resistance as to terrain. However, by 1700 hours both the 9th and 38th had reached the Chuchon River where swift waters and a lack of bridges delayed crossing. The engineers constructed a foot bridge for immediate use of the 9th and, in the 23d zone of advance, tanks of the regimental tank company were used to ferry people to the north bank.

Both units buttoned up for the night and prepared to continue forward in the morning.

The 9th Infantry ran into moderate resistance on 23 February but with all three battalions teaming up, an enemy force of 2,000 was routed, dispersed to the north, leaving their dead and wounded behind. The 23rd continued to slog out limited gains in the east. Back at Chechon the 38th Infantry, with the exception of "I" Company which was guarding supply trains from the south, was well into an intensive training program that was to continue for the rest of the month.

The Division became increasingly concerned with the almost insurmountable logistical problems which hampered its activities. The combined factors of weather, terrain and lack of supply routes finally prompted a request to X Corps for relief. The appeal asked for (1) Native bearers to establish a carrier supply network, (2) sufficient air drops to keep forward elements supplied, or (3) a halt in the advance of the Division until the necessary road network could be built. Corps replied that air drops could not be arranged but that bearers would be provided. In any case the attack was to continue.

Lengthy advances were recorded on 24 February although the 9th again encountered moderate resistance as did the 23rd. Liaison planes were used to supply the regiments deep in the rugged mountains, and the 3d Bn of the 23d detached a company to move to the rear and pack rations forward.

An enemy radio message intercepted by the First Battalion, 23d Infantry at 1400 hours on 25 February indicated the communist troops were critically short of ammunition and were planning to withdraw northward. The Division immediately set about to take advantage of the situation with both the 9th and 23rd moving out to set up blocking positions. Purpose of the moves was to deny the use of the east-west Hoengsong-Pangnimni road to the enemy.

The Second Batalion of the 23d, with the 37th FA Bn attached, moved east into the 7th Division zone on 26 February in preparation for an attack on the following day on Ungyo-ri, an important town on the Hoengsong-Pangnimni road. The 9th Infantry, after securing Haanhung-ni, west of Ungyo-ri, sent a battalion eastward along the road in anticipation of an enemy withdrawal from Ungyo-ri when the Second Battalion of the 23d launched its assault.

The 9th held its positions on 27 February; the First Battalion of the 23d established additional blocking positions around Ungyo-ri, and the Second Battalion of the 23rd jumped-off on its attack from the east and immediately tangled with an estimated enemy company dug-in around the objective. The fight continued throughout the day with all units buttoning-up for the night.

The First Battalion of the 23rd attacked Ungyo-ri early on the 28th of February and managed to secure the town although "A" Company was temporarily pinned down under intense fire. Air strikes and artillery were placed on the enemy positions and "A" was able to pull out of danger.

The evening of this last day of February found the 2d Division in positions astride the Hoengsong-Pangnimni road in its sector and preparing to continue its advance to Phase Line Arizona which paralleled the road roughly 7,000 meters to the north. Ahead of the Division were strong elements of the 197th and 198th CCF Divisions and lesser elements of the III and V North Korean Corps which were retreating slowly to the north in the face of the grinding X Corps offensive. Intelligence reports indicated the foe intended to delay the advance as much as possible while he prepared fixed defenses north of the 38th parallel.

The Division pressed forward the first days of March in an attempt to secure all the Arizona line. It was slow, rugged fighting, one ridge at a time.

"Award of the Distinguished Service Cross to Master Sergeant James J. Jovenall, Infantry, a member of Company G, 9th Infantry Regiment, for action against the enemy in the vicinity of Yongnangi on 4 March 1951. On that date, Company G was given the mission of assaulting a commanding terrain feature held by a well entrenched and determined hostile force. Three attempts were made to secure the objective, but each time the heavy volume of enemy fire forced the friendly forces to withdraw. In the fourth assault, Sergeant JOVENALL led his machine-gun squad across the fire-swept terrain and emplaced his weapons in an exposed position in order to bring effective fire to bear on the enemy forces. Despite the intense and accurate fire concentrated on him by the enemy, Sergeant JOVENALL fearlessly directed fire on the hostile emplacements. During this action, an enemy grenade landed near one of the machine-gun emplacements. Without hesitation, Sergeant JOVENALL hurled himself across the gunner and assistant gunner to protect them from shrapnel. Although painfully wounded, Sergeant JOVENALL refused medical treatment until the hill was secured."

Meanwhile, a new offensive was being planned, "Operation Ripper," designed to carry UN forces to the 38th Parallel. Similar to "Operation Killer," it aimed at maximum destruction of enemy personnel and equipment with minimum friendly casualties. To establish the units in the X Corps in the most advantageous positions for the coming operation, a shift in sectors was ordered by Corps. An operations order, implementing the shift, sent the 38th Infantry into Corps reserve and called for the rest of the Division to move to the west and assume responsibility for the 3rd ROK Division sector. The positions vacated by the 2d Division would be filled by the 5th ROK Division.

After several delays, the shift was completed on 6 March although the Second Battalion of the 23rd RCT was temporarily attached to the 7th Division until it could secure the Arizona line in its sector.

The westward movement of the Division front necessitated a change in the location of the Division Command post so on 5 March it displaced to Tudok which, although outside the Division zone, was the only suitable location for maximum control and communications. The left flank was hinged in the vicinity of Hyonchon-ni. All units prepared to jump-off on "Ripper" with the first objective being the town of Yudong-ni.

The days which followed were to be some of the most grueling the Division would face in Korea. It wasn't the character of the opposition so much, although at times throughout the month it was fanatic and as strong as any ever faced. It was the terrain, coupled with alternate spring thaws, rains and days of sub-zero freezes which hampered every activity and wrought unprecedented burdens on every unit and operation. The Division commander characterized it as some of the most easily defensible terrain in Korea, ideally suited to the enemy delaying tactics. Its acquisition, he commented, was undoubtedly one of the secondary aims of the January-February offensives on the Chinese forces.

"Operation Ripper" got under way for the 2d Division on 7 March from its positions on the Arizona line. Ahead of it lay other lines which, during the course of the month, would become bywords to everyone in the Indianhead Division. Familiar names, they were, too. Names like Pheonix, Albany, Reno, Idaho, Texas and Maine. Names that rang of home but in the rugged mountains of Korea represented only "one damn hill after another."

Initial resistance to "Ripper" varied from light to heavy. Abreast, the 9th and 23rd RCT's ground forward, the 9th concentrating on the trail to Yudong-ni while the 23rd assaulted an important hill mass about a mile west of Sanggung-ni. Stress was placed on lateral liaison with defense in depth. The narrow Division front made possible the massing of artillery fires and this advantage was called upon time and again to pound delaying groups of enemy.

"Award of the Distinguished Service Cross to Sergeant Houston D. Snowden, Army Medical Service, a member of Medical Company, 9th Infantry Regiment, for action against the enemy in the vicinity of Chigu-ri on 7 March 1951. On 7 March 1951, Sergeant SNOWDEN, a medical aidman, was attached to a rifle company which was advancing over mountainous terrain in an attempt to contact the enemy. As the company was making its way over the mountains, an enemy mortar barrage pinned down the leading platoon, inflicting heavy casualties. Without hesitation, Sergeant SNOWDEN made his way through the intense fire to reach his wounded comrades. While administering first aid, he was painfully wounded by mortar fragments but continued to treat the wounded. When the enemy barrage lifted, Sergeant SNOWDEN observed three wounded riflemen whom he had not noticed before and was moving forward to assist them when the concealed enemy opened fire on him with small arms and automatic weapons. Heedless of the hostile fire, he continued on to the wounded men and was administering aid when the enemy again delivered a barrage of mortar fire on the friendly positions. Shouting a warning to other members of the platoon, Sergeant SNOWDEN flung his body over the man he was bandaging. As he was shielding his wounded comrade an enemy mortar burst nearby and he was wounded for the second time. Although bleeding profusely, he continued to administer to the wounded. When he had ascertained that all of his wounded comrades had been properly cared for and safely evacuated, he proceeded to the aid station where his own wounds were treated. Then, although weakened from loss of blood, Sergeant SNOWDEN returned to the company and continued on the mission."

The 2d Reconnaissance Company screened the left flank of the 23rd to guard against bypassed and infiltrating enemy groups. "B" Company of the 72d Tank Battalion lent the weight of its guns to those of the 23d Tank Company in support of the 23d RCT's dogged attack. The 10th of March saw more climbing, digging the enemy out of one hill only to find him entrenched on the next, the North Korean troops holding on till the last minute and then falling back to more prepared positions.

The 38th Infantry returned to Division con-

trol on 10 March and sent its first battalion forward to reconnoiter the area of the 23rd Infantry.

A slight break in resistance occurred on the 11th when the enemy fell back more rapidly than previously, heading for Yudong-ni. Both the assaulting regiments pursued closely, taking advantage of every opportunity while the 23rd made plans to send an armor-infantry patrol into Yudong-ni itself.

And amidst the scrapping which characterized the action on 11 March came grand and welcome word—the Army was going to begin a rotation program. The news spread like a prairie fire throughout the Division. The Marines and Navy had already announced their own rotation plans and now the word was out that the Army, too, was planning ahead. It was destined to be a long time before sizeable groups were to leave but the mere announcement sent morale soaring.

Enemy mines became more and more a problem in the following days as mine casualties mounted rapidly. Booby-traps, too, hindered efforts to move forward and nature, itself, seemed to join with the enemy in dreaming up road-wrecking weather which confronted the engineers with almost insurmountable problems in keeping even the very vital supply routes open.

The 38th Infantry moved forward on 12 March in preparation to relieve the 23rd RCT. The units attached to the 23rd—37th FA Bn; "B" Battery, 82d AAA; "B" Company, 2d Engrs; and "B" Company, 72d Tk Bn—were notified they would revert to the 38th Infantry when it assumed responsibility for the 23rd's sector.

Relief of the 23rd took place on 13 March and the regiment moved back to set up blocking positions in the vicinity of Saemal. The 38th moved forward through Yudong-ni and halted on the Albany line prepared to move out to its next objective, the Reno line. The order directing the advance was published on the 13th and at 0800 hours on the 14th the troops moved out. meanwhile, heavy traffic on the trails leading to the 9th and 38th sectors turned them to ribbons of mud in which lay undiscovered mines which plagued vehicular movement. Engineers worked around the clock with all uncommitted line units furnishing additional labor in an attempt to keep traffic rolling.

The drive to the Reno line was completed against only moderate resistance by 14 March and plans for moving to the Idaho line were made. To bolster the 9th RCT, "C" Company of the 72d Tank Battalion was attached while "A" Company replaced "B" Company of the 72d in the 38th sector.

The push to the Idaho Line involved traversing a rugged, well defended pass on the Yudong-ni-Pungam-ni Road. Inteligence reports indicated the enemy would make a strong stand before falling back from the critical terrain feature for it was the last natural barrier to Pungnam-ni and once it fell the way would be open for unrestricted advance.

The Third Battalion of the 38th was to lead off in the attack up the pass with the Second Battalion following, sweeping laterally beyond the immediate ridges overlooking the rutted trail which served as the road through the pass. For the operation, the Third Battalion received as additional attachments "C" Company of the 2d Engineers and a psychological warfare team.

The attack to the Idaho line jumped off at 0730 hours with "L" Company on the immediate left and "K" on the immediate right of the road. The advance began easily but at 0815 the lead elements came under small arms fire. As the morning dragged on, the volume of fire increased and added to it was heavy and accurate mortar fire. The tank column, moving up the road, was delayed by mines and the engineer mine-sweepers, attempting to clear the road were forced back again and again as well entrenched snipers inflicted heavy casualties. Up on the hill, the elements of the Third Battalion faced a storm of fire from the well-entrenched enemy who seemed determined to hold the pass. Hill 570, a key terrain feature to the pass, was laced with concealed bunkers from which the enemy had unrestricted observation and fields of fire. Artillery and air were called in and "E" Com-

pany moved up behind the walking artillery barrage to join "L" Company in its assault on 570. "F" Company to the right of "K" on the east side of the road, moved forward to take another key hill, 719. "K" in the meantime, was digging the enemy out with bayonets, moving doggedly forward from bunker to bunker.

The terrain on the right of the road was secured, finally, but on the left where "F" and "L" battered against the enemy there was only difficult and slow progress. To assist, the 37th and

38th FA Bns laid down volley after volley of mixed HE, WP and VT artillery onto the hills. Nevertheless, the effort failed and all units adjusted their positions and buttoned up for the night.

A new attack plan was drawn up during the night and passed down to the units. The Second Battalion would assault with all its units down the left of the road and the Third Battalion would take the right. At 0730, the attack was launched, both battalions moving forward. The expected resistance had melted away during the night, only small forces clung to the positions and by mid-morning the pass was secure. The 9th Infantry, moving up behind because the narrow Division front was suitable for only regimental occupation, prepared to secure the recently won ground. The 38th assembled and moved forward, following up the advantage. "K" Company mounted the tanks of the RCT and together they rolled forward into Pungam-ni where, after receiving a few scattered long-range rounds, they secured the town and set up a perimeter for the night.

The Division consolidated its positions on 17 March while intelligence officers reported the continuing evidence of withdrawal of CCF and NK units to defense line north of the 38th parallel.

Sixteen Americans who had been Chinese prisoners were recovered by a patrol from "G" Company, 38th Infantry on 17 March. Four, who were seriously wounded, were evacuated by helicopter. The remaining were interrogated by intelligence officers before evacuation. All had been captured during the CCF advance on Hoengsong the previous month and were part of a group of 800 prisoners who were being marched northward. During a daytime stopover in a small village a bombing atack wounded several of the men including the 16 found by "G" Company and they were told they would be left behind. Letters furnished them by their captors directed other CCF and NK units not to molest them in any way. The letters proved effective for in the following days, several enemy groups questioned them but after reading the letters left them alone. The men remained in the house until found by the "G" Company patrol.

After securing the Idaho Line positions, the Division innaugurated extensive patrols to maintain contact with the withdrawing enemy.

The 9th RCT sent patrols to the Texas line for several days and then jumped-off to occupy defensive positions on the line the morning of 20 March. Light resistance was encountered and by evening the line was secure in the hands of the 9th.

Colonel Thomas E. DeShazo, former artillery officer for IX Corps, was assigned to the 2d Division on 20 March, replacing Brigadier General Loyal M. Haynes who received a new assignment in Japan. General Haynes had served the Division as artillery commander since its arrival in Korea.

The remainder of March saw the Division increase its patrol activities to the maximum, moving forward to occupy the Maine and finally the Cairo line paralleling a lateral road which intersected the Hongchon-Yanggu road at its midpoint. By far the most significant events of the closing days of March were the extreme efforts required to keep the Division supplied over the areas of mud which served as supply routes. Every conceivable type of transport was pressed into service. Stringent traffic regulations under the assistant division commander's personal supervision were further tightened as the Division barely surmounted the most terrific logistical problem it had encountered since arrival in Korea.

The Division comand post, which had been following the advance of the line units during the month, displaced to Salleyon on 27 March. The 38th Infantry, on the Cairo line, continued to send patrols out while the other units trained, patrolled and repaired roads. "Operation Ripper" came to a close on 28 March with the Division 30 miles north of the initial jump-off line. It was a battle-wise, victorious Division which had wrecked the remaining elements of the North Korean Divisions screening the withdrawal of the CCF. For the first time since its arrival in Korea, it was nearing authorized strength. Confidently it prepared for whatever the future might hold

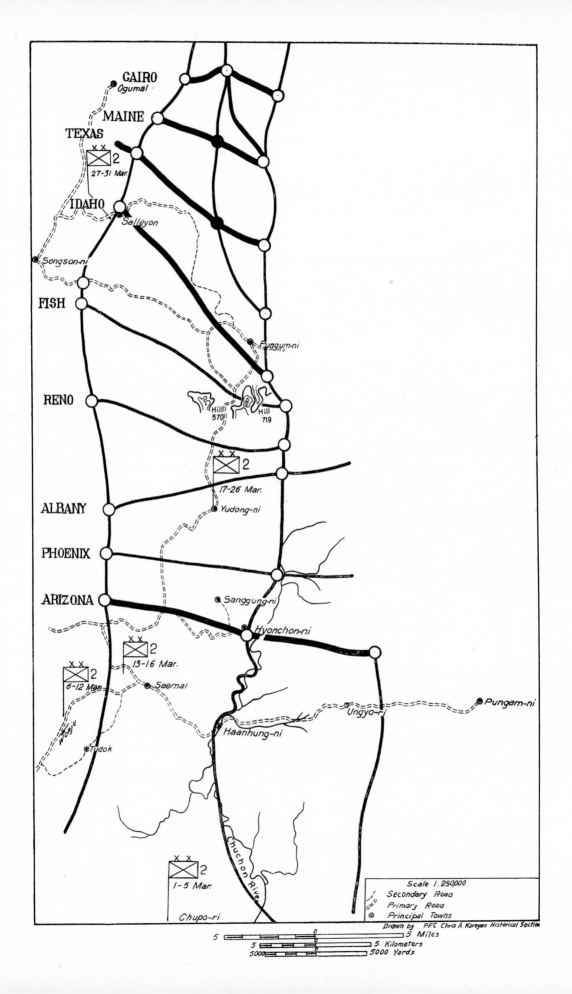

CAIRO
Ogumal
MAINE
TEXAS
XX 2
27-31 Mar.
IDAHO
Salleyon
Songson-ni
FISH
Pungum-ni
RENO
Hill 570
Hill 719
XX 2
17-26 Mar.
ALBANY
Yudong-ni
PHOENIX
ARIZONA
Sanggung-ni
Hyonchon-ni
XX 2
13-16 Mar.
XX 2
6-12 Mar.
Saemal
Wonju
Tudok
Haanhung-ni
Ungyo-ri
Pungam-ni
XX 2
1-5 Mar.
Chuchon River
Chupo-ri

Drawn by P.F.C. Chris A. Karayan Historical Section

Scale 1:250000
Secondary Road
Primary Road
Principal Towns

5   0   5 Miles
5   0   5 Kilometers
5000   0   5000 Yards

APRIL PRELIMINARY

The Eighth Army entered a new phase of the Korean campaign in April as it prepared to launch another northward drive to phase line Kansas with the goal of keeping the communists off-balance and preventing a successful build-up for another attack to the south. The 2d Division, fresh and experienced, laid plans for "Operation Rugged," which would, when completed, place its forces on the Kansas Line overlooking the waters of the Hwachon Reservoir.

On 1 April, the 23rd Infantry assembled in the vicinity of Hongchon, prior to relieving the 5th Marine Regiment. The 9th Infantry gathered its battalions near Sabangga-ri while the 38th patroled from the Cairo Line.

No enemy contact was reported on 2 April. However, from all along the front came reports of increasing vehicular traffic in North Korea. On 3 April, the Division FSCC reported a record number of sightings, while in Tokyo, General MacArthur revealed that 63 CCF Divisions were staging for a new attack.

The 23rd RCT, which had been reconstituted the previous day, moved northeast of Chunchon on 3 April. The First and Third Battalion took up positions on the north bank of the Soyang River while the Second and French Battalion remained on the south bank. "C" Company of the 2d Engineers, a part of the RCT, worked around the clock to improve the ford across the river and construct a bridge over which supplies could roll to support the planned attack.

The 9th Infantry went into Corps reserve on 4 April. The 38th prepared for its own relief by the 5th ROK Division. At the same time, the 23rd, having relieved the 5th Marine Regiment, struck out against the enemy defensive screen in its sector to secure jump-off positions for "Operation Rugged." Assisting the 23rd Infantry were "B" Company, 72d Tank Bn; "B" Battery, 82d AAA; and "C" Company, 2d Engineers. Moderate resistance was encountered but with the Second, Third and French Battalions attacking, the desired jump-off positions were secured on 5 April.

"A" Company, 2d Engineers, was attached to the 23rd RCT on 5 April to assist in engineering support and Division Artillery assigned the 15th, 37th, and 503d FA Bns to support the new offensive. At 2130 hours, X Corps ordered the attack to get underway the following day. After a night during which several enemy probing efforts were repulsed, the 23rd RCT moved out in its northward push at first light on 6 April.

The going wasn't too stiff the first day with the French securing Hill 785 by nightfall and the other battalions achieving their own first day objectives. Artillery and other supporting fires were utilized to the utmost as all efforts were made to inflict maximum enemy casualties at the least risk of friendly casualties. To the rear, the 38th RCT was reconstituted and together with the Ivanhoe Security Force launched patrols between the Cairo line and the Soyang River.

Increased enemy mortar and artillery fire harrassed the advancing 23rd as the attack ground forward the next day. Mines also hampered the advance and several tanks were disabled as they rolled up the road, keeping pace with the infantry. Hill 1039, dominating terrain feature between the 23rd and the reservoir was found to be bitterly defended by the enemy. The friendly forces fell back and, on order of the Division Comander, the supporting artillery plastered the hill and all the approaches to it. The infantry then moved forward and took the height with surprising ease.

"Award of the Distinguished Service Cross to Private Milton L. Cagle, Infantry, a member of Company G, 23d Infantry Regiment, for action against the enemy in the vicinity of Togol on 8 April 1951. On 8 April 1951, Private CAGLE's unit was assigned the mission of attacking a well entrenched and determined enemy force. As the men advanced, they were suddenly pinned-down by intense and accurate automatic-weapons fire from a comouflaged enemy emplacement. Realizing that his comrades were in danger of annihilation, Private CAGLE, despite the heavy volume of fire being directed at him, moved forward. Mortally wounded by the point-blank fire, he nevertheless crawled close enough to the enemy position to silence the weapon with grenades. The heroic action of Private CAGLE so inspired his comrades that they overrun the enemy positions and secured their objective.

Meanwhile, the Dutch Battalion, which had been guarding the railhead at Chechon, was released and began its journey northward to rejoin its parent unit, the 38th Infantry. Other unit shifts took place on 7 April as "A" Company of the 72d Tank Battalion was attached to IX Corps.

Far up in North Korea, a heavy ground haze reinforced by smoke from grass fires denied observation of enemy movements to air spotters but many signs pointed toward a buildup. Eighth Army troops advancing across the front pushed closer and closer to the Chinese forward supply area, meeting stiffer resistance with every forward move.

The next few days saw the 23rd scrapping forward with the help of heavy artillery support and the direct fire from tanks of "B" Company, 72d Tank Battalion. The 2d Reconnaissance Company, up from Division reserve, moved to the right flank of the 23rd to maintain contact with the 7th US Division on the right.

The southernmost tip of the reservoir was reached on 8 April by the French when they secured the town of Yuchon-ni. The other units of the regiment fought their way forward, slowly compressing the defending enemy into the narrowing area south of the reservoir. To maintain contact on the left with the 1st Marine Division, the 2d Reconnaissance Company and the Ivanhoe Security Force were shuttled to the west.

Plans for a final mop-up operation south of the reservoir were submitted to Division by the 23rd's commander, Lt. Col. John H. Chiles, on 10 April. Labeled "Operation Swing," the plan called for a double envelopment of Hill 796, just south of the reservoir, with the French Battalion wheeling around north of the hill and going east between it and the reservoir while the First and Second Battalions drove onto the hill from the south. The plan was approved and immediately put into operation. It worked to perfection and the driving infantry units, moving forward under the fire of the artillery and tanks, cleaned the pocket of enemy and firmly entrenched the RCT south of the reservoir. North Korean troops who tried to escape across the waters in boats were taken under fire by the 503d FA Battalion which had moved forward into positions from which it could cover the entire reservoir. Fighter strikes called by the FSCC sank 15 boats on 11 April. "Swing" was completed by 15 April and the 23rd turned its attention to the city of Yanggu, enemy anchor on the eastern tip of the natural water barrier. Patrols fanned out from the 23rd and succeeded in entering Yanggu and destroying a large enemy ammunition dump before returning to their own lines.

General James A. Van Fleet assumed command of the Eighth Army on 15 April, relieving Lieutenant General Mathew B. Ridgway who had gone to Tokyo to become Supreme Commander, Allied Powers, following the dismissal of General Douglas MacArthur by the President.

Relative quiet marked the sector of the 23rd the next few days. Patrols curling eastward around the reservoir, contacted small enemy groups who seemed to have little intention of holding their ground. But the lull was only temporary, concealing the frantic activity now confirmed to exist behind the enemy lines. To the west of the Division sector, strong spearheads from the Eighth Army pushed deep into the communist buildup areas, particularly in the "Iron Triangle", and super-sensitive screening screening forces furiously resisted UN efforts.

Elements of the First Battalion of the 23rd with "B" Company of the 72d attached rolled along the south bank of the reservoir daily, moving east and contacting elements of the 7th US Division although they frequently had to run a gauntlet of heavy mortar and long-range automatic weapons fire along the way. The 9th and 38th continued training and girding themselves for the test which seemed imminent.

By 22 April, the Kansas line had been completely secured and organized by the 23rd. A patrol the previous day had contacted a small sized enemy group north of Yanggu so the First Battalion lashed out around the east tip of the reservoir and using close air and artillery support swept to the crest of Hill 386, denying the enemy his vital anchor on the reservoir. The Third Battalion moved up from reserve and took positions behind the newly won hill.

The early evening hours of 23 April were quiet on the Division front but from the west came rumblings of an enemy offensive. By midnight, the rumblings turned to a roar as the entire I and IX Corps front burst into flames in face of the long expected Chinese "5th Phase Offensive" and, although the 2d Division was spared the attack in its sector, one unit of the Indianhead Division found itself in the path of the heaviest communist push. It was "A" Company, 72d Tank Battalion commanded by 1st Lt. Kenneth W. Koch which had been attached to IX Corps earlier in the month and further attached to the 27th British Brigade. Positioned with the Australian and Princes Pat Battalions behind the 6th ROK Division north of Kapyong in Central Korean, the 2d Division tanks found themselves with their infantry the only barrier to a successful enemy penetration which would have split the Eighth Army front. The 6th ROK Division collapsed in face of the Chinese onslaught, falling back south thru the Kapyong valley in which the tankers from the 2d Division were in a blocking position.

The hordes of Chinese followed on the heels of the retreating ROK troops and before midnight the tanks in the valley floor were surrounded. After suffering serious casualties in the initial assault, the tanks adjusted their positions in the path of the advancing Chinese and., together with the troops from Australia and Canada who held the high ground on either side, stood firm while the tide of the red sea dashed against their positions. All night the battle raged and morning found the force intact but cut-off from the rear. Remaining in position, the force denied to the enemy use of the route which would have carried him behind the hard-pressed UN lines. For three days and two nights the British Brigade, reinforced by the 2d Division tanks, held the ground, battling with every ounce of strength they could muster and inflicting terrific casualties on the fanatic Chinese During the day, the tanks fought back through the road-blocks to the rear with loads of wounded, re-fueled, resupplied and returned along the flaming corridor to the beleagured positions, transporting ammunition and rations for the defending infantry The stand enabled the flanking divisions to pull back and set up a new defense line. When the positions held so enaciously could be relinquished without further danger of the divisions holding the shoulders of the penetration being outflanked, the tanks moved forward once again, with their tremendous fire power engaging the enemy while the infantry withdrew, then pulling back in a fighting, rearguard action

"Award of the Distinguished Service Cross to First Lieutenant Wilfred D. Miller, Armor, a member of Company A, 72d Tank Battalion, for action against the enemy in the vicinity of Cheryong-ni on 23 and 23 April 1951. On the night of 23 April, a fiercely determined and numerically superior enemy force launched a sudden attack against Company A's position. The leading tank platoon of the company bore the brunt of the assault and the platoon leader was killed and three of the tank commanders were wounded. After receiving heavy casualties, the platoon began to fall back. Lieutenant MILLER, advancing with his own platoon, observed that the withdrawal was threatening to become disorderly. Quickly, he jumped from the protection of his own tank and ran forward halting the tanks and directing them to alternate defensive positions. The rapidly advancing enemy however, suddenly rendered these positions untenable and Lieutenant MILLER, realizing that the tanks would now be exposed to devastating anti-tank fire, ordered them to fall back. Then, although exposed to the concentrated, close range fire of the enemy, Lieutenant MILLER managed to fight his way back to his own platoon. On the following day he led his platoon, time and time again, through through enemy territory to reach beleaguered friendly infantry units with critically needed ammunition and supplies. On each of these trips he had the tanks loaded with wounded and repeatedly broke through the enemy encirclement to carry them to safety. Finally, he placed such devasting fire on the enemy that the withdrawal of the friendly units was successfully covered.

The stand of the British Brigade and "A" Company, 72d Tank Battalion permitted the serious breakthrough to be contained

Th struggle at Kapyong against the Chinese offensive was typical of the battles which raged all along the I and IX Corps front.

The 1st Marine Division, in position on the left flank of the 2d Division, was required to pull back its lines in order to avoid being outflanked as the lines further west in IX Corps dropped back to cover penetrations To maintain contact with the 1st Marines, Task Force Zebra was formed by the 2d Division and dispatched to the extreme left flank of the Division sector Composed of the French Battalion, 2d Reconnaissance Company, Netherlands Battalion. Reconnaissance Platoon and a platoon from "B" Company from the 72d Tank Battalion, the force was commanded by Lt. Col E. W. Brubaker, commanding officer of the tank battalion. It took up positions south of the reservoir and established the vital lateral contact between the Indianhead Division and the Marines.

On 25 April, with the gradual southward displacement of the I and IX Corps Line, the 23rd RCT was ordered to pull south of the reservoir and concentrate its defenses of the left flank. A minor enemy buildup was reported at Yuchonni near the junction of the 1st Marine and 2d Division boundry and was leveled as tank and artillery fire were placed on the enemy troops who were dispersed before the buildup could become threatening.

General Van Fleet ordered no more withdrawals anywhere in the Eighth Army under any circumstances. All units were to button up prior to darkness, organize their defenses in depth and, if any penetrations were made, they were to be contained until daylight when they were to be eliminated.

The 38th RCT moved forward to man the old Cairo line on 25 April.

Orders went out to the 23rd and Task Force Zebra to install tactical wire and defense mechanisms in anticipation of an enemy attack in the Division sector and to prepare to fall back behind the positions to be prepared by the 38th.

Plans were initiated to establish a strong defensive line in X Corps and after several locations were suggested and rejected, a stretch of hills with a comamnding view of the terrain to the north was selected and designated "Noname" Line. Here the Division would stand and hold together with the other elements of the Eighth

Army who were also selecting final defensive lines.

Preparation of defenses on the Noname Line began on 27 April as the 38th Infantry moved into position. The 23rd, still on line, reported moderate contact as it prepared to fall back through the 38th when the order was given. And, although pressure against the entire front began slacking off on the 27th, all non-tactical equipment was sent south. Division artillery moved up into new positions from which it could mass its fires anywhere in front of the new defensive line.

The 23rd commenced its withdrawal on 28 April together with the elements of Task Force Zebra, passing through the 38th Infantry which had its First, Third and Netherlands Battalions on the Noname Line with the Second Battalion in reserve. The 9th Infantry moving from Corps and Division reserve went forward to "back-stop" the 38th.

Enemy contact on 28 April was light as the 23rd RCT and Task Force Zebra completed their withdrawals.

The enemy began to break contact all along the front on 29 April but every intelligence report bore out the fact that, though badly battered, the major force of the Chinese attacking armies was still intact and possessed the capability of renewing the offensive at any time they so desired.

Occupation and preparation of the Noname Line was complete on 30 April. The Second Battalion of the 38th, in order to keep contact with the enemy, moved forward of the line and set up an advance patrol base with "F" and "G" Companies reporting minor contacts during the afternoon. Further knowledge of enemy movements was limited as haze and smoke from grass fires continued to obscure the vision of air observers.

Division liaison pilots, ranging far behind enemy lines in their newly acquired L-19's had little to report.

Task Force Zebra was reformed on 30 April to take up blocking positions near Hangye on the MSR leading Northeast from Hongchon where it relieved the 31st Regiment of the 7th US Division. Utilizing "B" Company, 9th Infantry; 1st Ranger Company; "F" Company, 38th and the 72d Tank Battalion (—), it served as the tie-in unit between the 38th Infantry on the Noname Line and the 5th ROK Division which had moved in on the right flank of the 2d Division replacing the 7th US Division.

April closed with the Division digging into position to meet whatever new moves might be brewing under screening smog which blanketed movements of the enemy lurking, still powerful, in the north.

"MAY MASSACRE"

The 2d Infantry Division receives the Distinguished Unit Citation streamer from the hands of Vice President Alben Barkley during a presentation ceremony held at Kapyong, Korea, in November 1951. Major General Robert N. Young, division commander, and his aide-de-camp, First Lieutenant Kenneth Miller, assist the Vice President in securing the streamer onto the Division colors.

Distinguished Unit Citation

In the name of the President of the United States as public evidence of deserved honor and distinction the 2d Infantry Division is cited for extraordinary heroism and outstanding performance of duty in action against the armed enemy in the vicinity of Hongchon, Korea, during the period 16 to 22 May 1951.

Defending the critical sector of the Eighth Army battle front, the 2d Infantry Division and attached units faced a hostile force of 12 Chinese Communist divisions with an estimated strength of 120,000 troops. The Third Chinese Communist Army Group drove the full force of its savage assault against the 2d Infantry Division with the specific mission of annihilation of the unit. The right flank of the unit was completely exposed when enemy pressure broke through adjacent United Nations elements. Pressure increased and each night enemy forces by passed the staunch defenders and occupied positions to their rear areas. Tactical units of the 2d Infantry Division launched fierce counterattacks which destroyed enemy penetrations, successfully extricated themselves and through readjustment of positions stopped the onslaught of the Chinese Communist forces. Executing planned withdrawals and extending their flank eastward over extremely rugged, mountainous terrain, the 2d Infantry Division contained and held all enemy attempts to envelop and destroy the Eighth Army. The heroic and determined stand by the 2d Infantry Division and attached units provided critically required time for other Eighth Army units to regroup and block the attempted enemy envelopment. Without thought of defeat, this heroic unit demonstrated such gallantry, determination and esprit de corps in accomplishing this extremely difficult and hazardous mission as to set it apart and above other units participating in similar operations. Its sustained brilliance in battle, resolution and extraordinary heroism reflect unsurpassed credit on those courageous soldiers who participated and are in keeping with the finest traditions of the United States Army, the United Nations Forces and their own homelands.

TERRAIN SKETCH

The battle scene was dominated by a long, massive ridge line running generally southwest and northwest. This ridge forms the Eastern rim of the CHUNCHON BASIN. Its towering main peak, KARI-SAN, from a height of 1051 meters looks down on the two road nets which bound it and other hill masses that were of lesser heights. The steep slopes were covered with heavy timber, and undergrowth, and the ridges were barren rock. Both roads were of great importance and they were to be the victor's prize. The enemy controlled one, the CHUNCHON-YANGGU road, while the one running between HONGCHON and HANGYE, lay in our hands. These roads were first class routes, wide, hard surface of earth and gravel, and capable of moving military equipment. Thus, the battle swirled around the heights dominating these routes. To the east, the lonely spire, known as HILL 683, also assumed a great importance. It overlooked, and thus controlled, the two lateral roads converging on PUNGAM-NI. The village and road junction of HANG-YE assumed importance as the apex to the defensive line which finally held the attack, and from which the successful counter-offensive was launched. From this point the lines sloped to the southeast and southwest. The defensive positions to the east had a narrow, rutted dirt road as a lateral means of supply and evacuation. This road ran east from SONGSAN-NI to PUNGAM-NI. Here again the narrow twisting valleys served as the means of advance and supply to the final defensive positions.

The armies of Communist China were far from defeated when they backed-off in the final days of April from the bent, but still-solid defensive lines, of the United Nations forces in the west. Turning away from battle, the endless columns of brown-clad soldiers dog-trotted through the mountains to the north, little knowing where they were headed but thankful to be out of range once more of the crashing of massed artillery. Thousands of their dead lay behind them, concealed in hastily-dug graves scraped out of the slowly warming hillsides of central and west Korea.

Two massive enemy groups, the 20th and 27th Armies of the IX CCF Army Group, shifted eastward from their positions west of Chunchon in the early days of May. Moving like a muddy tide under cover of cloudy skies, three more battered but powerful armies, the 12th 15th and 60th of the III CCF Army Group, flowed northward from their positions above Seoul. As they flooded into the newly captured country south of Chorwon, their leaders turned them eastward and south once more. Jogging back to battle through the mountains, the weary but obedient soldier could see dusty clouds rising from the highways snaking through the valleys below as trucks of supplies moved forward with him.

Political leaders told of great new victories ahead. Warnings to conserve the newly issued rations—dried corn, fried flour cakes, kaoliang and rice—were accompanied by stories of great fleets of planes and masses of tanks which would support the forthcoming drive. The great Second Impulse of the Fifth Phase Offensive was soon to begin, the men from the plains of China learned. The old enemy, the US 2d Division, would be destroyed and the ROK Army units on both sides would crumble and the route to the south would be open. The long-promised victory was soon to be realized.

And along the strangely quiet battle front, Eighth Army intelligence Officers pondered the lull and speculated on the sudden disappearance of the still-powerful Chinese masess. Air observers over the front tried to pierce the foggy blanket screening the movements they knew must be taking place below. Occasional glimpses told of many vehicles and troops moving away from the former battle area but then came word of the heavy movement to the east instead of continued movement north.

Destroyed bridges across rivers opposite the X Corps front were being repaired, friendly agents reported. Smoke pots were being fired day and night to produce the screening smoke which kept away the planes of the United Na-

tions. Here and there a prisoner was captured and questioning confirmed the southeastward movement. A communist medical officer, captured far in the west near Seoul, confessed that the 2d US Division, which had disrupted so many former CCF plans, was to be destroyed and the ROK Divisions to the east were to be swept aside in the new offensive.

Each day produced more evidence that the X Corps and the Indianhead Division were the final goal for envelopment by the human rivers which curled east and south through the rugged hills.

And in the sector of the 2d Division, feverish preparations were underway to place the Division in positions from which it could absorb any attack. Two new artillery units, the 96th and 196th FA Battalions, were put in general support of the Division.

Operation plans based on every conceivable type of emergency were drawn-up and distributed throughout the Division.

A special Roger Line was established by the 2d Division 4,000 yards forward of the constantly improving Noname Line, and from it the 38th Infantry sent patrols which met little resistance from enemy groups who seemed prone to turn and flee at the approach of the friendly force.

In a further effort to seek out the enemy, General Ruffner sent the 9th Infantry, less the Third Battalion which was in Division Reserve, to attack forward of the Roger Line. Moving northwestward against no opposition while a force from the 1st Marine Division advanced to the west, the 9th seized and occupied Hill 899, only five miles from Chunchon from which all movement in the town and on the surrounding plain was normally visable. However, the maddening haze reduced visability and no significant sightings were made.

With the 9th Infantry (—) forward of the Roger Line, the Second Battalion of the 38th, which had occupied the Roger Line, withdrew to positions behind the Noname Line and became part of the Division Reserve.

Task Force Zebra, blocking on the northeastern sector of the Noname Line, sent its tanks on patrol far as Ungnam-ni without enemy contact.

Harried intelligence officers at every level of command struggled to piece together the puzzle which faced them. Patrols were sent out and each day met increasingly heavy resistance but each, in turn, confirmed the presence of Chinese troops where before had been only pasively defensive North Koreans.

Night photographic reconnaissance planes

crossing the X Corps front, flew low over enemy lines and hurried back with their films. The story they revealed was one of heavy traffic where little or none had been before, hastily concealed supply dumps, and the mounting concentrations of Chinese soldiers.

One of these concentrations reported by air observers was in hilly terrain east of Chunchon and as a threat to the forward bases of the 2d Division, was brought under heavy artillery fire and air strikes. "A" Company of the 9th Infantry attacked the enemy-held ridge position on 10 May but an estimated 150 Chinese, deeply entrenched and employing streams of automatic weapons fire forced the company to disengage and return to its base. Another enemy force of 300 was discovered by a patrol in bunkered positions on the hill mass east of Chunchon and near the important East-West lateral road. "G" Company attempted to force an enemy withdrawal but, again, fanatic resistance foiled their efforts. And as "G" Company broke contact, it came under long-range fire from another source, a new enemy group on an adjacent hill mass.

By the morning of 11 May, an entire enemy battalion was entrenched on the high ground south of the Soyang River, dominating the north-south road leading through Anhyon-ni and denying its use to friendly forces.

The 9th Infantry continued to send out power patrols and in an effort to seize hill 699, an important terrain feature in the hill mass southeast of Chunchon, "E", "F" and "B" Companies were sent forward. "E" and "F" were to attack from the west while "B" moved up from the south. The attack progressed slowly against fierce resistance and, finally, with "E", the closest company, still 1,500 meters from the crest by late afternoon the Division commander ordered the attacking force to return to its base. That night a terrific artillery concentration was laid on the hill and all approaches and in the morning patrols from "G" Company went forward and reported the enemy still on the hill but not in such force as before.

Prisoners taken on 13 May confirmed the Chinese buildup in the Chunchon area.

Patrols from the 38th Infantry made only light contact on the 13th. The regiment, itself, was strengthened by the return of the Second Battalion, released from Division Reserve, and "F" Company, detached from Task Force Zebra.

Task Force Zebra received two added units on the 13th—the 3rd Bn, 36th ROK Regiment and the 2d Bn, 23rd Infantry. The ROK unit relieved the Ivanhoe Security Force which went into blocking positions between Task Force

Zebra and the 38th Infantry on the Noname Line. Meanwhile, the 9th Infantry pulled its advance patrol base south of the Roger Line.

The Division front on the night of 13 May was manned, from left to right, by the 9th Infantry, 38th Infantry and Task Force Zebra. The 23rd Infantry designated as Corps Reserve, had its French Battalion at Hangye as Division Reserve, prepared to counter-attack anywhere in the Division sector. The Second Battalion was with Task Force Zebra, having relieved the French Battalion on 12 May.

Patrols continued throughout the 14th with stiff resistance encountered in the vicinity of Hill 699. Air observers, late in the afternoon of the 14th, reported masses of enemy troops moving southeastward along a trail between Naepyongni and Sapkyo-ri, headed for the 2d Division positions. Immediately the entire 503d FA Battalion, two batterys of the 196th and one battery of the 38th FA Battalion were shifted to cover the area and opened fire with heavy concentrations.

New enemy sightings reported by air observers on the 15th were further confirmation of a Chinese buildup south of Yanggu and large movements through Yuchon-ni, along the south shore of the Hwachon reservoir.

All units were again cautioned that, in event of attack, they were to hold positions at all costs during the hours of darkness. Warnings were issued that any movement during darkness would be considered hostile unless the moving unit were properly identified and frontline units had received prior notice of the move.

As every indication pointed to an imminent mass attack, the Division readied itself to meet the onslaught. Division artillery continued to pound the valleys and draws suspected to be assembly points. Tanks from the regimental tank companies and the 72d Tank Battalion were located so they could be employed in indirect fire missions as well as direct. These, together with the other available supporting weapons, brought to 300 the total of artillery pieces which could be brought to bear on the 2d Division front. Ammunition was stockpiled and every precaution was taken to insure a continuous supply of artillery ammunition.

The night of 15-16 May, the Communists launched their preliminary attack against the 5th and 7th ROK Divisions on the 2d Division's right flank. An enemy force, trying to infiltrate between Task Force Zebra and the 38th Regiment, walked directly into the blocking positions of the Ivanhoe Security Force. And, although the determined Chinese pressed their attack until daylight, they were forced to withdraw and were observed moving into the village of Hachon which was immediately subjected to a heavy artillery concentration.

The attack in the ROK sector was launched at 0300 hours on the 16th and continued throughout the day. By 1800 hours, the entire ROK front was under heavy attack and all units were forced from their positions. Withdrawing south of the Inje-Hongchon road, the ROK's laid bare the entire east flank of the 2d Division.

And as this threat developed, contact patrols from the 38th Infantry and Task Force Zebra, reaching out after beating off attacks of the previous night, quickly encountered enemy groups, withdrew and called for artillery to breakup the concentrations they had discovered.

As dusk approached, the tempo of battle sharpened as reports from across the front revealed increasingly numerous heavy clashes and focused attention on the worsening situation to the east where ROK units were falling back.

By nightfall it was apparent the long-expected offensive had begun. Later intelligence reports revealed the full extent of the assault. Four Chinese Armies rolled forward in the 2d Division zone. The 12th aimed to penetrate the ROK positions on the right then turn in behind the Indianhead Division and envelop the right flank. The 15th Chinese Army was to make the frontal assault then split and move onto the flanks while the 60th CCF Army passed through in a column of divisions in a thundering

assault designed to hammer the lines against the enveloping 12th Army. The 27th Army was to follow up in the area north of Pungam-ni in conjunction with the 12th. In all, twelve full-strength divisions came screaming out of the night in the initial moves to annihilate the 2d Division. In immediate contact were the 31st, 34th, 35th, 44th, 45th, 181st, 80th, and 81st Divisions. Subsequently, dead from the 29th, 179th, 180th, and 79th were identified in front of the 2d Division lines.

The 38th Infantry stemmed repeated attacks early in the night with the Second Battalion coming under the brunt of the enemy effort together with "A" Company which clung to its positions atop Hill 1051, a main anchor on the Noname Line. Through the darkness, the confident enemy masses broke their endless columns against the positions of the 38th with "E" and "G" Companies fighting to hold their positions. Artillery, crashing into the ground forward of the lines, took a terrific toll of the attackers while other hundreds died in the mine-fields checkered with barbed wire. The groans of the wounded, screams of the attackers and the blast of bugles mingled with the clattering roar of battle as waves of Chinese pushed against the lines.

The Noname Line was secure at 0100 hours on 17 May but was afire throughout the zone of the 38th and Task Force Zebra. The Third Battalion of the 36th ROK Regiment, part of Task Force Zebra, fell back, but hastily organized provisional companies composed of headquarters and engineer troops were thrown into the breech and kept the line intact. Searchlights were turned on to illuminate the battle area and aid the defenders in locating and slaughtering the onrushing Chinese.

By 0230 hours, 17 May, bloody, reckless attacks by the Chinese had overwhelmed the positions of "E" Company of the 38th Infantry and the entire Second Battalion was under extreme pressure and was ordered to pull back. Word was sent to the 9th, also heavily engaged but holding in the face of slightly less-furious attacks on the left, that the withdrawal of the 38th was a planned one and not a cause for undue alarm.

Daylight revealed continued raging battle, the Chinese absorbing staggering losses from rolling barrages of artillery and the coordinated fire of the defenders. The situation was serious in the 38th sector with "A" Company clinging to the crest of Hill 1051 while on all sides the Chinese pressed upward. The French, ordered out of Division Reserve, were sent forward into the 38th area to attempt to close the gap which opened with the withdrawal of the 2d Battalion. Fighting forward, the French made contact with Chinese troops within 3,000 yards of the MSR and immediately pitched in to stop their advance. Up on Hill 1051, "A" Company was finally overcome, blanketed in swarms of Chinese who stormed the surrounded company until there was no hope of the company holding any longer.

"Award of the Distinguished Service Cross to Sergeant First Class Dellno Horne, Infantry, a member of Company A, 38th Infantry Regiment, for action against the enemy in the vicinity of Panmegi-ri on 18 May 1951. On 8 May 1951, Company A was deployed in defensive positions near Panmegi-ri when a numerically superior enemy launched an attack against the company positions. As Sergeant HORNE was about to launch a counter-attack with eight men against a high hill held by the enemy, his weapon was shot from his hands. Undaunted though unarmed, Sergeant HORNE gallantly led his men in a daring frontal assault on the hill. His fierce attack took the enemy completely by surprise and they were forced to flee, thereby enabling Company A to establish more favorable positions. A short while later three members of the company were observed to be surrounded by enemy troops on a nearby hill. Sergeant HORNE, with a machine gun that he had acquired, rushed to the assistance of the beleaguered men. Although fully exposed to intense enemy small-arms and automatic-weapons fire, he calmly delivered a steady stream of fire on the enemy, thereby drawing attention from the surrounded men and enabling them to break through the encirclement and rejoin the company.

As Hill 1051 fell, Division artillery, anticipating such a loss, shifted their guns and immediately began pounding the crest. But below, the thick crowds of dusty, determined Chinese flooded through the gap in the line, jogging over the bodies of the hundreds of dead, cut down by the murderous artillery fire.

At 1130 hours, the Corps commander granted an earlier request from Division and released the 23rd Infantry (-1st Bn) from reserve. Immediately it began moving forward into an assembly area two miles north of Hangye on the MSR. Col. Chiles, commander of the 23rd RCT, assumed comamnd of the Task Force Zebra and despatched his Third Battalion into the east sector of the zone and the French Battalion was ordered to continue to attack to secure the west sector. Assembling on a trail west of Hangye were the First Battalion, 23d Tank Company,

Heavy Mortar Company and the Medical Company.

All day the battle raged with increasing pressure on the right flank as the ROK's rattled to the rear leaving a yawning gap in the Army line exposing the 2d Division. Intercepted CCF radio messages indicated every Chinese unit was being directed into the gap near Hill 1051. It became imperative that the gap be plugged or sealed off and General Ruffner ordered the Dutch Battalion to prepare for an attack to close the dangerous hole.

The General, anxious to see the attack by the Dutch first hand, took off in his helicopter and headed for the area. Just prior to 1500, the copter's motor failed and the frail craft plunged earthward, crashing in a rocky crag. By some miracle both General Ruffner and his pilot escaped unhurt except for bruises although the craft was completely demolished. The General's first question was of the progress of the attack. Assured that it had jumped-off at 1515, he returned to his forward command post to continue directing the magnificent stand of his Division.

"Award of the Distinguished Service Cross to Major General Clark L. Ruffner, United States Army, Commanding General, 2d Infantry Division, for action against the enemy in the vicinity of Hangyi and Umyang-ni during the period 16 through 24 May 1951. On 6 May, after an ominous build-up of strength, the Chinese Communist Forces launched a massive offensive against the 2d Infantry Division and two Republic of Korea divisions of the United States X Corps with a force of an estimated 96,000 troops. Although the attack was expected and enormous casualties were inflicted on the enemy, the situation became critical on 18 May when the Republic of Korea forces, overrun by a numerically preponderant enemy force, collapsed and exposed the right flank of the 2d Infantry Division. At this juncture, General RUFFNER personally visited the most forward positions to rally his troops and reorganize the defense of a new line. Through his coolness, efficiency and indifference to danger, he assisted in extricating several units which had been cut off, narrowly escaping death on one occasion when the helicopter in which he was was riding crashed on a mountain peak within sight of the enemy. On 20 and 21 May, General RUFFNER moved his division in a difficult lateral maneuver across the battlefront, then personally led a counter-attack against the enemy. As a result of this brilliantly executed counter-attack, the hostile forces were routed

after suffering losses 30 times as great as those sustained by the 2d Division. On 24 May, General RUFFNER organized and led a special task force to seize and secure a bridgehead across the Soyang River and sever enemy escape routes to the north. When the troops were stopped by enemy mortar fire, General RUFFNER, with complete disregard for his personal safety, drove his jeep near the head of the tank-infantry column over a road that had not been swept for mines and through the area of the hostile mortar fire. This fearless action so inspired the officers and men of the task force that they mounted their vehicles and immediately resumed the advance. By his brave and daring leadership, the objective was secured in minimum time, thus putting a force 12 miles deep into the territory held by the enemy force and severing two of its main avenues of escape to the north.

All limits on artillery ammunition were lifted

59 days on frontline
Bob JAMES 51
KOREA
SEPT. 1951

on the 17th by General Van Fleet as the entire Eighth Army watched the defense put up by the 2d Division against overwhelming odds. More than 137,000 Chinese and 38,000 North Korean troops were being hurled against the front manned by the Indianhead Division and the ROK Divisions on the right. On their success depended the course of the war for it was an all-out effort on the part of the Communists to smash and destroy the 2d Division, thrust

through the ROK's and outflank the entire 8th Army line. The ROK's had already fallen back, but the 2d Division holding the shoulder of the penetration was resisting every effort to be thrown back. Already the 3rd US Division, which had been in Army Reserve, was preparing to move into the gap caused by the collapse of the ROK's. It remained for the 2d Division to cling to its ground and await the commitment of the 3rd and the entire situation would be greatly improved.

The 2d Division was doing its job. Fighting cooly, professionally, it lashed at every Chinese column, turning them back at the line with bloody casualties; piling up the dead in front of its positions and refusing to yield in face of tremendous odds. The only serious break in the line was being sealed up with artillery fire as more than 30,000 rounds had been fired in the first 24 hours of the attack. But even this was not enough, the hordes of enemy continued to stream through, overcoming every effort the Dutch could muster to stem the tide.

At 1633 hours the First Battalion of the 23rd was released from Corps reserve and now the entire 23rd was available to its comamnder. Immediately he shifted more weight to his right, which was also the east flank of the Division, where every effort by the communists to blast behind the Noname positions was beaten off. As nightfall approached, Division artillery reported every available piece firing into the gap in the lines while, overhead, B-26 bombers unleashed tons of bombs to reinforce the rain of death dealing missles which poured onto the masses of troops streaming through the break.

The Third Battalion of the 9th Infantry was alerted the evening of the 17th to prepare for commitment in the sector of the 38th. The First Battalion of the 23rd, still at Hangye, readied itself for a counter-attack. The 38th fought to hold the shoulders of the gap and continued to inflict maximum casualties on the hordes which poured through below.

By early morning of 18 May, the situation in the sector of the 38th Infantry had become critical with many of the units fighting Chinese on all sides. The First Battalion of the 38th was in particularly dangerous shape with the main enemy penetration between "A" and "B" companies. It was evident that help would have to be provided, so, at first light the Second Battalion of the 9th shifted eastward behind the 38th and attacked northeastward while the Third Battalion of the 9th launched a drive to the north. The purpose was to seal off the enemy who had succeeded in bursting through the lines.

The maneuver enabled the 9th to establish a line of blocking positions behind the embattled 38th. "G" Company of the 38th was utilized to hold the center of the line which, when secure, permitted the Division Commander to place the sector of the 38th under control of the 9th Infantry.

By 1030 hours, 18 May, communications were re-established with the First and Second Battalion of the 38th and arrangements were made to air-drop urgently needed supplies to the units that had been cut off. Both battalions had suffered heavy casualties and were extremely short of ammunition and rations.

The eastward shift of the 9th Infantry was made posible by a boundry charge which brought the 1st Marine Regiment into the sector formerly occupied by the 9th. When the Marines closed into the area, the First Battalion of the 9th moved out and went into blocking positions between the already emplaced Second and Third Battalions. This formed a strong defensive line anchored on Hill 442. Instructions went out to the First and Netherlands Battalions of the 38th to break contact and withdraw southward. The Second and Third Battalions were also ordered to break contact and pull back through the newly established positions of the 9th Infantry.

Meanwhile, the 23rd was under attack all along its front with particular pressure on the right flank against "I" Company. An enemy roadblock had been set-up at Yongnae-re by infiltrators and another enemy force had succeeded in infiltrating to Tappung-ni, threatening the entire Division right flank. Aware of the danger this posed, General Ruffner requested permission to modify the right flank of the Noname Line so the 23rd could deny its flank to the enemy who had streamed through the abandoned ROK positions. Corps granted the request and orders went out to Col. Chiles to commence the readjustment.

It was a difficult maneuver for the enemy was established and growing stronger in positions between the 23d's location and the new defensive line hinged below Hangye. Nevertheless, the regiment began imemdiate movement, the Second Battalion started south along the high ground on the west of the MSR and the Third Battalion along the east. "K" Company, six platoons from "B" and "C" Companies, 72d, and the wheeled vehicles of the regiment moved down the road. The enemy made every effort to stop the maneuver and succeeded in knocking out two tanks near Yongnae-ri, blocking the road for wheeled vehicles. Enemy mortars began shelling the column immediately, disabling

many of these vehicles. The tanks pulled off the road, established a 2,000 yard fire line and took the roadblock under fire. The Second Battalion joined by the men from the stalled wheel column crossed the road and joined the Third Battalion on the east. The battered group then fought a wide sweeping action, circled the roadblock while the tanks occupied the enemy and by 2200 hours had succeeded in withdrawing to their new defensive area. The tanks, after providing covering fire for the foot troops, continued south down the river bed and cleared the trap.

The Second and Third Battalions of the 23rd were joined by the First at Hangye and immeately the regiment set up its new defensive line with the Third Battalion on the left of the road, tied in with the 9th Infantry, and the First and Second Battalions on the right. The French went into blocking positions on the MSR and by midnight the line was secure, the adjustment complete and the enemy thwarted in his efforts to outflank the Division.

About that same time, the Division received word that the 3rd Division was going into positions to the east with the 15th RCT moving up through Pungam-ni.

As there was no reserve available to the 23rd, the Division commander attached the strongest company remaining in the Second Battalion of the 38th to the 23rd as reserve. It was "E" Company, then composed of one officer and 94 enlisted men. The enemy hurled fresh waves of troops at the modified Noname line shortly after midnight on 19 May. The fire of battle raged for 90 minutes with the Third Battalions of both the 9th and 38th bearing the 'brunt of the assault. Five battalions of artillery kept a stream of high explosive shells in the air, cutting down the attackers as they flung themselves against the barbed wire, mines and rain of fire poured on by the men of the 2d Division. In one eight minute period, more then 2,000 rounds of artillery were fired in front of one company alone, "K" Company, 38th Infantry.

This suicide attempt to breach the Indianhead positions failed. Although the troops didn't know it at the time, it was the last major attack against that section of the line. The line the men now held was never to be penetrated in force.

Eastward, the 23rd Infantry with "B" Company, 72d, in support, was battling equally as well, blunting repeated attacks against its new position. ROK troops jammed the MSR and hindered resupply efforts, but with the aid of superb air and artillery support the attacks were thrown back and by 1200 the weary troops realized the latest assault was defeated.

Late in the afternoon of 19 May, the pressure eased considerably all along the front. With the Marines firmly entrenched on the left and the 15th RCT moving up on the right, the Division began shifting its line eastward. The 9th Infantry pulled out of line, the gap filled as the Marines extended right and the First Battalion of the 23rd extended left. The Manchu regiment crossed over behind the 23rd and moved into positions on its right, tieing-in with the 15th RCT. The 38th Infantry (minus the Netherlands Battalion now serving as reserve for the 23rd in place of "E" Company, 38th) withdrew and went into Corps reserve at Chudong-ni. The Division CP displaced to Yudong-ni to be in a position to control action better in the new sector.

The crisis appeared to have been passed. The thinned but powerful ranks of the 2d Division steadied in their positions. The artillery, which had displaced eastward to maintain positions from which it could continue its support, kept up the terrific rate of firing. It reported an expenditure of more than 44,000 rounds in the previous 24 hour period, a major contributing factor in the sucecssful defense.

The Chinese kept pressure across the front during the night of 19-20 May but it was not nearly as intense as it had been previously. However, the First Battalion of the 9th came under platoon size attack about 0300 hours with the enemy force increasing in power as daylight drew near. While this action took place, the First and Third Battalions of the 23rd gained the high ground overlooking the Naechon River where they could observe large bodies of enemy troops concentrating and moving out to attack. Calling on the ever-ready artillery, the forward observers witnessed such accurate artillery fire that for the first time in the Korean war major forces moving out on the attack were disorganized and repulsed before reaching the lines. Follow-up fire forced the enemy to retreat in disorder before firing a shot at the ground troops.

And while the 23rd watched the butchery of the Chinese in the Naechon Valley, the First Battalion of the 9th was pitched in combat with the force which had attacked it earlier and which had now grown to battalion size. Again the artillery was called upon for fire support and by 1500 hours the combined efforts of the infantry and artillery had repulsed the attackers. The disorderly retreat was turned into a rout as the heroic defenders rose from their holes, moving forward in pursuit as the controlled fire from the big guns in the rear preceeded them. The vicious counter-attack continued until dark when, after inflicting tremendous casualties on the enemy, the First Battalion returned to its defense line for the night.

By nightfall both the 9th and 23rd were secure on their line. The 15th RCT, now a part of the 2d Division, was attacking north of Pungamni, digging the enemy troops from their entrenchments on the Division right flank. The re-spuplied, reorganized Third Battalion of the 38th, meanwhile, moved up from the south and went into reserve positions south of Pungamni where it also served to block any possible wide enveloping movement the enemy might try to launch.

General Ruffner sent a "Well done" to the artillery for its tremendous support of the line troops. To Colonel Thomas E. DeShazo, Division Artillery commander, the General despatched his compliment, "A magnificient job."

As the Division dug-in for the night, X Corps notified the commanding general that it planned to commit the 187th Airborne RCT in the Division zone on the following day and that plans were being made for a massive counterattack to rock the stunned communist forces back from their gains.

May 21st was a highly successful day. All front-line units, their defenses secure, lashed out in limited atacks at the hesitant, bewildered enemy. "G" Company of the 23rd lead a Second Battalion attack to secure hill positions south of the Naechon. Fixing bayonets, it slashed to the top of the crest killing a counted 300 enemy dead. By nightfall it was secure. "L" Company of the 15th, spearheading to Hill 592 killed a counted 142 enemy in capturing the height. "G" Company of the 9th on patrol to seek out the enemy, repulsed a company-sized attack, killing 25 CCF soldiers in the process.

And while all units reported successes in their sectors, the 38th Infantry left Corps Reserve and moved north to Sokpyokkol on the Division right flank where it went into blocking positions. As it came onto line, its Third and Dutch battalions reverted to its control.

The enemy made an attempt to penetrate through the positions of the 23rd Infantry at 0200 hours on 22 May. But front line troops laid down their prearranged cross fires and the shells from four battalions of artillery crashed down from above, forcing the shattered attackers to pull back. Daylight patrols, ranging 1,000 yards forward, reported no contact.

Patrols also went out at daylight from the 9th Infantry sector and encountered little opposition. The time appeared ripe for the planned counterattack and all units inched forward, securing positions for the expected order to take the offensive.

A hastily-organized assault group, Task Force Yoke, commenced a limited northward drive to keep the enemy forces off-balance while the counter offensive was being racked up. Composed of the 2d Bn, 38th Inf; 72d Tk Bn (—); a platoon from the 38th Inf Tank Co; a battery of Division Field Artillery and a tactical air control party, the mobile force moved northwest from Pungam-ni toward Habae-jae.

To the west, along the familiar Hongchon-Inje road, the 187th A/B RCT passed north-ward thru the lines of the 23rd picking up "B" Company of the 72d and securing the high ground around Hangye by nightfall thereby permitting the 23rd to fall back to an assembly area in the vicinity of Hongchon to prepare for its part in the coming counter-offensive.

And as Task Force Yoke and the 187th A/B RCT sent twin-pronged drives short distances northward, the 9th Infantry, operating between the two forces, jumped-off for two objectives—Hill 592 and Tappung-ni, former roadblock area. With the First Battalion on the left and the Second Battalion on the right, the Hill was secure by nightfall and the regiment buttoned up for the hours of darkness. The Third Battalion, relieved in its former area, went into blocking positions between the First and Second Battalion. The 38th RCT relieved elements of the 3rd Division on line and established blocking positions north of Pungam-ni.

The anticipated order for the counter-offensive was issued at 1900 hours on 22 May. To go into effect the following morning at 0800, it set the capture of Inje as its objective with the mission of cutting-off and slaughtering the 30,000 Chinese who still remained in front of the lines of the 2d Division. Task Force Yoke was dissolved, all its units returning to their parent organizations. The 15th RCT was detached from the 2d Division, reverting to its own 3rd Division where it would form the nucleus for a strong thrust to the east of that planned for the Indianhead Division. The 38th Infantry assumed responsibility for the sector formerly held by the 15th. The 187th A/B RCT was attached to the 2d Division for the pending operation.

The attack order set-up a three phased operation. The 187th RCT was to make the main thrust up the Hongchon Road toward Inje. The 38th supported by "B" Company, 72d Tk Bn, was to advance northward on the road network paralleling the Inje road to the east. It's route would take it Northeast to Hyon-ni then Northwest to Inje. The 9th Infantry was to sweep the area between the two powerful armored fists until it had secured the high ground overlooking the Hongchon River.

The 2d Division front was comparatively quiet on the night preceding the offensive. The only enemy activity reported was a probing attack of about 50 enemy against the positions of "C" Company, 9th Infantry, which was quickly driven off.

At 0800 hours on 23 May, the 2d Division initiated its aggressive offensive, one of the most remarkable and spectacular of the war. For six days, the Division had fought a determined enemy, giving ground slowly while inflicting casualties estimated at 10,000 for each day of the Chinese offensive. Throughout the period, the Division had maintained its tactical unity and freedom of maneuver. Now it turned and drove against the desperately tired enemy who no longer had the numerical strength or supplies to continue the pressure. The heroic stand of the previous days and the sudden reversal of tactics embodied in the new offensive marked one of the most dramatic achievements of the Korean War.

The attack moved out on schedule against light resistance. Both the 9th and 38th Regiments secured their first-day objectives. The 187th A/B RCT, making the main thrust, battled stiff resistance as it advanced along poor roads, ringed with enemy-dominated peaks.

A bridgehead was secured on the Soyang River on the second day of the attack by a tank-tipped spearhead moving up the main axis. The mobile force was made up of the 2d Bn, 187th; "B" Co, 64th Tk Bn; "B" Co, 72d Tk Bn; "C" Battery, 674th FA Bn; and "A" Company, 127th Engineers. Consolidating its bridgehead, the force prepared a crossing while the 23d Infantry made ready to follow-up the gains by sweeping the same route from the south. Meanwhile, both the 9th and 38th met heavy resistance. The 9th, especially, had difficulty in dislodging a strong delaying force from three large hills which stretched across the route of advance. At one time the Second Battalion took the hill only to be pushed off. However, a counter-attack regained the height and by nightfall it was secure as artillery pounded the fleeing enemy. The First Battalion of the 38th had the heaviest resistance in the regimental sector but by night had secured its objectives.

The night of 24-25 May was quiet except for the ambush of a supply train belonging to the task force holding the bridgehead. Three battalions from the 23rd were ordered to clear the area and at 0710 the Second, Third and French Battalions commenced sweeping northward against heavy resistance which was methodically put-down. By 1500 hours they had contacted the bridgehead force. Both the 9th and 38th, meanwhile, continued battling forward during the day.

"Award of the Distinguished Service Cross to Private First Class Murray T. Manning, Jr., Infantry, a member of Company I, 9th Infantry Regiment, for action against the enemy in the vicinity of Sogong-ni on 25 May 1951. On 25 May 1951, two squads of Company I had the mission of assaulting Hill 800 while the remainder of the company furnished covering fire for the operation. Private MANNING, a member of one of the squads, was in the leading element of the assault when intense enemy fire temporarily halted the advance. With complete disregard for his personal safety, Private MANNING moved up the fire-swept slope until he could bring effective fire on the hostile element holding up the advance. When he had killed six enemy riflemen with accurate fire from his M-1 rifle, the assault was able to continue. Observing the automatic rifleman of his squad fall from exhaustion, Private MANNING rushed to the fallen man, pushed him to a safe position behind a rock, then picked up the automatic rifle and continued advancing up the hill. As the squads reached the hill top, the enemy launched a vicious counter-attack on the friendly forces, forcing them to withdraw. Heedless of the intense enemy fire, Private MANNING led the attack, moving relentlessly forward in the face of withering enemy fire. The aggressive actions of Private MANNING so inspired the men around him that they followed him to the crest of the hill, engaged the numerically superior enemy troops in hand-to-hand combat and forced them to flee in disorder, leaving numerous dead and wounded on the hill.

Patrols sent out the night of 25-26 May found little evidence of enemy activity as it became apparent that the Chinese and the screening North Korean forces were bent on escaping from the trap being closed around them.

On 26 May, the 9th Infantry reverted to Corps reserve, moving back to Hangye. The 23rd commenced relief of the 187th and continued northward in conjunction with a rapid advance by the 38th to the right against slight resistance.

The converging attacks by the two regiments continued on 27 May with the 38th surprising a large enemy force scurrying out of Hyon-ni. The First Battalion rolled into positions overlooking the town and opened fire on the fleeing enemy. Tanks from the regimental tank company and "B" Company, 72d Tk Bn, roared into the milling frantic enemy and the combination was too much. More than 300 enemy were killed and 156 prisoners were taken before the combat team set up its primeter for the night.

Westward, the 23rd encountered increasingly stiff resistance as the enemy fought to protect the main body of his retreating troops. To give added strength to the 23rd, the Second Battalion of the 9th, operating under corps control, relieved the French battalion at the bridgehead site, enabling it to move forward in support of the rest of the regiment.

The 23rd secured Inje, spearheaded by armor from "C" Company, 72d, in conjunction with the 187th on 28 May while the 38th advanced northwestward to effect a junction with the spearhead. The 23d Infantry sent patrols north of the town to clear the high ground of the enemy troops still holding out.

Intermittent mortar and artillery fire fell on the 23rd Regimental CP on the Inje airstrip during the night of 28-29 May.

The 38th reached the Inje road on 29 May, contacting elements of the 2d Reconnaissance Company and completing the pincers movement which had brought death or capture for hundreds of the enemy. Both regiments spent the final few days of May consolidating their positions, sending out patrols to locate and destroy the enemy and calling down artillery on the fleeing Chinese. The 23d prepared to continue its attack north of Inje.

A final enemy reaction was registered on 1 June when an estimated regiment struck briefly at the troops of the 35th ROK Regiment, attached to the 2d Division, and succeeded in disorganizing them causing them to abandon their defensive positions east of the Soyang bridgehead. The 9th Infantry was ordered to send a battalion into the area and at 1000 hours the Third Battalion commenced its sweep. It returned at 1600, having cleared the area. The other two battalions of the 9th moved into position in the Division area, relieving elements of the 187th A/B RCT still present.

The Division was given one more offensive mission by Corps and then informed that it would go into reserve for a well-earned period of rest, reorganization, training and re-supply. The objectives for the mission were commanding peaks in the rugegd hills forward of the Inje-Soyang bridgehead and the moves to take them were initiated early on 2 June. For three days,

paced by energetic attacks of all the regiments, the offensive continued and by 5 June all the objectives were secure.

This latest flurry brought to a close the most notable period of the 2d Division's actions in the campaign. It brought forth, for the first time, a powerful counter-attack which followed on the heels of one of the most spectacular defensive stands of the war. It was a counter-attack which not only killed thousands of enemy troops, caught completely off-balance, but proved that the 2d Division could absorb the pounding of overwhelming numbers of enemy forces only to turn and cut them to ribobns. In the twenty day period preceeding the conclusion of the final attack the Indianhead Division had killed more than 65,000 enemy soldiers, the cream of the armies of Red China. Ten enemy divisions had been comimtted against the 2d Division with soldiers from an additional 2 communist divisions identified among the thousands of dead who littered the battle-field. It was a major defeat for the Chinese and North Korean forces. Their ranks were decimated, entire divisions rendered useless. They had flung themselves in an all-out atempt to annihilate the 2d Division and had failed under the merciless pounding of hundreds of thousands of rounds of artillery, tons of bombs and millions of round of small arms ammunition thrown at them by the determined, steadfast and victorious men of the 2d Infantry Division.

On 5 June, the Division began its movement into reserve in the vicinity of Hongchon and by 11 June the move was complete. The relief from combat was utilized for the needed training and reorganization accompanied by corps command inspections of all the units. It was to be the longest non-combat period enjoyed by the Division since its arrival in Korea and it was the unanimous opinion of all that no division deserved it more.

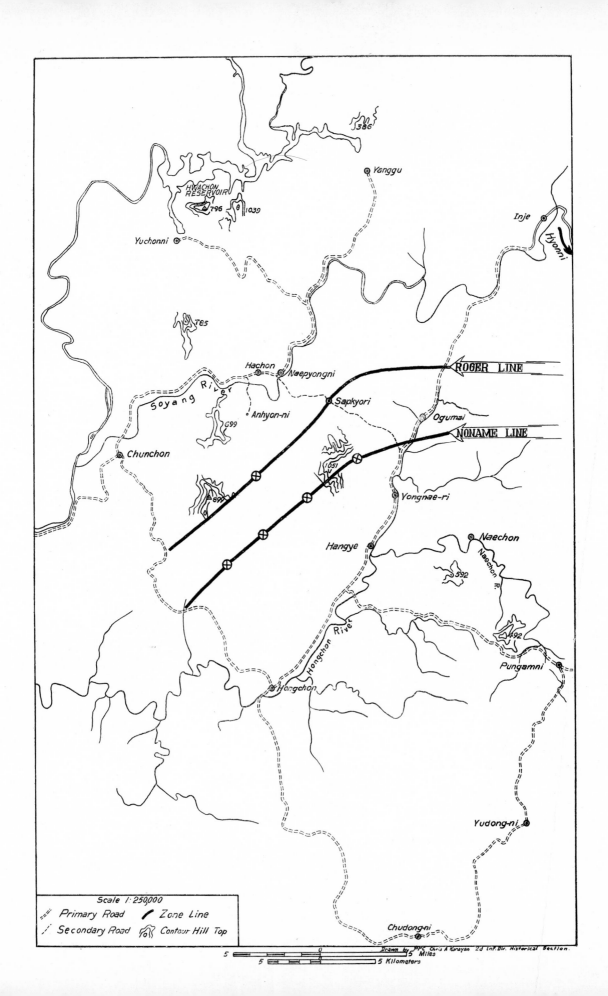

Scale 1:250,000

Primary Road — — — Zone Line ▬▬▬

Secondary Road · · · Contour Hill Top

Drawn by PFC Chris A Karayan 2d Inf. Div. Historical Section.

5 ▭▭▭ 0 5 Miles

5 ▭▭▭ 5 Kilometers

HWACHON RESERVOIR

Yanggu

Inje

Hyonni

796 1039

Yuchonni

785

ROGER LINE

Hachon Naepyongni

Soyang River

Sapkyori

Ogumai

NONAME LINE

699

Anhyon-ni

1051

Chunchon

Yongnae-ri

899

Naechon

Hangye

592

Naechon R.

Hongchon River

492

Pungamni

Hongchon

Yudong-ni

Chudong-ni

386

Typical of the destruction in Korea.

Corporals Joseph M. Capral, Harry L. Huges and Frank White of "D" Company, 9th RCT with an old friend near Chungju.

*The ROK soldiers were still with the Division in late December of
'50. This is Private John F. Angle on guard with Shin Chon Suk.*

*A Manchu Regiment convoy crosses a river near Chungju
in December 1950.*

An all-denomination service is held for Headquarters Company of the 9th RCT in December.
It was cold on Christmas eve but that didn't hamper Pfc Jesse C. Arriagz's appetite.

A 9th Infantry Tank
Company M-4 in posi-
tion for fire support.

Corporal D. J. Broshanahan spins the prop while Corporal Charles W.
Cathcart mans the controls of the Division observation plane.

An "E" Company, 9th Infantry patrol passes the frozen bodies of a Korean family.

Shaving water was a bit chilly in early February so Sfc August Hart and Sgt John J. Gabriele of "A" Company, 23rd Infantry settle for a quick hot shower.

The First National Bank of Wonju is taking an extended "bank holiday."

The paddies were still frozen enough to permit these "C" Company tanks from the 72d to move across them in support of a 23rd Infantry assault.

Pfc Edmund Saldana stayed
beside two wounded buddies
although they were deep behind enemy lines and went
for three days without food
before being rescued by helicopter.

General Matthew B. Ridgway troops the line during presentation ceremonies of the
Distinguished Unit Citation to the French Battalion.

The 2d Engineers were at this kind of work 24 hours a day to make possible the supply and transport of the Division. It was a never-ending job done well.

The remains of a few of the thousands of Chinese dead who tried in vain to capture Chipyong from the 23rd RCT.

It's a lot harder to pick-up than it is to drop but it has to be done just the same.

The body of an American soldier and one of the many Chinese attackers he killed before he himself was mortally wounded. Both were found after the 23rd RCT had repulsed one of the many attacks on its Chipyong perimeter.

Sgt Carl B. Grothe, on the right, plays a rough hand with a straight faced buddy. The buddy was a dead winner.

The Wonju air strip was littered with fallen parachutes during February as C-119's did their best to help keep the Division supplied during the heavy February battles.

Sfc Charles R. Brown proudly points to the record of his old tank 22, one of the few remaining original tanks which "C" Company of the 72d boasted by June of 1951.

One way to get the shells out a little further is to nose into a rice-paddie bank for more elevation.

Did you ever feel as big as a Mack truck in the middle of a football field? This man from the 23rd Infantry does and chances are he doesn't like it.

No comment.

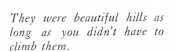

They were beautiful hills as long as you didn't have to climb them.

*...contractor from the 23rd
...antry construction com-
...y hard at work on the
...ndation for a temporary
...et.*

*This crater from a 500 pound bomb undoubtedly served as a command post for
advancing 38th Infantrymen north of Hangye.*

Services in the field found a ready audience.

A river bed this smooth was like a four-lane highway anywhere else. This is a tank from "C" Company, 72d.

TAEU SAN

The 2d Division had made good use of the well-earned period in reserve when, on 8 July, it received notice to prepare for relief of the 1st Marine Division between 15 and 17 July. All units has been reorganized and resupplied. Rotation had gotten into high gear and, as a result, training was speeded up to prepare incoming replacements for the days which lay ahead. Special service shows had been sandwiched in between training problems and the other activities of the period. Many of the officers and men had the opportunity to see Jack Benny for the first time in person when he brought his troupe to the Division Command Post for a show.

But with the alert order in the hands of the units, all efforts were turned to put the finishing touches on the training program. Reconnaissance parties went out to view the Kansas line where the active defense would be undertaken. Teams from the 9th Infantry also toured the Wichita Line, south of the Kansas Line, which it was to prepare and organize as a secondary defensive position. Division engineers, who had been devoting their efforts to improving the roads in the reserve sector, shifted northward on 13 July and began extensive surveys and work on the roads in the new sector.

The X Corps commander, Lt. Gen. Edward M. Almond, was succeeeded on 15 July by Maj. Gen. Clovis E. Byers who took command of the corps as the 23rd Infantry initiated relief of the 5th Marine Regiment. By 1300 hours of the 15th, the French and Third Battalions of the 23rd were entrenched on the Kansas Line. The following day, the 38th, with the Third Battalion of the 9th Infantry attached, had relieved the Korean Marine Corps and the 1st Marine Regiment. To the rear, the 72d Tank Battalion and the 9th Infantry (—) went into Division Reserve with the 9th occupying and improving the Wichita Line.

Patrols were immediately dispatched from the Kansas Line to feel out enemy positions. Their reports revealed the North Korean troops were using a prominent hill mass, centered on Hill 1179, from which to observe all movements of the Division on the Kansas Line and 20,000 meters to the south. Plans were immediately drawn up for an assault on the hill mass. Running north and south, the whole hill complex cut through both the enemy Main Line of Resistance and our own positions. The side having control of it possessed a definite advantage over the other.

Patrols went out across the entire front in the succeeding days so as not to tip off the enemy to the forthcoming attack. The 23rd Infantry, operating on the right flank of the line, sent patrols into the "Punchbowl,' a marked depression in the hilly terarin of the area situated east of Hill 1179 and Hill 1100, another prominent section of high ground which controlled the approaches to 1179.

The attack was scheduled for 26 July and the 38th Infantry was named as the attacking element. The 23rd Infantry was to launch a series of diversionary attacks to seize three objectives in the "Punchbowl" from which it could cut-off escape of enemy elements from 1179 and also provide fire support for the 38th.

Air and artillery pounded the enemy positions on the 25th in preparation for the assault the next morning. Fifty-four air sorties were directed against the objectives and 7,000 rounds of artillery were hurled onto the well-bunkered positions.

At 0615 hours, 26 July, the First Battalion of the 38th Infantry moved out in a dense fog to take Hill 1179, known to the Koreans as Taeu San, then known to the Americans as "Fools Mountain." Supporting by fire, although hampered by poor visibility were all the weapons of the 38th Regiment plus the Heavy Mortar Company of the 9th Infantry. "C" Company lead the assault. "A" and "B" Companies followed as they inched forward up the ridge east of the objective. Until 0930 hours, the slowly advancing infantrymen met no resistance. Then the enemy opened up. From deep entrenchments and bunkers providing interlocking fields of fire came solid streams of automatic weapons fire. The troops crawling up the sheer heights were alternately pinned down or driven back, but each time they moved out again and each time gained a little more ground as air and artillery fired in maximum support.

Dutch troops, attacking Hill 1100 from the south, were also stopped and failed to make any gains after 1100 hours.

To the west, tanks from the 38th Regimental Tank Company and "A" Company, 72d Tank Battalion nailed thousands of rounds into a carpet of steel against the sides of adjacent hills to prevent reinforcement of the North Korean garrison from the west. Eastward, the 23rd Infantry attacked its three objectives and met with heavy resistance.

As evening approached, plans were made to have the First Battalion of the 38th hold-up for the night near "Cathedral Rock," a ragged mass of rock east of 1179. However, a tragic error forced alteration of the plans. During an air-sortie, one of the aircraft released its Napalm on

"C" Company, the lead element, inflicting severe casualties and disorganizing the unit. This required the First Battalion to pull back from its hard won gains where it went into a perimeter defense.

The first day's action sketched the picture of the enemy defenses. He was determined to stay on 1179 at all costs. His elaborate preparations, plentiful supply of ammunition and determined resistance in face of terrific concentrations from all the supporting fire weapons including nine Battalions of artillery indicated the fight for Taeu San would be more difficult than first anticipated.

That night, the skies were kept a flaming red as the artillery fire was intensified. Dust from the roads swirled hundreds of feet into the air as trucks rolled around the clock to provide ammunition for the barrage.

Mist again filled the air as dawn broke on the 27th of July, and attacking through the haze and streams of enemy tracers came "B" Company of the 38th in its renewed attempt to take Taeu San. Close behind were "B" Company of the 9th, and "A" and "C" Companies of the 38th. Bitter fighting raged throughout the day, even super-human effort and courage failed, but by 1530 hours, with "B" of the 9th in the lead and the battered remains of the First Battalion of the 38th in support, a new attack began. Moving forward with the two "B" Companies in a line of skirmishers athwart the ridge and "A" of the 38th flanking in a column to the right, the heroic force inched upward. Suddenly the sun broke through the clouds, giving artillery and mortar observers a clear view of the enemy and immediately crashing salvos of exploding shells were called on the defenders. The infantry surged forward, following the artillery bursts within 75 yards, tossing hand granades and firing every available weapon. By nightfall the inspired foot soldiers had battled to within 50 yards of the crest of the un-numbered hill east of 1179 and there they halted, digging in to wait until daylight for the final assault.

Meanwhile, the Second Battalion of the 9th relieved the Third Battalion of the 38th which then began moving forward to join the First Battalion. Eastward, "K" Company of the 23rd was struggling to take Hill 1059 and by nightfall its every attempt had been repulsed for the enemy, hanging onto 1059 to keep open his supply route to Hill 1179, was determined to stay. "K" pulled back and the 23rd made plans for a renewed attempt the following day.

Throughout the night, the big guns laid a protective screen of steel around the weary infantry clinging to their slim foothold just short of the crest of the un-numbered hill. At first light on 28 July, with "B" of the 9th again in the lead, the First Battalion of the 38th moved forward to take the peak guarding the natural, east approach to 1179. Braving a rage of machine gun, mortar and small arms fire, they finally were successful and by evening the hill was secure. The Third Battalion arrived soon afterward and reinforced the ranks of the First Battalion for the night's vigil.

And as the fanatic enemy persisted in his attempt to hold Hill 1179, equally determined North Koreans held-out against every attempt by the 23rd Infantry to take Hill 1059. The commanding general ordered the slopes covered with tank and artillery fire and a renewed atetmpt was drawn-up for the following day.

The expected counter-attack against the hill held by the 38th came during the night of 28-29 July but the forces refused to yield and repulsed the North Korean troops with heavy losses.

The 38th, reinforced by "B" Company of the 9th, spent the morning and early afternoon of 29 July in preparation for another attack on 1179. Murderous artillery concentrations were laid on the slopes and at 1600 hours, "I" and "K" Companies struck out in face of the enemy cross fire. The assault was carried out with such vigor that the crest was reached and Hill 1179 was in the possession of the 2d Division by evening. The enemy fortress fell after some of the most intense offensive fighting the Division had undergone in months. The fanatic defenders had to be dug out of their deep entrenchments and it was a slow, bloody, body-tiring job. But it was done. The enemy was pushed off suffering more than 2,000 casualties with the annihilation of one complete regiment and the crushing of another. The decimated North Korean 27th Division withdrew, its thin ranks in disorder after the onslaught of the 2d Division attack. An attempted counter-attack by an estimated battalion was disorganized the following day when a six battalion artillery TOT slaughtered the enemy before he could get in range of the 38th's troops.

More than 115 tons of bombs had supported the attack on Taeu San. A total of 74,823 rounds of artillery had been hurled onto the hill and added to that were more than 49,000 rounds of mortar which had been fired in the assault.

Taeu San had been taken, another step on the ladder to the north up which the 2d Division was slowly but certainly climbing.

"BLOODY RIDGE"

The first days of August found the 2d Division adjusting its positions and preparing defenses along the Kansas Line. Hill 1179, firm in the control of the 2d Division, had eliminated enemy observation of the Kansas Line activities in the east. However, three hills overlooking the western portion of the line—983, 940 and 773—were now being used by the enemy as observation posts. Patrols from all three regiments, now on line, ranged out to determine the extent of this new threat. Tanks from the 38th Tank Company and "C" Company, 72d, kept up continual concentrations on the forward slopes of the hill to prevent the enemy from constructing bunkers and observing our movements. Meanwhile, the Netherlands Detachment was released from the Division and passed to 8th Army Control for shipment to Pusan where its veteran members were to be rotated and replacements were to be brought in to fill the ranks.

Reports coming from the regimental patrols revealed the enemy planning no offensive action but busily engaged in preparing defenses along the 983-940-773 terrain complex. Greatly increased use of artillery by the enemy covered these preparations and hampered patrol activities of the Division. Not only combat and reconnaissance patrols were harrassed by the enemy artillery, but also engineer working parties striving to maintain and improve the road network behind the Kansas Line came under repeated concentrations. Finally, in an attempt to cut down the number of casualties, the Division Engineer was ordered to suspend work within range of the enemy fire on days when mist or rain prevented observation of the suspected enemy artillery positions.

Instructions from 8th Army directed that every effort be made to reduce the number of casualties in the period of the cease-fire negotiations. Offensive operations were to be undertaken only when, in the long run, such operations would ultimately reduce the number of casualties suffered over a given period. Consequently, all operations were conducted with the thought of incurring a minimum number of casualties and friendly artillery was utilized to a maximum.

Extensive rains throughout the first half of August worked a great hardship on the Engineers, especially in regard to bridges and roads which ran parallel to and on a level with the many streams in the area. Only extensive work and maintainance activity served to keep the roads in usable shape.

Information gathered on the enemy defenses on Hills 983-940-773 pointed to an increasing urgency that these heights be captured by friendly forces for they posed a serious threat to the Kansas Line and also served as observation posts from which the enemy called down increasing amounts of artillery fire.

On 12 August, the Division received word that plans for an attack on the enemy hills were being considered. The following day, shortly after midnight, the Division was directed to prepare plans for seizing the hill mass and submit them to X Corps. That same day, a boundry change was received which narrowed the Division front, delegating the portion it had been reduced to the 7th ROK Division.

Late in the afternoon of 14 August, G-3 was notified by X Corps that orders were being cut for the operation to take Hills 983-940-773. The 36th ROK Regiment was attached to the Division for the forthcoming attack.

The operation order from X Corps was received late in the afternoon of the 14th. It directed the 36th ROK Regiment to make the assault. In support of the attack, each of the 2d Division's organic regiments was also given a mission. The 38th Infantry, in addition to maintaining one battalion on 1179 was to occupy two hills northeast of the ROK objectives from which it could support the ROK attack by fire and prevent enemy counter-attack or reinforcements. The 23rd was to launch a diversionary attack on Hill 1059 and send reinforced patrols across the "Punchbowl". The 9th was to organize fire support teams to support the ROK attack. Air and artillery priority was given to the South Koreans.

The night of 15-16 August, twenty-eight close support air sorties were flown in the Division sector. Fighter bombers napalmed, rocketed and strafed enemy installations along the ridgeline dominated by the three objectives and one radar-controlled B-26 dropped eight 500 pound bombs to the rear of the three hills. "B" Company, 72d, was attached to the 7th ROK Division and in two weeks fired 3,069 rounds of fire in support of its operations.

And as the Division prepared for this new maneuver, Brig. Gen. George C. Stewart, who had served as assistant division commander since 16 December 1950, left the Division for rotation to the states. Brig Gen. Haydon L. Boatner, chief of staff for the Chinese Army in India during World War II, arrived to fill the newly vacated position.

The attack by the ROK Regiment was set for 18 August and the 2d Division air and artillery were ordered to do their utmost to soften the way for the attackers.

All the supporting fires of the 2d Division

were utilized in the pre-assault softening-up of the ROK objectives on 17 and 18 August. As the fires were lifted, the ROK regiment moved out at 0600 hours and in the initial stages of the attack met only light resistance. Mid-morning, as they advanced up the slopes of 983-940-733, the South Korean troops encountered heavy fire from enemy small arms, automatic weapons and mortars. An estimated two North Korean battalions were entrenched on the hills in well-bunkered positions and they hotly resisted the advance. On several ocacsions, they rose from their holes and battled hand-to-hand with the attackers, using bayonets and grenades.

The fire became so intense that the ROK attack was stopped in the late afternoon but the South Korean comamnder notified the 2d Division he planned a night attack. General Ruffner alerted the 9th Infantry to be ready to move out and hold the hills if the ROK's succeeded in taking them.

CHOI-SANGRYONG
OUR HOUSEBOY
KOREA JAMES '51

The 23rd Infantry, making a diversionary attack in the east, met heavy resistance and, although "G" Company succeded in securing the heights of Hill 1059, "E" Company was forced to pull back after being subjected to an intense artillery barrage. The 38th Infantry occupied its objectives on the high ground northeast of the ROK objectives and immediately had its fire-support team in action.

The ROK night attack was pressed with deter-mination but both the Second and Third Battalions were stopped within a few hundred yards of their objectives. The assaults were continued doggedly the next day and in face of intense fire the South Koreans inched forward to within 50 meters of the crest of Hill 940 and within 200 meters of the crests of 983 and 773. The 38th Infantry, supporting the ROK's by fire, came under heavy artillery and mortar fire during the period but held its positions.

August 20th witnessed the ROK's hurling themselves up the crests and finally, by 1800 hours, Hill 773 was in their hands. The enemy on the other two peaks were being mauled by the ROK's and the heavy supporting fire from the 38th and the 9th Infantry. A North Korean counter-attack on 773 that night was repulsed.

All the objectives of the ROK regiment were taken on 21 August. Hills 940 and 983 fell under combined assaults from the 36th Regiment and a total of 30 prisoners was taken as well as large stores of ammunition and supplies being captured. Col Rupert D. Graves, 2d Division chief of staff who was serving as Gen. Ruffner's personal representative with the attached ROK Regiment, reported a determined counter-attack by the enemy might succeed for the ROK's were short of food and ammunition. Immediately the 38th Infantry was alerted to send reinforcements.

The night of 21-22 August passed without incident and plans were made to exploit the success of the ROK units by having them continue forward and capture three hills just north of their newly won positions. Designated Objectives "A", "B" and "C", the heights were a continuation of the sharp hill masses which dominated the area north of the Kansas Line.

The attack by the ROK's on their new objectives proceeded slowly for the next two days with the enemy resisting with all his forces and utilizing his artillery to the maximum. And as the South Koreans moved forward, the regiments of the 2d Division all sent out patrols which reported light contact. Then, on 24 August, the North Koreans counter-attacked and stopped the ROK drive. At the same time, enemy troops struck at patrols of the 38th and engaged 2d Division elements of Hill 1059 and the surrounding area.

It appeared as though the ROK's would be unable to take all three of their objectives so they were ordered to concentrate on "C", an un-numbered hill north of the ridgeline connecting Hills 940 and 773. The 9th Infantry, meanwhile, moved out and established contact with the 36th ROK Regiment on the southwest slope of 983 and the 38th Infantry did the same near the crest of 773.

The next day, 25 August, was relatively quiet with Division patrols reporting no contact and the ROK's continuing to press against Objective "C" but without success.

The quiet was shattered at 0245 hours, 26 August, as two North Korean battalions hit Hill 983 from the north while other company-sized elements executed an enveloping maneuver on the height. The attacks were accompanied by assaults of other North Korean units which successfully installed themselves on the saddle between Hill 940 and Hill 983 from which they put heavy pressure onto the ROK elements on Hill 940. By noon of the 26th, Hill 983 was completely surrounded and by 1430 hours those South Korean troops who had not been killed or wounded were forced to give themselves up. Meanwhile, "F" and "G" Companies of the 38th Infantry were under heavy attack in their positions north of Pia-ri and were forced to withdraw 1,000 meters south of the town where they were joined by "E" Company, sent forward from the Kansas Line for reinforcement.

Immediate plans to retake Hill 983 were made by the Division. The 9th Infantry was given responsibility for securing, occupying and defending the 983-940 hill mass and was directed to launch a counter-attack in conjunction with the remaining elements of the 36th ROK Regiment which still held Hill 940. The 38th Infantry was directed to give fire support to the ROK's who would move westward along the ridgeline extending between Hills 940 and 983.

At 2250 hours on the same day, the Second Battalion of the 38th was ordered to move to Hill 773 to bolster the ROK's who had defended it successfully against several North Korean attacks during the daylight hours. Both the 36th ROK Regiment and the 35th, which had arrived at Tokko-li, were placed under the operational control of the 38th Infantry.

The 9th Infantry launched its attack the morning of 27 August. Fierce fighting throughout the day failed to net any gain and by nightfall, 983 was still secure in enemy hands. That night, Division artillery unleashed the most intense artillery barrage of the war on the slopes of 983 as more than 22,500 rounds were sent screaming into the hillsides during the hours of darkness.

The Division delegated to the 9th Infantry the sole responsibility of retaking Hill 983 and on 28 August, the Third Battalion prepared to pass through the Second Battalion to press the attack. The Second had been badly battered in the pre-

vious day's assault. The First Battalion was still in positions on the Kansas Line, securing it against any enemy thrust.

Heavy rains turned the roads and trails leading to the battle area into rivers of mud on the 28th and, as a result, it was not until noon that the Third Battalion was in position to move forward. It had no sooner jumped off, however, than at 1300 hours it met with heavy resistance. "I" and "F" Companies bore the brunt of the fighting during the afternoon and nightfall revealed them still a few hundred meters short of the crest. There, with darkness upon them, they set up a perimeter defense for the night.

A terrific rain, which had fallen intermittently during the day, built up to a virtual flood that night as more than four inches of rain coursed down the hills, filling the gulleys and making roaring rivers out of the mountain streams. Bridges over which poured the constant flow of supplies to support the attack were washed out. The Ladue bridge, largest double-span Bailey in the world bridging the Soyang near Division CP, was damaged when a washed out pontoon bridge struck one of the supports and disabled the northern-most span. G-4 hastily arranged to have ammunition, fuel and supplies trucked from Chunchon, reducing the traffic load over the seriously weakened span. The 8229th Mobile Army Surgical Hospital serving the Division was isolated when the pontoon bridge leading to it was washed out and all seriously wounded patients had to be routed to Chunchon.

The bloody fighting on the scarred hills continued during the following day and Division released the First Battalion, 9th Infantry from the Kansas Line to reinforce the other two Battalions who had battered against the enemy positions. Someone, somewhere coined the inevitable GI nickname for the barren battlefield and it was only a matter of time before "Bloody Ridge" was known, not only to the weary, wet and miserable attackers, but to all at home who read the news reports of the gallant struggle.

Plans were drawn-up on 29 August for a new "limited offensive" for all units in the X Corps. Scheduled for 0600 hours, 31 August, it called for an attack to the newly designated "Hays Line." The principle objective of the 2d Division was a north-south hill mass extending 3,000 meters in length in the eastern portion of the Division zone, and dominated by Hill 1243, a rocky, craig-covered peak, honeycombed with enemy bunkers. On the east, the 5th ROK and the 1st Marine Divisions would push out to take the extension of the hill mass which, in their sectors, curved into the east-west ridge which lined the northern rim of the "Punchbowl." In anticipation of the new attack, the Division front was greatly narrowed, excluding the "Punchbowl" from the 2d Division zone.

The attack plan called for the 9th Infantry to assault and seize Hills 940 and 983 then move north and secure the ROK's former Objective "C". The 23rd Infantry would keep one battalion to maintain the Kansas Line and hold two other battalions in reserve for commitment anywhere in the Division zone. The 38th Infantry was given the mission of seizing Hill 1243. All units began immediate preparations for the offensive.

The 9th Infantry renewed its efforts to retake the 940-983 hill mass in the early morning hours of 30 August. And as the First and Second Battalions moved out on the attack, the Third Battalion went forward to relieve ROK Army elements supposedly holding Hill 773. However, as the Third Battalion moved up the slopes of 773 it became engaged with a large enemy force and in the ensuing fire-fight was forced back down the hill. It returned to its base in Worun-ni, reorganized and stepped off again to try and reach the crest of 773 which had been given-up by the ROK's. And again their efforts failed and nightfall found the entire 'Bloody Ridge" still in enemy hands. The First and Second Battalions had tried to take the western portion of the ridge but fire from 1,000 enemy reinforcements had repulsed their attack. It had been a day of bitter battle with heavy casualties on both sides. Night brought little relief for both sides knew the assaults would be renewed at daybreak.

Eastward, the 38th Infantry under command of Colonel Frank T. Mildren girded itself for a new offensive. And back at Division headquarters, Brig. Gen. Thomas E. DeShazo, commander of 2d Division Artillery prepared to replace Major General Clark. L. Ruffner, the commanding general. General Ruffner, who had come to the Division from X Corps in mid-January, had received orders to a new post in Washington. Destined to depart the first of September, he could look back on more than seven months during which he had piloted his troops through some of the bitterest battles of the Korean War, leading them to their greatest victories climaxed by the overwhelming defeat of the Chinese during the Battle of the Soyang River which won for his Division the Presidential Unit Citation. Even as he prepared to leave, his men were struggling forward, welded into a completely professional, well-trained army which attested to his leadership.

The 9th Infantry had an advance taste of success as August faded into its final days. The First Battalion launched a new assault on Hill 773 in the early hours of 31 August. With "B" and "C" Companies hurling themselves upward against the fire of the entrenched North Korean troops on Hill 773, the crest was over-run at 2130 hours. All available troops in the battalion moved upward and in a matter of minutes the position was organized, a perimeter thrown up and the first of three peaks in "Bloody Ridge" was again ours. It never fell to the enemy again.

The 38th Infantry, having readied itself for days, was prepared to move out against one of the most rugged, inaccessible peaks it had encountered in Korea—Hill 1243. Towering high in the distance, its top shrouded in clouds and mist, the objective was the northernmost crest of a string of hills jutting northeast from Taeu San. Like an arrow, it penetrated into the heart of the enemy defenses but the stepping stones along the shaft were formidable goals in themselves—Hills 892, 1059, 1181 and finally, 1243, called Kachilbong by the Koreans.

The supply problem, alone, was almost insurmountable and only ingenious and full ex-

ploitation of every possible method of resupply enabled the attack to be carried out. Personnel from Headquarters and Service Company, the Tank Company (for the terrain precluded use of the regiment's tanks), and the mortar sections were pressed into service as carriers, augmenting and supervising the Korean carriers. Each infantryman carried with him three mortar rounds or a round of 75 mm recoiless ammunition as he toiled up the sheer heights for hours before even reaching the line of departure. The medical company, reinforced by additional personnel, performed miracles of recovery and casualty colelction. The signalmen overcame immense difficulties to keep all the advancing elements in contact with headquarters. And to the foot soldier goes credit for an endurance and fortitude which has few records of equal, even in Korea. To all these went the signal to attack at first light on 31 August.

The First Battalion took the lead, moving upward against light resistance until, at 0920, "C" Company, spearheading the advance, became engaged with two enemy companies on the approaches to Hill 992. Immediately "A" Company swung to the side to attempt an enveloping maneuver and "B" Company moved forward to add its support to that of "C". The fighting raged until dusk without appreciable progress and all units broke contact and went into positions for the night.

Next morning, the attackers moved out again. Calling on massed artillery, utilizing every weapon, the atacking elements forced their way forward. The enemy could not withstand the assault and slowly gave ground as he took casualties which would have sapped the strength of any force. By 1100, the First Battalion had scaled the peak of Hill 1059 and rolled on up the ridgeline in pursuit of the withdrawing enemy. By 1900 hours, Hill 1181 was in the hands of the 38th and the entire attacking force swung into a perimeter for the night, more than half-way to their objective at the end of two days of assault.

The 38th followed up its original success on 2 September. From their consolidated positions on Hill 1181, the troops moved up the last long ridgeline leading to the objective. Enemy mortar and artillery fire hindered the initial moves and as the men toiled closer to the crest the added fury of small arms and automatic weapons fire joined in the chorus. The Third Battalion, leading the assault, continued struggling forward, digging the defenders out of their holes and annihilating those who tried to resist the advance. The fight raged throughout the day

and after dark. Finally, at 2145, the exhausted, shaken but victorious troops cleared the crest. Around them lay the bodies of 152 enemy dead. Behind them lay the tortoruous route over which they had fought for three days. Ahead and on both sides was the enemy. Dog-tired, the men organized the crest for the long night.

The 9th Infantry was far from idle as the 38th thrust deep into the enemy defensive line. After securing Hill 773 on the last day of August, it struck anew at the two remaining peaks on "Bloody Ridge," Hills 983 and 900. Both the heights were bare now. All vegetation had long since withered under the constant pounding of artillery and tank fire. Now only dusty, rock studded, brown silt remained. Trees, twisted and scarred, criss-crossed the steep slopes, obscuring the pock-marked faces of the lower portions of the hills. Here and there dark holes marred the highest reaches, the only evidence of bunkers until the sharp, rattle of the "burp" guns cut loose. Sweating, heart pounding heavy-footed soldiers dragged their throbbing legs up these tortured, vertical hills. Those who succeeded in grasping their way close to the bunkers were greeted by the crump and shower of black smoke, dirt and sharp steel as grenades were tossed down upon them. Dirty, unshaven, miserable they backed down, tried again, circled, climbed, slid, suffered, ran, rolled, crouched and grabbed upward only to meet again the murderous fire, the blast of mortar and whine of bullets and jagged fragments. Minutes seemed like hours, hours like days, and days like one long, terrible, dusty, blood-swirled night-mare. Shiver at night, sweat clogged at day, racked with chills one minute, stewed in their own juices the next.

It was like that for days. The First Battalion tried to reach the top on 1 September but never had a chance. It was the same on the 2nd of September, and the 3rd. Each day locked in struggle and each day stopped short of the crest which meant an end, at least temporarily, to the endless fight. Then came 4 September. Everything was told to hold where it was. Plans for an all-out attack were coming up. Air and artillery spread new destruction and havoc on the slopes of the blood-stained ridge. Constant pounding of shells, bursting of bombs, the "whoomp" of napalm, long roar of rockets and the muffled clatter of aircraft machine guns comprised the preparation for another trip upward on 940 and 983. But there was additional help for the 9th this time. The 23rd Infantry made ready to move around to the west and tackle the ridgeline stretching north from 983 to Hill 778;

objective "N" was its name. And the 38th Infantry was now in position to offer fire support and block reinforcements from the northeast for on 4 September it moved westward and captured Hills 754 and 660 overlooking the MSR north of Pia-ri. All was in readiness as 4 September faded away.

The climax was almost anti-climax. After the struggle of the past weeks, the First and Second Battalions of the 9th moved out on 5 September. Their goal was Hill 940. It was tough going but not to be compared with the previous, frustrating efforts. At 1400 hours, the troops of the 9th Infantry were on the crest and the enemy, those that remained, were fleeing to escape the trap. Hundreds of North Korean dead were strewn on the hill, surorunded by their ammunition and supplies. Later it was revealed more than 4,000 enemy troops had fallen under the attacks and an additional 7,000 had been badly wounded in the vain attempt to defend the hill. It had been a fierce battle and the rutted, dirty razor-back now supporting the exhausted soldiers who had wrested it from the enemy well-deserved the title "Bloody Ridge."

The supporting attack of the 23rd Infantry proceeded equally as well as that of the 9th. By 1615, the Second Battalion, advancing under accurate and devastating fire from "B" and "C" Companies of the 72d Tank Battalion, had secured Objective "N". Fifteen minutes later the First Battalion was on the uppermost height of Hill 618, a knobby lump of land which blocked the northward curl of the MSR west of "Bloody Ridge" and forced it to curve to the east.

The 9th Infantry began moving out of the line on 6 September to reorganize, resupply and intergrate replacements after the days of battle preceeding the fall of Hill 940. The 23rd Infantry moved up to relieve the 9th, assuming responsibility for its sector. The 38th Infantry continued organizing defensive positions along ridge running north from 1179 to 1243.

During the day, the 23rd moved out from Objective "N", sending "E" Company to occupy Hill 785 and "F" Company to Hill 778, two peaks northwest and northeast from Objective "N", respectively. "I" Company repulsed a counter-attack at 2130 by an estimated enemy company from its positions on Hill 618.

The 2d Division zone of responsibility was shifted westward 900 meters on 7 September, the 5th ROK taking over the hard-won ridgeline from the 38th Infantry. To better control the Division, the Commnd Post moved up to a valley north of Yanggu off the eastern tip of the Hwachon Reservoir. Patrols, meanwhile, reported contact with enemy groups on Hill 868, west of Hill 1181, and on Hill 702, the next high ground north of Hill 660 which was in the hands of the 38th Infantry.

Major activity for units of the Division on 8 September was centered in the artillery and the tank battalion. DivArty turned its guns loose to fire in support of an attack by the 5th ROK Division on Hill 1211, next peak northward in the 1179-1243 ridgeline. The 72d Tank Battalion furnished fire support for the 7th ROK Division trying to take Hill 883. Neither attack was successful, however, in spite of the fact that they continued for two days running. On 9 September, "B" Company of the 72d fired over 800 rounds direct fire.

Plans for putting the 38th Infantry into reserve were drawn-up on 9 September. Details called for the 9th Infantry to relieve the 23rd in place with the 23rd then shifting eastward, relieving the 38th which would then go into reserve. The move was to be initiated on 13 Sept. Meanwhile, both sides continued probing activity with an unsuccessful attempt by the First and Second Battalion of the 38th to occupy positions on the ridge branching west off Hill 1181.

Evidence of enemy infiltration was revealed the same day as the abortive attempt by the 38th to move out the spur of 1181. Two tanks from the 38th Regimental Rank Company on patrol along the Pia-ri—Worun-ni road were disabled by mines obviously planted by infiltrators.

The 38th launched a heavy assault on Hill 868 the following day which raged for three days.

"A" and "G" Companies spearheaded the attack the first day and though they succeeded in moving up the slopes, they were unsuccessful in nearing the crest in any force. On 11 September, "A" and "G" Companies struck at the hill from the northeast while "E" Company swung up from the southwest and by 1830 'E' was within 50 meters of the peak when a tornado of grenades rained down upon it and the company was forced to withdraw temporarily. In a renewed attempt, both "A" and "G" were within five feet of the top when they were stopped and forced to withdraw down the slope and set up a perimeter for the night. The next morning all units moved out once again, this time joined by "F" Company. Finally, by 1500 hours on the 12th. the hill was taken and secured.

Meanwhile, the 9th Infantry began the relief of the 23rd, the First Battalion relieving the First Battalion of the 23rd before nightfall on the 10th.

Relief of the 23rd was completed on 11 September with "B" Company, 72d Tank Battalion reverting from the 23rd to the 9th and continuing in its mission of fire support. The 23rd then began relieving elements of the 38th not engaged on Hill 868. This phase of the relief was completed by 1200, 13 September when the hill was secure and the 38th free to go into reserve.

Another peak was snatched from under the noses of the North Koreans on 12 September when "B" Company of the 23rd took Hill 702 with surprising ease. By 1530 the crest was secure.

The firing for "Bloody Ridge" had scarcely died in the distance when rumblings of a new and equally epic struggle were heard. With the 2d Division organizing its newly won ground and jabbing out to find enemy weaknesses to its front, the North Koreans decided to made a new stand and stop the 2d Division's grinding offensive. From their rear areas and from the shattered ranks of the recently defeated defenders of "Bloody Ridge," the enemy formed three new battalions which he placed in column along the new area he chose to hold—the important north-south ridge dominated by Hill 851 on the north, 931 in the center and 894 on the south. The long slopes jutting down from 894 curved southwestward and ended in a series of small hills clustered around the village of Tutayon on the west MSR. The ridge line was ideally suited for defense, as was the entire area. The most important portion of it was that extending from Hill 894 north to Hill 851. It was to be the scene of bitter fighting for many weeks. Little did anyone know that in a short time the people of the free world would be well acquainted with the ragged peaks of "Heartbreak Ridge."

"HEARTBREAK RIDGE"

TERRAIN SKETCH

"Heartbreak Ridge" is a narrow, rocky, mountain mass running north and south with HILLS 931, 894, and 851 dominating the MUNDUNG-NI and SATAE-RI Valleys. The south and east slopes were extremely steep. From these slopes the "Punchbowl" and HILL 1179 could be seen in the distance. Both prominent objectives had already fallen into our hands. Initially heavy vegetation covered the slopes of Heartbreak Ridge but air strikes and artillery destroyed all individual concealment. In each valley bordering the ridge were two important roads and stream beds. The roads were secondary class routes, but a road capable of moving military equipment was built in a short time. Also, a twisting, boulder-strewn stream bed in each valley furnished an approach for tanks. Narrow gorges and deep defiles presented difficult engineering problems which were overcome during the engagement. Enemy bunkers guarded the key ridges of approach. Due to a moderate slope to the west and north, the enemy supplies were moved up in positions with a minimum amount of labor.

The battle for "Heartbreak Ridge" started on 13 September with the 9th Infantry launching an attack on Hill 728, west of the main objective, and giving fire support to the First and Second Battalions of the 23rd who jumped off onto Hill 931, central peak of three heights on the ridgeline. The 38th Infantry, meanwhile, had gone into reserve with its relief by the 23rd.

The first day's fighting for Hill 931 brought little success as the well-entrenched enemy called upon artillery and mortars to held repel the attackers. His stiff resistance was bolstered on the 14th as both the 9th and 23rd continued their assaults in the vicinity of Hill 894. "B" Company of the 72d Tank Battalion was able to support the 9th from positions on the MSR to the west and their high-velocity tank fire proved effective in knocking out the enemy bunkers exposed to the direct fire of the tank guns.

The Second Battalion of the 9th moved out against 728 and by noon was on the southeast slope of Hill 894. However, an order came down directing it to change its original objective and swing northward to assault Hill 894 from the south while the 23rd Infantry continued atetmpts to overcome it from the north. The pincers attack was pressed all afternoon and by 1700 hours the Second Battalion of the 9th was within 650 meters of the crest but there it was stopped. The 23rd, meanwhile, had succeeded in gaining the crest of the ridge which joined Hills 931 and 851 and at 1900 hours it set up defenses for the night.

The enemy reacted quickly to the 23rd's gains which succeded in blocking the ridgeline connecting his garrisons on 851 and 931. Strong probing attacks were flung out as the North Koreans attempted to reestablish their net-work of entrenchments but the 23rd succeeded in repulsing them all.

The 9th Infantry jumped off again to gain Hill 894 at 0700 hours on the 15th. Fighting fiercely against determined resistance, the Manchu regiment gained the crest by 1445 and immediately sent strong forces down the ridgeline south and west from the peak and northeast toward Hill 931. The forces rushing south secured the entire ridgeline, stopping on an unnumbered hill overlooking the village of Tutayon near the western MSR. A platoon from "L" Company of the 9th was unable to overcome strong resistance on Hill 485, western anchor of the ridgeline running southwest of 894.

The troops from the Second Battalion, 9th Infantry who moved north from Hill 894 dug-in on positions 400 meters north of their newly captured objective.

And while the 9th was successful in securing the southern and southwestern portion of the important ridgeline, the 23rd sent its Second and Third Battalions in a coordinated attack to take Hills 931 and 851 while the French Battalion launched an attack on Hill 841, a peak east across the MSR from the regiment's foothold on "Heartbreak Ridge". All these efforts met with no success in spite of close air and artillery support. The enemy utilized every weapon in his arsenal, fighting with furious determination in his effort to keep control of the vital ridge.

All limits on artillery ammunition expenditure were lifted by Eighth Army on 15 September as it offered every support to the 2d Division in its attempts to take "Heartbreak Ridge."

The 23rd Infantry renewed its slamming attacks against 931 and 851 on 16 September but made little gain during the day. Nightfall saw the tired, chopped ranks of the 23rd again going into perimeter defenses to protect themselves from the inevitable enemy probes. The air was thick with the blue smoke of artillery, the peaks churned into pulverized dust. The ridge had the appearance of a forest following a devastating fire as only twisted gaunt remains of trees and shrubs gave evidence of the once heavy underbrush which had carpeted the sheer slopes before the battle.

The enemy threw light probing attacks against the elements of the First Battalion, 23rd Infantry shortly after midnight. The North Korean garrison on 931 was strong although the positions of the First Battalion, 23rd, astride the ridge running south from 931 made re-supply and reinforcement impossible. The men of the 23rd readied for a new assault which the probes had signaled. The anticipated thrust came at 0300 hours. Two enemy companies struck at "C" Company from the north. Hardly had the attack begun than an entire North Korean battalion was screaming down from 931 and "C" Company's positions were penetrated. At 0730 hours, "A" Company was pushed through the dogged "C" Company and together the two units hit the wall of attackers, forcing them back and regaining the lost positions. The enemy hurled another battalion-sized atack against the First Battalion at 1300 hours. Immediately a devastating rain of 2d Division artillery was called in and the big guns thundered in the rear, their shells plowing gaping holes into the ridge-line. "A" Company counter-attacked again, pushing north onto the ridge-line. At the same time, the Second and Third Battalions struck again toward Hill 851, clawing their way through a curtain of flying mortar to gain positions 1,000 meters from the crest. By this time, night had fallen and all three battalions dug-in to hold their gains.

The first faint streaks of dawn were hardly visible on 18 September when the 23rd renewed its efforts on the ridgeline. Two enemy regiments were now defending "Heartbreak" to the death. No amount of artillery fire could drive them from their bunkers on the rear slopes where they took refuge until the artillery lifted and the infantry assault began. It was a question of digging them out, one at a time. The 23rd attack was met with immediate resistance, fierce and determined. All day it raged with every foot forward paid for in human life. By nighttime, the First Battalion was within 500 meters of 931 when the enemy counterattacked again. Determined to hold, the 23rd called again on the superb artillery support and watched as the explosions shook the hill and turned the North Koreans back. The Second and Third Battalions, after dueling with the enemy all day, decided on a night attack against 851. Under cover of darkness they moved forward as the artillery rolled ahead of them. Assaulting the enemy in his foxholes, terrifying him with flame-throwers, the attackers crawled upward, not to be denied. Success was theirs at last. Shortly after midnight, the lead elements crawled to the top, exhausted but in weary high spirits for Hill 851 was theirs.

But the feeling of accomplishment was short lived. At 0100, an enemy company struck at "L" Company on the crest. By 0200, the enemy force had grown to battalion size and though the valiant troops clung to their hard-won positions for hours in face of violent attack, daylight found them being forced off their peak, pulling back under fire cover from the remainder of the Third Battalion. At 1230 hours, the Second Battalion, passing through the Third, counter attacked and attempted to retake Hill 851. Individual, hand-to-hand fights raged all over the crest as hand grenades exploded, throwing their dirt and steel like rain along the peak. And as the troops of the 23rd and the North Koreans grappled, a strong, reinforcing enemy descended and counterattacked in the early morning hours. "L" Company's ammunition became exhausted and the enemy surged forward, overrunning four machine guns. Still the company stood until the entire foot-hold was overrun. The company commander Lieutenant Pete Monfore stayed with the last of the defenders until he fell, mortally wounded among his men.

Meanwhile, in clearing weather that aided both air and artillery observation, both the First and Third Battalions of the 9th Infantry and the First Battalion of the 23rd slammed anew at their objectives. Thirty seven fighter bombers roared out of the sky and covered the Third Battalion of the 9th as it struck at the 485-728 hill mass north of Imokchong on the west MSR while the First Battalion of the 23rd again pushed up the unbelievably steep slopes of 931. Neither battalion was successful. Minefields, covered by fire from both 485 and 728 stopped the Manchu Battalion. The First Battalion of the 23rd, clawing upward in an inspired attack, fought to within 300 meters of the crest of Hill 931 but again was stopped. Again they were forced to pull back, digging-in to await the dawn.

Westward, a patrol from the Third Battalion, 9th Infantry moved onto Hill 1024 to engage and determine enemy defenses, returning before nightfall.

The Indianhead Division was in contact with four North Korean Divisions on 20 September when Major General Robert N. Young arrived to replace Brigadier General Thomas E. DeShazo —due for rotation to the states—as commanding general. The former assistant division commander of the 82d Airborne Infantry Division, General Young took over the helm of the 2d Infantry in the midst of one its most rugged offensive actions. General deShazo, with a long and spectacular record of action in Korea as a super-artilleryman and strong advocate of extensive use of forward observers bid farewell to the Division which he had served so well.

The fierce struggle for "Heartbreak Ridge" continued unabated throughout the day and again the two enemy regiments resisting the efforts of the 23rd Infantry were successful in repelling all attacks. The 9th Infantry west of the vital ridge reported all its patrols in contact with the enemy. "A" Company on 867 was engaged all day before returning to its base.

Action on the entire Division front was quieter on 21 September than it had been in weeks with the enemy putting up only a passive resistance to patrols sent out from the regiments. All units gathered themselves for new assaults.

Battles flared again on 22 September as the First and Second Battalions of the 23rd launched another coordinated attack on 931, center of "Heartbreak Ridge." Fiercest yet of all the assaults, both battalions were on the crest of the hotly contested height several times during the day only to be thrown off as the enemy attacked through his own mortar fire, hurling grenades and directing streams of machine gun fire forward of his advance. The First Battalion of the

9th became engaged in this same action and was unable to break contact although it was headed for an assault on Hill 728. Finally, plans to take the peak that day were abandoned and all three battalions took up blocking positions on the ridgelines extending from 931 in both directions.

The 15th North Korean Regiment crowded a strong counter-attack against the 23rd Infantry during the night supported by heavy mortar concentrations which churned the dirt on all sides of the defenders. Fighting fiercely, the 23rd repulsed the attackers and sent them scurrying back to the protection of their bunkers.

The 23rd and 24th of September developed into a tragic act which helped to give further backing to the label "Heartbreak Ridge." Desperate to end the continual fighting, the First Battalion of the 23rd again forced its way up the slopes of Hill 931. There it grappled with the enemy, cut into his ranks and inflicted severe casualties, all the time moving upward. At 1400, "A" Company found itself within 50 meters of the crest. It called upon every reserve of energy and courage it had and flung itself upward but was battered back. Again and again it tried to make the grade, in spite of mortar, grenade, and bullet it crept and crawled forward only to be shoved down again. A fourth assault met with failure and summoning unbelievable guts the dauntless men moved out again and by sheer dint of courage scaled the peak. 931 had been taken. It was ours. And the First Battalion of the 23rd found it hard to believe but the presence of the men of "A" Company on the peak confirmed the fact which they hardly dared to believe. Hastily setting up a defense, the handful of men remaining in the First Battalion dug-in on the crest, surrounded by the aftermath of battle. The anticipated enemy counter-attack came at 0220 hours on the 24th. Maddened screaming, animal-like the North Koreans charged the positions in mass, hurling grenades out of the night and directing their murderous fire into the bunkers which they had built and knew so well. It was too much for the thinned, battle-weary men to resist and at 0330 hours the remaining few were forced from the crest. At 0445, with "A" Company again in the lead, the First Battalion counter-attacked. At 0610 hours, "B" and "C" Companies were engaged with 200 enemy pouring down from 931 and from the northwest, repulsing the enemy efforts to annihilate them. The fighting continued throughout the day until at nightfall the heroic men of the 23rd went into positions for the hours of darkness during which they turned-back countless enemy probes.

The heart-rending story of frustration was repeated in the sector of the 9th Infantry during the same two-day period. An attack by the First Battalion to take Hill 1024 met with failure with the attackers going into perimeter defense 300 meters northeast of the crest. An attempt on 24 September by the First Battalion of the 9th to take Hill 728, again bypassing Hill 931, also was repulsed.

For eleven days, now, the two regiments had given every ounce of energy and reserve they possessed to take their objectives. Time and time again they had met with failure at the hands of the North Koreans. Each day was like the last—fight, suffer, meet or escape death, sweat-out the nights only to move out each new day to climb and battle up the endless hills. Victory almost in hand for a second only to see it swept away again. But like all war, there was no rest. The objective had to be taken.

And so it was that the 9th and 23rd Infantry Regiments again moved into battle on the 25th of September. While in the valleys below the trees turned autumn golden and red and leaves littered the ground much as they did back home, on the hills there was only the pock-marked hard and dusty earth littered with steel and blood and the remains of men who had given all they possessed.

One success will often keep men going long after the time they could be expected to drop. And so when the First Battalion of the 9th Infantry met with success that day on Hill 1024, the news was a stimulant to all. Lead by "A"

Company attacking from 800 meters below the peak, the lead elements of the Battalion were on the crest at 1145 hours. And moving up amid resistance from a heavy enemy mortar barrage, the rest of the Battalion was on the hill by 1500 hours and four hours later was tied in with ROK units on the left.

The French Battalion relieved the Second Battalion of the 23rd over on the ridgeline south of Hill 851. The Second Battalion then moved down into an assembly area at Imdong-ni, well south of Worrun-ni and well out of contact with the enemy. There its tired remnants were to gather themselves together, be resupplied, reorganized and readied for new commitment.

The Ivanhoe Security Force took over surveillance of the Kansas Line on 25 September and the 38th Infantry prepared to move forward for future action. Poor visability hindered all actions.

The next day, 26 September, the French tried their luck against Hill 931 and found it no better than had the rest of the regiment. The First and Third Battalions remained in position, kept close into their meager holes by continuous barrages of enemy artillery, mortar, automatic weapons and small arms fire.

The 9th Infantry consolidated its positions on Hill 1024, sending a patrol from "A" Company 300 meters north to flush and kill 45 enemy troops in bunkers on the ridgeline. The 38th Infantry sent patrols to the vicinity of Hills 1052 and 851 without contact.

The enemy made up for the relatively quiet day as darkness enveloped the rocky hills for the night. On Hill 1024, the First Battalion of the 9th Infantry contained strong enemy counterattacks while the Second Battalion repulsed equally strong attacks against its positions on Hill 582.

Morning of 27 September brought welcome relief to the First Battalion of the 23rd when it was pulled out of line, relieved by the refitted Second. Gladly the men came down from the hills into Worrun-ni where they, too, were given the opportunity to rest, bathe, get fresh clothing and resupply.

And the 38th Infantry became engaged on the 27th for the first time since its return from reserve. The First Battalion encountered enemy on the slopes of 1052 and a platoon from "M" Company became the center of attention for the entire Division when it inadvertently made a "wrong turn."

Moving up to furnish fire support to the Second Battalion in its attack on 1052, the platoon was headed for Hill 868. The platoon had left

its company area at 0500. Its instruction were to turn up a trail just beyond a certain tank which was blocking along the road. Unfortunately there was more than one tank in blocking position and it was at the wrong tank that the platoon made its turn. It walked into enemy infested territory until it reached a small footbridge 800 meters west of Satae-ri. At 0900, it became bitterly engaged with an enemy force deployed in bunkers on Hill 656, just north of Satae-ri. Word went back to Division and a rescue force was hastily assembled and sent forward. The units making up the force were mute evidence that everyone in the vicinity had been called upon for help. There was a platoon from "X" Company, French Battalion; two squads from "C" Company, 38th Infantry; a platoon from the Tank Company, 38th Infantry; and a platoon from the Tank Company, 23rd Infantry.

After several hours of hard fighting in the midst of the enemy infested area, the rescue force succeded in extricating the embattled platoon and making its way back to friendly lines at 1300 hours. There was some question as to who was the most surprised at the maneuver, the North Koreans or the "M" Company platoon.

The enemy made a concerted effort to recapture Hill 1024 from the 9th Infantry on 28 September. Thirteen separate counter-attacks were pushed against the First Battalion but all were turned back with heavy losses. Immediately afterward, a narrowing of the Division front placed the peak in the zone of the 7th ROK Division and at 1300 hours, ROK elements relieved the First Battalion of its responsibility for holding the crest. The Battalion then withdrew to an assembly position 5,000 meters south of the lines.

Ground activity elsewhere in the Division sector on the 28th was relatively light compared to previous days but clearing weather permitted a record number of air sorties. Under control of Division FSCC, 128 fighter aircraft were employed in the Division sector with excellent results. The planes were particularly effective ranging beyond the limits of artillery fire, destroying enemy gun positions, supply and assembly points.

Activity on 29 September was confined mainly to the 9th Infantry as the First Battalion, supported by fire from "B" Company of the 72d Tank Battalion and Division Artillery, moved out to make another attempt on Hill 867.

Lady luck favored the North Koreans on this day. Fog, ground mist and rain throughout the day greatly reduced the effectiveness of artillery support. No air support was available at all.

Initial contact was light as the lead elements closed to within 150 meters of the objective. But upon reaching this point, a hail of exceptionally intense mortar and artillery fire pinned the troops down. The concentration continued until 1725 hours when it suddenly lifted and the enemy launched a fierce counter attack. By 1800 hours, the 9th was ordered to break contact and return to its original positions.

The First Battalion, 23rd Infantry, relieved the Third Battalion on position during the day with the Third returning to Worrun-ni. The remainder of the regiment remained in place, organizing its positions as did the 38th.

All combat units of the Division were in contact with the enemy during the last day of Sep-

tember. In spite of every attempt by the Division to oust the entrenched North Koreans from their mountain strongholds, the fading September sun set on Heartbreak Ridge, Hill 1052, 867 and 728 and revealed them still in enemy hands. But the rock-like defenses for the North Koreans had been costly. Excluding air strike casualties, 7,256 enemy troops were killed during the month; 9,878 were wounded and more than 600 communists were herded into UN prison camps. With the air-inflicted casualties included, the enemy dead and wounded in September came to more than 20,000, a total the North Koreans could ill-afford to absorb.

Division casualties, though light by comparason, were the heaviest in months. In spite of the hopes for a truce, the war continued to rage at a heart-rending pace.

A plan for ending the seemingly endless struggles on the hills on and near "Heartbreak Ridge" was set forth at a staff briefing on 1 October by General Young. Anxious to bring the operations in the mountains north of Yanggu to a sucecssful conclusion, he directed the laying of plans for an all-out assault. Heretofore, the regiments had jumped-off on their own objectives one at a time. Consequently, the defending North Koreans were able to concentrate their fire support weapons, especially mortars, on the single attacking element of the 2d Division. Added to the determined defensive attitude of the communists and the ideal defensive terrain, this had been enough to repulse almost every effort of the 2d Division in the preceeding weeks unless we were willing to pay more than a reasonable price in casualties.

The plan put forth by General Young envisioned all regiments attacking simultaneously on the Division front with a strong tank-infantry attack up the Mungdung-ni valley on the west coupled with an armored task force foray up the Saete-ri valley in the east. Purpose of these armored ventures was to break behind the enemy lines, disrupt his defenses and inflict the greatest number of casualties.

The advantages of the operation were threefold. First, the enemy would be forced to disperse his mortar fire over a wider front thus reducing the volume of fire he could place on any one particular area. Second, a line established on the salient terrain features designated as objectives for the attack would require fewer troops to secure than the jagged front now maintained. Third, a considerable saving of manpower would be realized by withdrawing and placing into reserve the units holding the hills which were dominated by the objectives of the proposed operation.

Citing the idea behind the three-regiment attack, the General emphasized the importance of the tank-infantry spearheads up the Mung-dung-ni and Saete-ri valleys. Such an operation would not only put the forces into positions from which they could disrupt the enemy defenses from the rear and inflict heavy casualties but also would relieve a great deal of pressure on the Indianhead regiments making the assaults on the hills.

Target date for the attack was 5 October 1951; H-hour, 2100.

Plans to provide the immense logistical support required of such an operation were immediately drawn-up by G-4. Every available truck was pressed into service and by 1800 hours, 5 October, more than 45,000 rounds of artillery ammunition, 10,000 rations, and 20,000 gallons of gas were stockpiled in supply dumps in the valley of the west MSR.

As the trucks hauled load after load of supplies, the regiments moved into positions from which they could advance on the offensive when the word was given. Operation Order 37 setting up the attack plan was published on 2 October. The 9th Infantry was given the mission of attacking and securing Hills 867 and 1005, dominating the ridgeline north of Hill 1024 to the west. The 23rd Infantry was to secure Hill 931 on "Heartbreak" and the ridgeline running west from that peak. It was also to be prepared to assist the 38th Infantry in taking Hill 728 and Objective "C", an unnumbered ridgeline which jutted south from Hill 851. The 38th Infantry, in the center of the Division sector, was to assault Objective "C" and Hill 485, a small hill south of Tutayon on the west MSR. The 38th was also to provide infantry support to the 72d Tank Battalion which was to be prepared to make an armored thrust into Mung-dung-ni. The 2d Engineer Battalion was to exert its maximum effort on the valley road below Mundung-ni, attaching "C" and "D" Companies to the 38th Infantry, "A" to the 9th and "B" to the 23rd. One platoon of "D" Company of the Engineers was to support the tank thrust up the valley.

The tank-infantry task force to operate in the east valley of the Division sector was commanded by Major Kenneth R. Sturman of the 23rd Infantry. This force subsequently bore his name. Raiding thrusts were initiated into the enemy lines on 3 October and were conducted daily for the remainder of the period during which the Division operated in the area north of Yanggu. Composed of the 23rd Infantry Tank Company,

2d Reconnaissance Company and the Combat Company of the Ivanhoe Security Force, the task force proved to be highly successful in knocking out enemy emplacements, inflicting casualties and diverting a portion of the enemy strength from the western half of the Division front. It complemented the stronger tank force operating in the Mundung-ni valley to the east.

By 1800 hours of 4 October, all units of the Division were in position for the attack scheduled for 2100 hours the following day. One fortunate break occurred during the early hours of the 4th when a patrol from "F" Company of the 38th Infantry reported Hill 485 unoccupied. The remaining elements of "F" Company immediately moved onto the hill, securing it and thus placing one of their objectives in their pocket before the main assault had begun.

The tempo of 2d Division air and artillery support picked-up during the daylight hours of 4 October as the enemy continued to throw in harrassing mortar and artillery fire on friendly positions. Small enemy probing attacks were repulsed during the night.

The first indication of the reappearance of the Chinese Communist Forces into the X Corps zone came from prisoner of war reports on 5 September, the day the offensive of the Division was scheduled to get underway. One PW picked up by the Division reported a Chinese reconnaissance party on Hill 931. Later in the day, X Corps intelilgence officers relayed a message from the 8th ROK Division that two civilians had been picked up in its sector who admitted being CCF agents. These reports were the first of CCF troops so far eastward since their disastrous May offensive.

At 2100 hours, 5 October, "Operation Touchdown" moved out with all regiments on line. In the 9th Infantry sector in the west, the First and Third Battalions moved toward Hill 867 as the Second Battalion remained in reserve. By nightfall, after a day without enemy contact, the two attacking battalions were secure on the high ground south and east of their objective and prepared to make their main assault the next day.

The Second Battalion of the 23rd Infantry moved from its positions on Hill 894 and under enemy mortar fire advanced toward the ridge-line jutting west from Hill 931, the battered crest which had been wrestled momentarily from the enemy on the 23rd of September. By 0300 hours on 6 October, the Second Battalion turned into the southernmost knob of the 931 Hill mass and immediately became engaged with elements of an enemy battalion which stubbornly resisted the attack. After a brief but sharp fire-fight, the enemy withdrew from the hill and the Second Battalion moved onto the peak. By 0630 hours, it had tied in with the French Battalion and the hill was secure as a result of the outstandingly successful night attack.

Over in the sector of the 38th Infantry, the First Battalion, less "B" Company which remained on Hill 778, moved out toward Hill 728 overlooking the west MSR. Only light opposition was encountered and the objective was taken with little trouble. "A" Company then extended north and east and tied in with elements of the 23rd Infantry on the ridgeline west from Hill 894.

Down in the valley which lead out into the heart of the enemy defensive garirsons, the 2d Engineers began the tremendous task of making a passable route for the tanks to advance north to Mundung-ni. Apparently the enemy had anticipated such a maneuver and had mined and cratered the road more heavily than any the Division had previously encountered. Tremendous boulders blocked the mountain stream paralleling the road, making the use of that normally passable avenue out of the question. Enemy mortar and automatic weapons fire poured into the area, seriously hampering but failing to stop the engineer effort. "B" and "C" Companies of the tank battalion stood by, firing in support of the attack on the hills overlooking the road and awaiting the opportunity to break through the obstacles which the engineers were clearing.

The 38th Infantry was given three new objectives on the 7th of October. They were Hills 905, 974 and 841, all in the central sector of the Division zone, and they comprised the next ridgeline north of that under attack by the 9th Infantry. A fourth hill, 605, was also assigned to the 38th Infantry. It was on the left of the MSR about 1,800 meters southwest of Mundung-ni.

South of the newly assigned ridgeline objectives of the 38th Infantry, the Third Battalion of the 9th moved onto Hill 867 against little opposition and made immediate plans to continue its advance the next day to the unnumbered hill between 867 and 1005. The Second Battalion, sweeping through the 8th ROK Division zone on the west, succeeded in cutting the ridgeline between Hills 867 and 1005. It then set out to the northwest toward Hill 1005. Initial resistance was light but it increased with every move upward. The advance continued throughout the 7th and 8th and the morning of the 9th found the Second Battalion near its goal

but held up by a death-stand resistance by the North Koreans. Fixing bayonets, the lead elements rushed forward and routed the enemy, digging the individual soldiers from their caves and by late afternoon the hill was secure.

The First Battalion of the 9th, during the actions of the Second and Third Battalions, had begun a move up the valley and on 8 October was occupying the high ground northeast of Hill 867 with a platoon on Hill 666. Plans were made to pass the First Battalion through the Second on Hill 1005 and then continue the attack to the northwest against the next peak, Hill 1040. Early on 10 October, the First Battalion made its move and against moderate resistance inched up the slopes. The enemy, unable to mount his usual last-stand defensive actions after his defeat on 1005, was overcome by 1610 hours and the 9th Infantry was then in full possession of the 867-1005-1040 ridgeline, sometimes spoken of as the Kum Il Sung ridge.

With the important Kum Il Sung ridge held by the 9th, the situation was ripe to launch the 38th in its assault on the next northerly line of crests dominated by Hills 606, 905 and 974. The way was also clear to move onto Hill 605.

Hill 636, the gateway to the ridge objectives of the 38th, was stubbornly defended by the enemy and the initial attempt by the Second Battalion to wrest it from the enemy failed. Another atetmpt was made immediately and although the crest was occupied by nightfall on 9 October, the enemy clung to his foothold and battled the troops into the hours of darkness before relinquishing his positions. The following morning, moving out from 636, the Second Battalion headed for Hill 905 and the high ground to the north east. Again the going was extremely rugged and the enemy resisted every foot of the way. A strong North Korean counterattack forced the battalion to hold-up its advance on the afternoon of the 10th but as soon as it died down the attackers moved out again. Finally, the Second Battalion battled its way to the top of 905 on the 11th and there pulled into a perimeter for the night.

Back in the valley, the Third Battalion of the 38th was moving north to launch an attack on Hill 605 which, if successful, would place it closer to Mundung-ni than any major friendly element had yet been.

Further south, the engineers toiled day and night, blasting through the blockaded roadway which prevented the tanks from thrusting into Mundung-ni itself. Enemy mortar continued to fall into the hive of activity in an effort to prevent a breakthrough.

The Third Battalion of the 38th continued to slog forward up the valley in face of enemy mortar and artillery fire. After two days of dogged advance supported by fire from the 38th Regimental Tank Company, the Third was able to move onto Hill 605 and secure it against counterattack. The Netherlands Detachment tied in on the left and "L" Company tied in with the 72d Tank Battalion on the right. "L" was to remain attached to the tank battalion for the duration of the operation.

The situation in the western valley proceeded in heartening manner while in the east, the 23rd Infantry continued its bitter three week battle for Hill 851, the northernmost objective on "Heartbreak Ridge." With Task Force Sturman making repeated slashes into the enemy lines near Satae-ri, the remainder of the 23rd fought the North Koreans who seemed destined to remain in their deep, protective bunkers forever. On 7 October, the First Battalion prepared to attack the hill once more from the south while the Second Battalion moved northwest from newly won Hill 931 to tie-in with the 38th Infantry which was securing the left flank of the 23rd. The Third Battalion, in conjunction with the moves of the other two units, began an attempt to cut the ridgeline jutting west from 851. The attempt proved successful as the infantrymen managed to fight their way to a point on the ridgeline only 1,000 meters west of the crest. Determined to follow-up their advantage, both the First and Third Battalions inched their way nearer their long-sought objective on the 8th. The enemy fought back furiously, utilizing every weapon he possessed. But the attackers managed to make substantial progress in spite of the resistance and by nightfall they were in a position to dig-in to await morning and a renewal of the attack.

Task Force Sturman made its greatest effort to date on 9 October, ranging deep behind the enemy lines and pouring its high velocity fire into the bunkers on 851 and seriously hindering the enemy's efforts to make repairs.

The Second Battalion of the 23rd was diverted from its attentions to Hill 931 on 10 October when it was ordered to seize a new objective— Hill 520, the end knob of a long ridgeline running west from 931. The battalion moved swiftly down the crest of the spur, flinging aside the defenders, and by 1800 hours was secure on the objective, digging-in at the same time as the Third Battalion of the 38th secured Hill 605.

The Second Battalion of the 23rd tied-in on its left with the 72d Tank Battalion in the valley below, completing a defensive line across the high ground separating the two valleys in the Division zone. Thus, the high ground on both sides of the Mundung-ni valley was secure from the positions of the 23rd and 38th Regiments southward. The stage was set for the armored thrust into the town itself.

B. Smith

The chief obstacles to the armored penetration had been the natural and man-made barriers in the defiles north of Imokchong. Since the start of "Operation Touchdown," "D" Company of the 2d Engineers had been blasting for mines, filling craters, grading the rocky road carved from the hillside, building by-passes and diverting streams in an effort to clear the way for the tanks. Thirty three tons of high explosives had been used in the operation. Finally, after laboring day and night, the defile was clear enough for tank passage. The commanding general ordered the waiting armor to be prepared to move out at first light on 10 October.

The long planned tank-spearhead rolled north through the newly constructed gateway into enemy territory at 0630, 10 October. "B" Company of the 72d Tank Battalion led the raid with "L" Company, 38th Infantry aboard to give added weight to the punch. A platoon from "D" Company, 2d Engineers, accompanied the group to give its assistance in clearing obstacles along the route.

The armored fist burst through the enemy positions and deep into the valley which served as his supply route. Mundung-ni was entered and bypassed as the lead elements of the tank force advanced 1,200 meters north of the town to place fire on the hills. One section turned west into the valley fronting Hill 841 and was able to strike at the reverse slopes of the enemy hills.

Eastward in the Satae-ri valley, Task Force Sturman made another surge north and wrought similar havoc on the disorganized enemy. The two tank assault groups forging up the twin valleys found the enemy unprepared and hundreds of casualties were inflicted beore the communist troops could find cover from the ranging fire.

Meanwhile, the commanding general ordered the 38th Infantry to hold up its advance once it reached Hill 905. Purpose of this was to avoid placing the 38th in a position exposed to possible enemy attack from three sides. Thus, the left flank of the Division was to be, for the moment, along a line connecting Hills 1040 on the south, 905 in the center of the flank, and 605 at the top side. From there the front extended east across the MSR along a line generally 1,000 meters south of Mundung-ni. Once the 8th ROK Division on the left flank of the 38th Infantry pulled onto line, then plans were to be made to be made to move out to take Hill 974 and 841.

Indications of an entrance of Chinese Communist Forces into the 2d Division zone had been increasing during the preceeding few days operations. Finally, on 10 October, a patrol from "G" Company, 38th Infantry, captured a prisoner who was identified as being from the 204th CCF Division. Interrogation officers drew from him information that the CCF was planning a counter attack against the 2d Division within two days after the relief was complete.

The capture of the Chinese soldier formed the last piece necessary to complete the order of battle picture along the Division front. It was now evident that the 68th CCF Army had relieved the V North Korean Corps with the limiting point for the CCF and NK forces the northward projection of the Mundung-ni Road. Thus, the 2d Division faced CCF troops on its left front and North Korean on its right.

The relief of NK troops by those of China was conclusive and decisive evidence of the staggering casualties suffered by the North Koreans in the operations along "Bloody" and "Heartbreak" ridges.

The night of 10-11 October was quiet except for a heavy clash by a Division patrol which ran into an enemy battalion in the vicinity of Hill 851. During the hours of darkness, the First Battalion of the 38th moved up from reserve into an assembly area in the vicinity of Kongdong.

The 23rd Infantry had spent all day of the 10th in another attempt to take Hill 851. This enemy stronghold continued to be defended with every weapon and man the North Koreans could muster and the determined assaults by the 23rd were again repulsed.

Fighting flared anew on 11 October as the Second Battalion of the 38th struck out toward Hill 905 from its positions on Hill 636. The First Battalion, moving up from Kongdong, was following behind prepared to exploit whatever success the Second Battalion achieved. Forging upward against moderate resistance, the Second Battalion secured Hill 905 and the First Battalion passed through and took the high ground between the newly won objective and Hill 974 to the north.

That night, "B" of the 38th secured the high ground between the two hills and "A" and "C" pulled back onto 905.

Plans for extending the holdings of the 38th Infantry were inaugurated on 12 October with a boundry shift to the west which placed Hill 1220 in the Division sector. The Division commander directed the 38th to prepare to take to take Hill 1220 after the 9th Infantry moved up to secure the terrain adjacent to the west MSR, freeing the 38th for the operation. The 23rd Infantry was directed to make a new assault to wrest Hill 851 from the North Koreans. The 72d Tank Battalion reverted from the 38th to the 9th Infantry and was to continue its daily thrusts into Mundung-ni.

At 1300 hours on the 12th, the First Battalion of the 38th moved out against light enemy resistance and in two hours had secured Hill 974, thus placing it in a position for its later attack on 1220. The 9th Infantry organized on its newly occupied positions and the 23rd made preparations for hitting 851 the following day.

Both Task Force Sturman and the 72d Tank Battalion made new forays into the enemy lines on the 12th and again inflicted heavy casualties and wrought extensive damage to the enemy rear areas. One platoon moved up the deep westward draw to a point almost directly north of Hill 841 and slammed its effective, high velocity fire into the Chinese bunkers on the reverse slopes of that enemy-held height.

The tanks of Task Force Sturman again concentrated on Hill 851 where the enemy had resisted every effort of the 23rd Infantry to reach the crest.

As nightfall descended on the rugged peaks, the 23rd Infantry launched a night attack on Hill 851. The North Koreans threw arcs of fire down the slopes, adding hand grenades as the attackers pressed upward. The battle raged throughout the night and at 0530, the First and French Battalions sumomned their last reserves of strength and launched a final assault on the crest. Digging upward in face of murderous enemy fire, they managed to throw the defenders from their peak and by 0630 they were in possession of the long-sought crest. For more than a month, the 23rd Infantry had battered against the enemy on this northernmost height of "Heartbreak Ridge." Once it had been in their hands for a few hours until a powerful counter-attack forced them back. Now it was again in their possession and this time it was theirs to keep.

Reconnaissance of 'Heartbreak Ridge" after its capture revealed why it had been so hard to take. Hill 931 itself was the center peak of three that were within small arms range of each other. While continuing to hold it the enemy could put down well aimed and observed fire on the neighboring two peaks. But what added even more to its strength for the North Korean defenders was the fact that its slope on the eastern side facing the 2d Division troops was rocky and almost perpendicular for the last 250 to 300 yards. Ascent by foot troops was necessarily slow. On the reverse or western side, the slope was less steep and was of dirt. Into this slope, the enemy had dug his many bunkers of such strength as to resist even a direct hit from our 105 mm howitzers. These bunkers, only twenty five to thirty five yards from the topographical crest of the hill, were numerous enough to provide complete protection to some 400 to 500 men. During artillery or air bombardments, the enemy troops would leave their entrenchments and communications trenches on the crest for the protection of their strong bunkers. Yet, when the artillery or air attacks were lifted, they had ample time to return to their positions before our troops could scale the last very steep and rocky 200 to 300 yards on the attacking side.

"Heartbreak Ridge" had fallen but westward, the First Battalion of the 38th was unable to take Hill 1220 despite the slugging fire support from the regimental tanks in the valley to the north. The attackers dug-in for the night while the Netherlands Detachment, relieved by the 9th Infantry, moved up behind to make the assault the next morning.

The Dutch troops moved out at first light against Hill 841, the peak flanking 974 to the north, and against moderate resistance they were on the crest by 1430 hours. Simultaneously, the First Battalion made another lunge up to Hill 1220 with fire from all the supporting weapons in the regiment. By 1430 hours, the assault ele-

ments were within 250 meters of the crest but further efforts to advance upward were repulsed and the battalion dug-in for the night. The Third Battalion had moved up during the attack and at dusk tied in with the First Battalion on the ridgeline leading to 1220.

The first light of dawn was just appearing in the skies on 15 October when the Third Battalion of the 38th Infantry passed through the blocking positions of the First Battalion and moved out to take Hill 1220. Moderate resistance was encountered but by pressing their attack under cover of heavy artillery fire support the attackers were on their objective by mid-afternoon and soon afterward the newly won hill was secure.

The fall of Hill 1220 brought the Indianhead Division abreast of a new line of defense. Stretching from that peak in the west, it arched eastward across the now quiet peaks of "Heartbreak Ridge", Hill 1243, and thence into the northern rim of the "Punchbowl".

The struggle to secure this new line had been one of the most vicious offensive actions the 2d Division had ever undertaken. The deeds which brought it to a close constituted a shining chapter in the history of the United States Army.

The days following the end of "Operation Touchdown" were relatively quiet. Task Force Sturman continued its end runs into enemy territory as did the 72d Tank Battalion but the main purpose of these strikes was to divert the enemy from the relief of the Division which was begun on 20 October. Elements of the 7th U.S. Division were already in the 2d Division area even as "Heartbreak" was falling. By 22 October they were entrenched in the old positions of the 2d Division and the men wearing the Indianhead patch were headed southward in trucks for a well-earned and much-needed period of reserve after 103 days of continuous combat.

The period just completed was truly one of heartaches as well as of Heartbreaks, but even more for the communists than us. The V North Korean Corps had been destroyed and replaced by the 67th CCF Army. The II North Korean Corps had also been decimated. On "Heartbreak Ridge" the 23rd Infantry had captured prisoners from six communist regiments. And all of this was taking place during the period when the truce talks had been suspended. Soon after these successes by the 2d Division, the communists agreed to resume the truce talks.

The sacrifices could not have been in vain if they were the moving factor in convincing the communists that their military defeat in battle was inevitable.

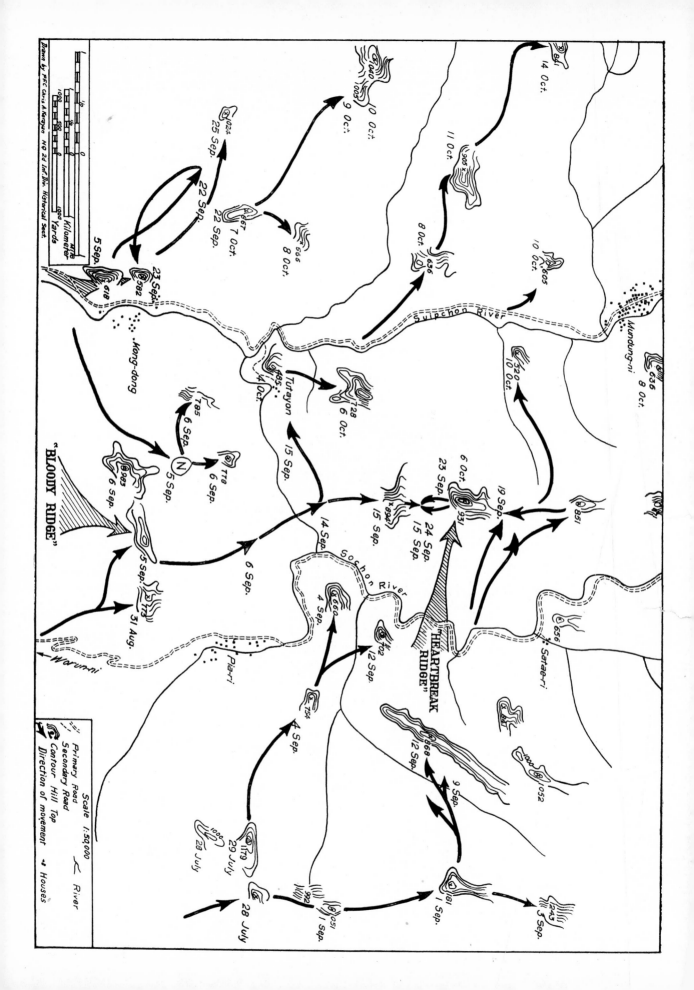

The autumn leaves were falling from the trees in the valleys north of Chunchon and Kapyong when the convoys bearing the 2d Division rolled to a stop. Tents were pitched, stoves were lit against the new cold, and plans were made for rugged training to bring the Division once again to its peak of combat efficiency.

South in Pusan and southwest at Inchon, heavily loaded ships arrived daily bringing new men to fill the ranks of the 2d Division. Waiting to occupy the berths on these now outbound vessels were the men who had earned ten times over the right to return to their homelands.

No one could say what the future had in store. The winds from North Korea brought the first bite of winter and also the sounds of continued battle. The frost which covered the ground in the early morning failed to hide the scars of war. Only the men around the conference tables and those who guided them could make the final decisions. But the men who trained from dawn to dusk and on into the night were preparing to give pointed evidence to the negotiators that whatever the future held, the 2d United States Infantry Division was ready.

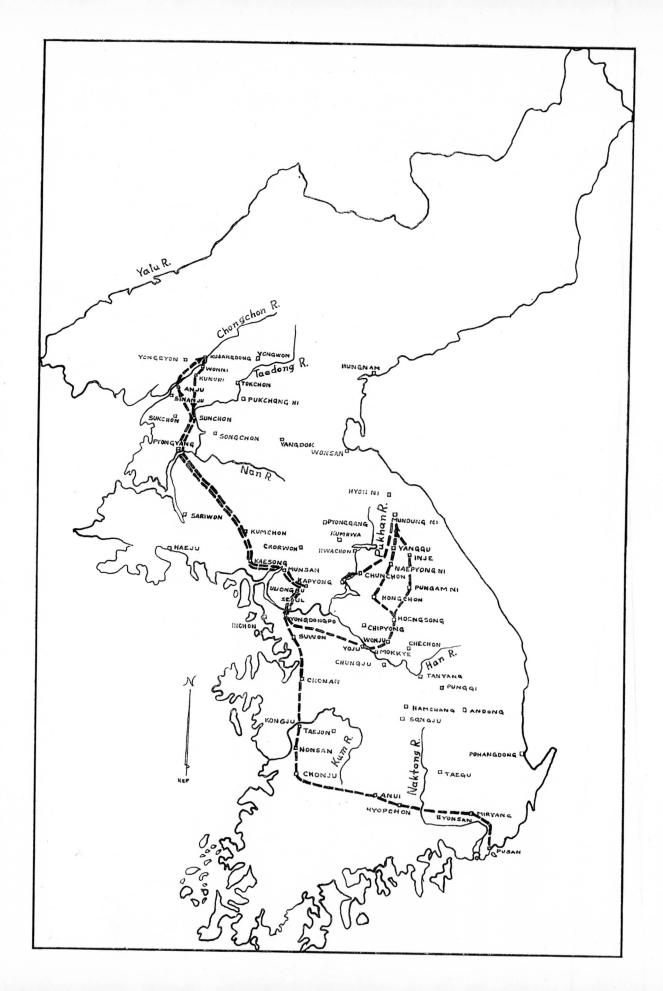

of "F" Company, 9th Infantry, constructing a new home in the residential area of
40 north of Yanggu.

*Chaplain Oscar M. Lifshutz
pauses at a United Nations
cemetery to offer prayer at
the grave of a Jewish-
American soldier.*

The road back down was tough enough when you were well, let alone when you were wounded. Both these shots were of men from the Second Battalion of the 9th Infantry.

It's a long way to the top and all you ever found was another hill just over the crest.

Observing the 9th Infantry's attack on "Heartbreak" Ridge are (left to right) Colonel Lynch, CO of the 9th; General Van Fleet, CG of Eusak; Major General Byers, CG of X Corps; Brigadier General Boatner, Assistant Division Commander of the 2d Division; Brigadier General Meade, Assistant Division Commander of the 3rd Division; and Lieutenant Colonel Pope of the 9th Infantry.

Major General Ruffner pins the Distinguished Unit Citation onto the colors of the Third Battalion, 23rd Infantry, for its action at Chipyong-ni.

"The Chapel on the Parallel" near the Division CP at Yanggu.

Even the Engineers were caught unawares when the heavens opened up and stranded a truck trying to release a Treadway bridge. "A" Company of the 72d Tank Battalion lends a hand in docking the flagship of the 2d Engineers.

General Ruffner sends the 37th Field Artillery Battalion's 250,000th round "on the way."

These 50 caliber barrels are guaranteed to weigh 500 pounds each by the time these men of the 9th Infantry reach to top of the hill. Doing the honors with the muscles are Pfc Bernard P. Arndt, Pfc Marvin Wallman and Sfc Gerald L. Huffman.

Hill 983 gets the heat treatment from the Air Force, deluxe edition.

Stamping-ground for the "Redlegs" of the 503d Field Artillery Battalion during the battle for "Bloody" Ridge.

"H" Company, 9th Infantry transportation corporation rests during a "slight" climb up the hills north of Yanggu.

An enemy WP shell tells these 2d Division tankers that their presence has not gone unnoticed.

Nobody has explained the wind sock hanging above this group of engineers but no explanation is needed to indicate that the rains came during the night.

If you can think of a better way to climb a hill . . .

Four months of life in the great outdoors enabled Sergeant Delbert C. Large of "E" Company of the 9th Infantry to raise this cultured growth of lip foilage.

When the reds dug-in deep they had to be blasted out and this eight inch artillery attached to the 2d Division helped to do the job. They're men of "B" Battery, 720th Field Artillery Battalion.

The Indianhead Division Band gives forth with "Stars and Stripes Forever" for the men of "L" Company of the 38th Infantry.

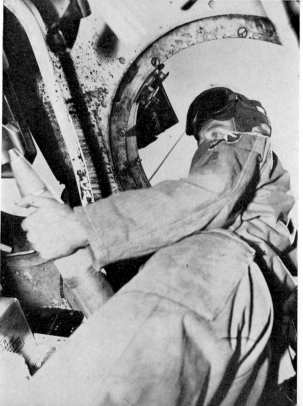

A driver's-eye view of the loader in an M-4 tank. In this case the view is of Sergeant Paul J. Fiest of "C" Company, 72d Tank Battalion.

Pfc Claude Coffey, "C" Company, 38th Infantry, attends to the wants of a wounded buddy after an assault on Hill 1171.

A mariner's view of the 23rd RCT command post after fall rains caused the Soyang River to go on a rampage. The points on this jeep got a little wet when they hit a deep spot duirng the crossing.

The shoe-shine boy stepped out for coffee but the customers stayed on in this barber-shop operated by "I" Company of the 23rd.

The walking-wounded of the 38th make their way down Hill 1171.

A 23rd Infantry carrying party makes its way along one of the better roads in the area north of Yanggu.

Major General Clovis E. Byers, X Corps CG, talks things over with Private Gilbert L. Mates and Pfc Alvin F. Mills of "L" Company of the 38th Infantry.

A faithful old M-4 of "C" Company, 72d Tank Battalion, lets loose with a round of 76 mm in the Inje sector.

Right after this shot was snapped, a Chinese soldier crawled out of the bunker to escape the effects of the WP grenade which had just been tossed inside. Needless to say, a reception party was on hand for the event.

It's never any trouble to gather a crowd for the chaplain in the hills of Ko

Men of "G" Company, 9th Infantry watch and wait atop "Bloody Ridge." Ahead of them are only more hills, each like last—steep, dirty and, sooner or later, ours.

Photo by Dave Cicero of International through courtesy of Newsweek.

AWARDS-DECORATIONS-CITATIONS

By Direction of the President, the Medal of Honor for conspicuous gallantry and intrepidity at the risk of life above and beyond the call of duty is awarded by the Department of the Army in the name of Congress to the following named officer and enlisted men:

FIRST LIEUTENANT FREDERICK F. HENRY, *Company F, 38th Infantry, for action against the enemy on 1 September 1950 in the vicinity of Am-Dong, Korea. His platoon was holding a strategic ridge near the town when they were attacked by a superior enemy force supported by heavy mortar and artillery fire. Seeing his platoon disorganized by this fanatical assault, he left his fox hole and moving along the line ordered his men to stay in place and keep firing. Encouraged by this heroic action the platoon reformed a defense line and rained devastating fire on the enemy, checking his advance. Enemy fire had knocked out all communications and Lieutenant Henry was unable to determine whether or not the main line of resistance was alerted to this heavy attack. On his own initiative, although severely wounded, he decided to hold his position as long as possible and ordered the wounded evacuated and their weapons and ammunition brought to him. Establishing a one-man defensive position, he ordered the platoon's withdrawal and despite his wound and with complete disregard for himself remained behind to cover the movement. When last seen he was singlehandedly firing all available weapons so effectively that he caused an estimated 50 enemy casualties. His ammunition was soon expended and his position overrun, but this intrepid action saved the platoon and halted the enemy advance until the main line of resistance was prepared to throw back the attack.*

SERGEANT FIRST CLASS LOREN R. KAUFMAN, *Company G, 9th Infantry, for action against the enemy on 4 and 5 September near Yongsan, Korea. On the night of 4 September, the company was in a defensive position on two adjoining hills. Sergeant Kaufman's platoon was occupying a strong point two miles away protecting the battalion's flank. Early on 5 September, the company was attacked by an enemy battalion and his platoon ordered to reinforce the company. As his unit moved along a ridge, it encountered a hostile encircling force. Sergeant Kaufman, running forward, bayoneted the lead scout and engaged the column in a rifle and grenade assault. His quick, vicious attack so suprised the enemy that they retreated in confusion. When his platoon joined the company, he discovered that the enemy had taken commanding ground and pinned the company down in a draw. Without hesitation, Sergeant Kaufman charged the enemy lines, firing his rifle and throwing grenades. During the action, he bayoneted two enemy and seizing an unmanned machine gun, delivered deadly fire on the defenders. Following this encounter, the company regrouped and resumed the attack. Leading the assault, he reached a ridge, destroyed a hostile machine-gun position, and routed the remaining enemy. Persuing the hostile troops, he bayoneted two more and then rushed a mortar position, shooting the gunners. Remnants of the enemy fled to a village and Sergeant Kaufman led a patrol into the town, dispersed them and burned the buildings.*

MASTER SERGEANT ERNEST R. KOUMA, *Company A, 72d Tank Battalion, for action against the enemy on 31 August and 1 September 1950 in the vicinity of Agok, Korea. His unit was engaged in supporting infantry elements on the Naktong River front. Near midnight on 31 August, a hostile force estimated at 500 crossed the river and launched a fierce attack against the infantry positions, inflicting heavy casualties. A withdrawal was ordered and his armored unit was given the mission of covering the movement until a secondary position could be established. The enemy assault overran two tanks, destroyed one and forced another to withdraw. Suddenly, Sergeant Kouma discovered that his tank was the only obstacle in the path of the hostile onslaught. Holding his ground, he gave fire orders to his crew and remained in position throughout the night, fighting off repeated enemy attacks. During one fierce assault, the enemy surrounded his tank and he leaped from the armored turret, exposing himself to a hail of hostile fire, manned the .50 caliber machine gun mounted on the rear deck, and delivered point-blank fire into the fanatical foe. His machine gun emptied, he fired his pistol and threw grenades to keep the enemy from his tank. After more than nine hours of constant combat and close-in fighting, he withdrew his vehicle to friendly lines. During the withdrawal through eight miles of hostile territory, Sergeant Kouma continued to inflict casualties upon the enemy and exhausted his ammunition in destroying three hostile machine gun positions. During this action, Sergeant Kouma killed an estimated 250 enemy soldiers. His magnificient stand allowed the infantry sufficient time to reestablish defensive positions. Rejoining his company, although suffering intensely from his wounds. he attempted to resupply his tank and return to the battle area. While being evacuated for medical treatment, his courage was again displayed when he requested to return to the front. Entered the military service from Nebraska.*

PRIVATE FIRST CLASS JOSEPH R. OUELLETTE, *Company H, 9th Infantry, for action against the enemy from 31 August to 3 September 1950, in the Naktong River salient near Yongsan, Korea. When an enemy assault cut off and surrounded his unit, he voluntarily made a reconnaisance of a nearby hill under intense enemy fire to locate friendly troop positions and obtain information of the enemy's strength and location. Finding that friendly troops were not on the hill, he worked his way back to his unit under heavy fire. Later, when an air drop of water was made outside the perimeter, he again braved enemy fire in an attempt to retrieve water for his unit. Finding the dropped cans broken and devoid of water, he returned to his unit. His heroic attempt greatly increased his comrades morale. When ammunition and grenades ran low, Private Ouellette again slipped out of his perimeter to collect these from enemy dead. After collecting grenades, he was attacked by an enemy soldier. He killed this enemy in hand-to-hand combat, gathered up the ammunition and returned to his unit. When the enemy attacked on 3 September, they assaulted his position with grenades. On six occasions, Private Ouellette leaped from his fox hole to escape exploding grenades. In doing so, he had to face enemy small arms fire. He continued his resistance despite a severe wound until he lost his life.*

SERGEANT JOHN A PITTMAN, *2d Platoon, Company C, 23rd Infantry, for action against the enemy on 26 November 1951, near Kujangdong, Korea. He volunteered to lead his squad in a counterattack to regain commanding terrain lost in an earlier engagement. Moving aggressively forward in the face of intense artillery, mortar and small arms fire, he was wounded by mortar fragments. Disregarding his wounds, he continued to lead and direct his men in a bold advance against the hostile strong point. During this daring action, an enemy grenade was thrown in the midst of his squad, endangering the lives of his comrades. Without hesitation, Sergeant Pittman threw himself on the grenade and absorbed its burst with his body. When a medical aid man reached him, his first request was to be informed as to how many of his men were hurt. This intrepid and selfless act saved several of his men from death or serious injury and was an inspiration to the entire command.*

PRIVATE FIRST CLASS LUTHER H. STORY, *Company A, 9th Infantry, for action against the enemy on 1 September 1950, in the vicinity of Agok, Korea. On that date, a savage daylight attack by elements of three enemy divisions penetrated the thinly held lines of the 9th Infantry Regiment. Company A beat off several "banzai" attacks but was bypassed and in danger of being cut off and surrounded. Private Story, a weapons squad leader, was heavily engaged in stopping the early attacks and had just moved his squad to a position overlooking the Naktong River when he observed a large group of enemy crossing the river to attack Company A. Seizing a machine gun from his wounded gunner, he placed deadly fire on the hostile column and killed or wounded an estimated 100 enemy soldiers. Facing certain encirclement, the company commander ordered a withdrawal. During the move, Private Story noticed the approach of an enemy truck loaded with troops and towing an ammunition trailer. Alerting his comrades to take cover, he fearlessly stood in the middle of the road and threw grenades at the truck. When out of grenades, he crawled to his squad, gathered up additional grenades, and again attacked the vehicle. During the withdrawal, the company was attacked by such superior numbers that it was forced to deploy in a rice field. Private Story was wounded in this action but disregarding his wounds, he rallied the men about him and repelled the attack. Realizing that his wounds would hamper his comrades, he refused to retire to the next position and remained to cover the company's withdrawal.*

When last seen, he was firing every available weapon and fighting off another hostile assault.

SERGEANT FIRST CLASS CHARLES W. TURNER, *2d Reconnaisance Company, for action against the enemy on 1 September 1950, in the vicinity of Yongsan, Korea. On that date, a large enemy force launched a mortar and automatic-weapon supported assault against his platoon. Sergeant Turner, a section leader, quickly organized his unit for defense and then observed that the attack was directed at the tank section 100 yards away. Leaving his secured section, he dashed through a hail of fire to the threatened position and mounting a tank, manned the exposed turret machine gun. Disregarding the intense enemy fire, he calmly held this position, delivering deadly accurate fire and pointing out targets for the tank's 75 mm gun. His action resulted in the destruction of seven enemy machine gun nests. Although severely wounded, he remained at the gun shouting encouragement to his comrades. During the action the tank received over 50 direct hits; the periscopes and antenna were shot away and three rounds hit the machine gun mount. Despite this fire, he remained at his post until a burst of enemy fire cost him his life. This intrepid and heroic performance enabled the platoon to withdraw and later launch an attack which routed the enemy.*

MASTER SERGEANT TRAVIS E. WATKINS, *Company H, 9th Infantry, for action against the enemy from 31 August to 3 September 1950, in the vicinity of Yongsan, Korea. When an overwhelming enemy force broke through and isolated thirty men of his unit he took command, established a perimeter defense and directed action which repelled continuous, fanatical enemy assaults. With his group completely surrounded and cut-off, he moved from foxhole to foxhole exposing himself to enemy fire, giving instructions and offering encouragement to his men. Later, when the need for ammunition and grenades became critical, he shot two enemy soldiers fifty yards outside the perimeter and went out alone for their ammunition and weapons. As he picked up their weapons he was attacked by three others and wounded. Returning their fire, he killed all three and gathering up the weapons of the five enemy dead returned to his amazed comrades. During a later assault, six enemy soldiers gained a defiladed spot and began to throw grenades into the perimeter making it untenable. Realizing the desperate situation and disregarding his wound, he rose from his foxhole to engage them with rifle fire. Although immediately hit by a burst from an enemy machine gun he continued to fire until he had killed the grenade throwers. With this threat eliminated, he collapsed and despite being paralyzed from the waist down, encouraged his men to hold on. He refused all food, saving it for his comrades and when it became apparent that help would not arrive in time to hold the position ordered his men to escape to friendly lines. Refusing evacuation as his hopeless condition would burden his comrades, he remained in his position and cheerfully wished them luck. Through his aggressive leadership and intrepid actions, this small force destroyed nearly 500 of the enemy before abandoning their position.*

For extraordinary heroism, the Distinguished Service Cross was awarded
to the following named members of the Second Infantry Division:

Bater, Lawrence H.	Headquarters, 9th Infantry
Bennington, Robert W.	"K" Company, 23rd Infantry
Beahler, Lee E. Jr.	"D" Company, 2d Engineers
Brazeal, Amos L.	"F" Company, 9th Infantry
Bradley, Joseph S.	Headquarters, 2d Division
Brown, Clarence G.	"L" Company, 23rd Infantry
Brown, James L.	"E" Company, 9th Infantry
Brownell, George R.	"K" Company, 38th Infantry
Burnette, James I.	"F" Company, 23rd Infantry
Gagle, Milton L.	"G" Company, 23rd Infantry
Carroll, Robert C.	"H" Company, 9th Infantry
Chamberlain, George	"K" Company, 23rd Infantry
Chiles, John H.	Headquarters, 23rd Infantry
Cooper, Robert	"L" Company, 23rd Infantry
Coughlin, John G.	Headquarters, 38th Infantry
Craig, Thomas K.	"I" Company, 23rd Infantry
Crow, Dalex J.	"G" Company, 38th Infantry
Crytzer, Robert E.	"A" Company, 9th Infantry
Edwards, James W.	Headquarters, 23rd Infantry
Emerson, John E. Jr.	"G" Company, 23rd Infantry
Ensley, Sherman W.	"H" Company, 38th Infantry
Falconer, John C.	"F" Company, 23rd Infantry
Fleischmann, Richard L.	Medical Company, 23rd Infantry
Freeman, Herbert H.	"A" Company, 9th Infantry

Freeman, Paul L.	Headquarters, 23rd Infantry
Gallardo, Robert	"E" Company, 9th Infantry
Gasquet, Andrew J.	"G" Company, 9th Infantry
Goode, John	"L" Company, 9th Infantry
Gray, Stephen E.	"L" Company, 23rd Infantry
Guerra, Juan F.	"F" Company, 23rd Infantry
Hall, Glenn M.	1st Ranger Company
Hanes, Wallace W.	Headquarters, 3rd Battalion, 38th Infantry
Horne, Dellno	"A" Company, 38th Infantry
Hutchin, Claire E. Jr.	Headqquarters, 1st Battalion, 23rd Infantry
Imrie, Robert K.	"F" Company, 38th Infantry
Jastram, Alan	Headquarters, 3rd Battalion, 38th Infantry
Joslen, Donald R.	"H" Company, 9th Infantry
Jovenall, James L.	"G" Company, 9th Infantry
Koch, Kenneth W.	"A" Company, 72d Tank Battalion
Koldenhoven, Richard A.	"G" Company, 38th Infantry
Kotite, Richard S.	"B" Company, 23rd Infantry
Lee, Chew-Mon	"H" Company, 9th Infantry
Lewellyn, Elmer E.	"E" Company, 38th Infantry
Lopez, Erasmo G.	"E" Company, 38th Infantry
Lowry, Leonard	"C" Company, 38th Infantry
MacDonald, Albert B. V.	"C" Battery, 37th Field Artillery Battalion
McDonald, John D.	"H" Company, 9th Infantry
Manning, Murray T.	"I" Company, 9th Infantry
Mathewson, Stanley A.	"I" Company, 38th Infantry
McCorley, James	Headquarters, 1st Battalion, 9th Infantry
Merkle, Howard P.	"G" Company, 38th Infantry
Messinger, Edwin J.	Headquarters, 9th Infantry
Miller, Wilfred D.	"A" Company, 72d Tank Battalion
Murphy, John M.	"G" Company, 9th Infantry
Nelson, John H.	"F" Company, 38th Infantry
Nesci, Joseph A.	"G" Company, 9th Infantry
Orig, Bruno R.	"G" Company, 23rd Infantry
Patten, Ralph E.	"G" Company, 23rd Infantry
Peploe, George B.	Headquarters, 38th Infantry
Picou, Wilfred J.	"K" Company, 38th Infantry
Rampendahl, Dieter W.	"I" Company, 23rd Infantry
Redman, Wilbur A.	"F" Company, 23rd Infantry
Rhotenberry, R. M.	"H" Company, 38th Infantry
Ruffner, Clark L.	Headquarters, 2d Division
Schmitt, Edward	"H" Company, 9th Infantry
Schauer, Ernest J.	"G" Company, 38th Infantry
Sherwood, Charles W.	"D" Company, 23rd Infantry
Skeldon, James H.	2d Battalion, 38th Infantry
Snowden, Houston D.	Medical Company, 9th Infantry
Stacy, James E.	3rd Battalion, 23rd Infantry
Stai, Melvin R.	"A" Company, 23rd Infantry
Taylor, Clovis R.	"H" Company, 9th Infantry
Trinen, William P.	"C" Company, 72d Tank Battalion
Truitt, Joseph M.	Headquarters, 9th Infantry
Tybroski, Max M.	"K" Company, 23rd Infantry
Walls, Claude R.	"C" Company, 38th Infantry
Wald, Oliver B.	"I" Company, 9th Infantry
Wall, Paul A.	"B" Company, 9th Infantry
Wallace, William C.	"B" Company, 9th Infantry
Westerman, Samuel V.	"A" Battery, 38th Field Artillery Battalion
Wynn, Ellison C.	"B" Company, 9th Infantry

THE SILVER STAR

For gallantry in action, the Silver Star is awarded to the following members of the 2d United States Infantry Division:

Captain Abanto, Rizalito
1st Lt Abare, Richard D.
1st Lt Abrams, Joseph T.
SFC Abbott, Francis M.
Cpl Abbott, Ray L.
Pfc Ackeret, Harry G Jr.
Cpl Acosta, Reynoldo E.
M/Sgt Acosta, Felix R.
Pfc Adams, Dennis L Jr.
Sgt Adams, Duane B.
1st Lt Adams, Marvin L.
Capt Adams, Royce F.
Pfc Adsem, Seymour.
M/Sgt Aguayo, Richard.
Pvt Albi, Carlo L.
Sfc Aldretem Joseph.
1st Lt Alfe, Norman M.
Major Aline, Robert F.
SFC Allen, Jackson.
M/Sgt Allen, Walter T.
PFC Allen, Warren R.
SGT Alston, James H.
Pfc Alston, Leslie E.
Pfc Alt, Dwain K.
Sfc Alvarez, Raymond L.
Sfc Ambrose, John A.
1st Lt Ancheta, Carlos F.
Cpl Ancheta, Enrique,
Pvt Anderson, Allan G.
Pfc Anderson, Robert A.
Cpl Anderson, Steven L.
2d Lt Anderson, William A.
1st Lt Anderson, William R.
Pfc Andrew, Joseph J.
Pfc Ashworth, Howard.
Cpl Atherton, Raymond
M/Sgt Atkins, Orman R.
Sgt Atkinson, Benny C.
Pfc Atwood, Russell A.
Capt Baca, Antonio L.
Pvt Bacon, Richard.
Cpl Bagley, Albert G.
M/Sgt Bagley, Henry C.
Sfc Bailey, Ford G.
Sfc Bair, Don C.
Sgt Baker, John W.
Pvt Baker, Paul E.
Pfc Baker, Robert J.
Sfc Baker, Samuel E.
M/Sgt Baker, Warren D.
Major Balldridge, James.
  1st OLC
SFC Ballinger, Everett M.
Pfc Balog, John.
Sfc Banks, Arthur
Pfc Banks, Clarence H.

Sgt Banks, Quincy G.
Cpl Banks, Robert L.
Capt Barata, Ventura
Sfc Barch, Fdward
Pfc Barcomb, Clayton P.
1st Lt Bard, Harry E.
Major Barneris, Cesides V.
  (1st OLC)
Pfc Barnes, Lewis R.
Capt Barnitz, Gerald W.
Pfc Barrow, Larence H.
Sgt Barry, Donald V.
Lt Col Barsanti, Olonto M.
Capt Bartholdi, Cyril S.
M/Sgt Bartlett, Russell V.
Cpl Bartlow, Roy E.
Pvt Barton, Eldon L.
Pvt Bass, Richard
Sgt Bates, Thomas W.
Pfc Bau, Robert K.
Sfc Bauer, Jack W.
Sfc Baxter, Jimmy L,
Pfc Beach, Donald J.
Pfc Beach, Tim M.
1st Sgt Beacham, Clarence L.
Sfc Beall, Phillip D.
Bear, James T.
1st Lt Beard, Robert A.
Capt Beaver, Alfred T.
WOJG Beckwith, Warren E.
1st Lt Becton, Julius W Jr.
Pfc Beebe, Donald L.
Sgt Beibuyck, Victor M.
Capt Bellamy, Freeling W.
Pfc Bender, James R.
1st Lt Bennett, Chancy Jr.
SFC Bennett, William S.
Cpl Benson, William A.
Sgt Berg, Elmer E.
Sgt Berg, Leonard
Pfc Berg, William Jr.
1st Lt Berger, Donald E.
Pfc Bergerson, Marion J.
Pfc Bernstein, Jack E.
SFC Beroth, Ernest
SFC Best, Billy J.
Sgt Bettencourt, Ernest D.
M/Sgt Billiingsley, Weyland
1st Lt Binkoski, Joseph J.
Cpl Birchfield, Edward D.
2d Lt Bird, David F, 1st OLC
Sgt Bird, Louis H.
Maj Bishop, Gaylord M.
1st Lt Bishop, Jesse L.
Pfc Bixler, Joseph R.
Pfc Bjerkebek, Orville C.

Sgt Blackburn, Thomas J.
Cpl Blackmore, LeRoy E.
Capt Blackstock, George B.
Capt Blackwell, John L.
Sfc Blevins, Leo
Sgt Bloom, Frank H.
Lt Col Boatwright, Linton S.
Sgt Bogdan, John
M/Sgt Bohn, Eugene E.
Cpl Bolden, Robert H.
Cpl Boring, Robert
Maj Boullion, Kenneth
1st Lt Bown, Henry E.
1st Lt Boyd, Cauthion T Jr.
Sgt Boyd, James A.
1st Lt Boyer, John L.
Cpl Boyle, Thomas G.
M/Sgt Bozarth, Grover L.
Sfc Braddock, William
Pvt Bradley, William J.
Capt Brady, Hugh W.
Pfc Brainthewaite, George J.
1st Lt Brandsford, Billy E Sr.
1st Lt Brantley, Charles S.
Sgt Braswell, Jimmy C.
1st Lt Braswell, Lee A.
Pvt Bray, Glen L Sr.
Pfc Brewer, Rosco E.
1st Lt Bright, Richard O.
M/Sgt Brinkley, Billy L.
Pvt Brisco, James E.
Pfc Broadus, Russell
Cpl Brock, Dennis
Cpl Brockband, Fred M.
Pfc Brodur, Louis H.
1st Lt Bromley, Bruce
Cpl Brooks, Richard H.
Cpl Brosnahan, Donald J.
1st Lt Brothers, Raymond R.
Sgt Brown, Charles R.
M/Sgt Brown, Dean
M/Sgt Brown, Elmos T.
Pfc Brown George W.
Capt Brown Jack D.
Cpl Brown, Jack P.
Cpl Brown, Kenneth J.
Cpl Brown, Kenneth L.
Pfc Brown, Luther J.
SFC Brown, Stanley A.
SFC Brown, William E.
Capt Brownell, George R.
Pvt Broyles, Bruce M.
Pvt Brubaker, Kenneth C.
1st Lt Brumet, Chester C.
Cpl Bruno, Gerald P
Capt Bryhn, Cornell B.

Pfc Bryson, Robert D.
Sgt Brukaty, Alfred M.
SFC Burciaga, Robert C.
1st Lt Burk, Eugene C.
Pfc Burkeen, Billie R.
1st Lt Burkett, Joseph W.
1st Lt Burkett, Ellwood W.
Capt Burla, William O.
Pfc Burton, Hughie W.
Capt Burton, Rhondal L.
1st Lt Burum, Peter F.
Sgt Buska, Richard J.
Sgt Bulter, Virgil E.
Col Buys, Joseph E.
Cpl Byrne, Joseph A.
Cpl Caballero, Albino
  (1st OLC.)
Pfc Cabell, William W Jr.
Cpl Cagle, Leslie H.
Maj Callum, John
Pvt Calvert, George E.
Pfc Calvey, Allen L.
Pfc Campbell, George B.
Pvt Campbell, Lloyd C.
Sgt Carey, Richard W.
Pvt Cargill, Kenneth E.
M/Sgt Cargle Leland L.
Capt Cariglia, Michael
1st Lt Carmichael, Turner F.
Capt Carn, Phil R.
Pvt Carpenter, Marion J.
Sfc Carter, Joe P.
Sfc Carter, Pinkie
Capt Casey, James J.
Cpl Casias, Nemecino L.
Pfc Castiglia, Anthony J.
Pfc Castillo, Augustine
Pfc Castro, Charles H.
Cpl Castro, Lavro G.
M/Sgt Causey, Clay H.
Sfc Cayer, Lucien J.
Cpl Ceckowski, William Jr.
Cpl Cena, Librado
Cpl Centeno, Manuel C.
Sfc Chamberlain, George
Sgt Chamberlain, Robert J.
1st Lt Champion, William H.
Sgt Chandler, Carl A.
Sgt Chapin, James R.
1st Lt Chapman, Herschel E.
Cpl Chapman, Randolph
1st Lt Chapman, Robert P.
Pfc Chapman, Virgil E.
Pfc Charnesky, Arthur A.
1st Lt Charnetski, Peter R.
Pfc Chase, Frederick E.
1st Lt Chateau, Louis A.
Cpl Cheppa, Michael
Pfc Chew, Charles A.
Cpl Chichester, Brent
Cpl Chisum, Gene H,
Pfc, Chiwiwi, Santow
Pfc Church, Paul K.
Pfc Church, Vernon J.
Sfc Churco, Benjamin J.
Cpl Cirimele, Jack J.
Pfc Clark, Henry D.
1st Lt Clark, Ralph T.
Pvt Clark, Robert L.
Pvt Clark, Warren M.

Capt Clark, William D.
1st Lt Clements, Robert C.
Cpl Clintsman, Leslie L.
Pfc Cochran, Sherley N.
Sfc Coiner, Philip L..
Capt Coker, Martin A.
Cpl Cole, Charles H.
Sgt Cole, William H.
1st Lt Coleman, Alfred I.
Sfc Colvin, Thomas E.
Cpl Comfort, James A.
Capt Cormier, Gustav J.
Cpl Commelly, Louis B.
Cpl Conrad, Martin
M/Sgt Conrad, Morris O.
Capt Conrad, Robert G.
Cpl Considine, William D.
Pfc Contreras, Liandro
Sfc Conway, Thomas
1st Lt Cook, Clifford J Jr.
Pfc Cook, Harold D.
M/Sgt Cook, Harry M Jr.
Pfc Cook, Lewis D.
Cpl Cook, Riley J.
Cpl Cooper, David W.
Sfc Cooper, Oren S.
2d Lt Corley, Pomp
Capt Cortez, Clyde A.
  1st OLC
  2d OLC
Pfc Costello, John T.
M/Sgt Costopoulos, Peter C.
1st Lt Cote, Raymond L Jr.
Col Coughlin, John G.
  1st OLC
Sfc Cox, Doyle A.
Sgt Cox, Robert H.
Pfc Crago, William E.
2d Lt Craig, Thomas K.
  1st OLC
Sgt Crary, William B.
Cpl Crawford, James A.
M/Sgt Crawford, Robert L.
Cpl Crawford, Walter K Jr.
Sgt Clayton, Junior,
1st Lt Cronin, Francis J Jr.
1st Lt Cronin, Gilbert F.
Pfc Crowie, Allan F.
Sgt Culp, Arnold D.
Capt Culpepper, Walter S.
Cpl Cummings, Martin
Pvt Cunningham, Daniel D.
Sgt Cunningham, John J.
Sfc Cunningham, Julius L.
2d Lt Currie, James D,
Pfc Curtin, Daniel V.
Pfc Curtis, Donald C.
1st Lt Curtis, Eugene L.
Pvt Curtis, James R.
2d Lt Curtis, Robert W.
Sgt Cushman, Richard G.
Cpl Cybulski, Edward F.
Cpl Da Fonseca, Rui M.
Capt Dallas, Bertram J.
Pfc Daniels, Bradley H.
Pfc Darling, Lewis R.
1st Lt Darner, Floyd W.
Sgt Davenport, Billy
2d Lt Davenport, Roy L.
2d Lt Davidson, Charles H.

Pfc Davis, Harold F.
Cpl Davis, Robert L Jr.
Sfc Davis, Wilbur B.
2d Lt Davis, Willie A.
Pfc Denffendoll, James S.
1st Lt Dehaas, George D.
Cpl Delage, Arthur H.
M/Sgt Della, Mele M.
1st Lt Del Plain, Theodore R.
M/Sgt DeMarie, Anthony J.
  (1st OLC,)
Sgt Dena, Librado
Sgt Dentale, Patsy J.
Brig Gen De Shazo, Thomas E.
Cpl Deshelter, Lambert W.
  (1st OLC.)
1st Lt Dewey, Carl C.
Pvt Dewey, John F.
Pfc Dewitt, Jack J.
M/Sgt Dick, Robert D.
Sgt Dickerson, Donald R.
Pfc Dienhart. Wayne E.
Pvt Dietz, Arnold
2d Lt Dimartino, Peter P.
1st Lt Doescher, George S.
1st Lt Dollings, James A.
Pfc Dominguez, Henry
1st Lt Donahue, John E.
Sgt Donatelli, Anthony J.
SFC Dorr, Earl L.
SFC Dotson, Virgil M.
Pfc Dougherty, Arthur
  1st OLC
M/Sgt Douglas, Glen
Pfc Downen, Jimmie L.
Cpl Dozier, Roscoe Jr.
Pfc Draper, James A.
1st Lt Drda, Robert J.
Pfc Driggers, Oscar
Capt Drowns, Norman
Pfc Dryden, Kenneth E.
Cpl Dube, Arthur J.
1st Lt. Dubois, McClellan A.
Pfc Duff, Glenn E.
Pfc Dugan, Lawrence E.
Major Duncan, James R.
  1st OLC
Sgt Dupont, Roland L.
Sgt Duryea, Harold S Jr.
WOJG, Dusseau, Ralph E Jr.
Sgt Dyer, Delmar J.
Cpl Easte, William C.
Pfc Ebarb, James R.
Pfc Edgecomb, Morgan J.
Pfc Edwards, George E.
Lt Col Edwards, James W.
  1st OLC
  2d OLC
  3d OLC
  4th OLC
Cpl Eggenberg, Vernon A.
Sgt Eley, Jackson R W.
Capt Elledge, John A.
  1st OLC
1st Lt Ellis, William R.
Capt Emerson, John E.
  1st OLC
Maj Engen, Millard C.
  1st OLC
  2d OLC

Pvt Enger, Albert H.
Pfc Enos, George W.
1st Lt Ensley, George H.
Pfc Eppler, Clarence K.
Capt Erdesky, Joseph L.
  1st OLC
  2d OLC
M/Sgt Ermini, Americo
Sgt Erndt, John A.
Sgt Eskew, Paul F.
1st Lt Euell, John H Jr.
Capt Evers, Francis D.
Sfc Eversoll, Harvey C.
Capt Fair, Robert L.
Sfc Fahey, Francis R.
Pfc Falvay, George N.
Cpl Fanning, Joe
Maj Farley, Clare F.
Cpl Farnham, Donald T.
2d Lt Faulkner, Bruce W.
Cpl Feinstein, David
1st Lt Fenderson, Maurice
1st Lt Fern, Albert J.
M/Sgt Ferrell, Leonard T.
  1st OLC
2d Lt Finn, Kenneth G.
Sgt Finney, Frank
1st Lt Fischer, Albert C.
M/Sgt Fischer, Albert D.
  (1st OLC.)
Cpl Fischer, James F.
Cpl Fitch, Donald R.
1st Lt Fitspatrick, William
M/Sgt Fitzgerald, Robert J.
Cpl Flores, Frank G Jr.
Pfc Foley, Charles T.
1st Lt Ford, John N.
Sgt Forney, Jason E.
Sgt Forshaw, W M.
Sgt Fortune, Richard L.
1st Foulk, Elden K.
SFC Foster, Leon H.
SFC Fox, Edward E.
1st Lt Fox, Harley C.
1st Lt Fox, John
  (1st OLC)
Cpl Foy, Grover J.
Major Fralish, John C.
M/Sgt Franklin, Vernon E.
Pvt Frazier, Arthur C.
1st Lt Francioni, Francis T.
Sgt Fredericks, John L.
Col Freeman, Paul L.
  (1st OLC.)
Cpl Fricke, Ervin A.
M/Sgt Fridrikksson, Thorvaldur
Capt Froment, Howard H.
1st Lt Frost, William R Jr.
Major Fry, Charles A.
Capt Fuller, Ellis L.
Sgt Fuller, Robert E.
M/Sgt Fultz, John
Cpl Gaines, Obie M.
Cpl Galindo, Joe
2d Lt Gallardo, Robert
1st Lt Gallivan William
Capt Games, William J.
Pfc Gomez, John
Pfc Lt Gandy, John E.
  (1st OLC)

Sfc Garcia, Cayetano
Sfc Garcia, Elizio
  1st OLC
2d Lt Gardner, Frank H Jr.
1st Lt Gadner, George W.
1st Lt Garner, Frank R.
Sfc Garner, Reginald M.
Sgt Garrett, Joseph T.
Sfc Gaspard, Steven
2d Lt Gatrell, Wallace B.
Sgt Gatson, Bernard H.
1st Lt Gehm, Robert J.
Cpl Geissler, Richard J.
Pfc Gentry, James D.
Sgt George, Francis J.
2d Lt Genuario, Louis V.
Lt Col Gerot, Joseph O.
Pfc Gerstner, Robert
1st Lt Gibbons, Benjamin F Jr.
  1st OLC
Pfc Gibson, George
Cpl Gibbons, Leroy
Pfc Gibson, George
Pfc Giellis, John N.
Pfc Gill, Irving L.
Pfc Gilleland, William D.
Pfc Gillespie, Larry L.
1st Lt Gilliland, Charles E.
Sgt Gilstrap, Robert D.
2d Lt Gipson, William H.
Sgt Girolimo, John D.
Sgt Glasby, Thomas C.
1st Lt Glasgow, William M Jr.
Sfc Glassman, George H.
Pvt Glaymiller, Russell
2d Lt Gleason, George M.
Cpl Glover, Lawrence U.
Pfc Goan, William E.
Sgt Godeaux, Lionel
2d Lt Golden, Peter T.
Sfc Goldsmith, Charles H.
1st Lt Gombos, Nicholas
  1st OLC
Pfc Gomez, Joseph
Pfc Gonzales, Alfonso
Cpl Gonzales, Tony
Sgt Good, Leonard P.
Cpl Goode, Bobbie E.
Col Goodrich, Walker R.
Pvt Gordon, George L.
Cpl Gordon, Donald A.
M/Sgt Gordon, Roy T.
Cpl Gossett, James A.
1st Lt Gould, Dudley C.
Pfc Gow, Walter W.
  1st OLC
Sfc Goyer, Merrill
Cpl Graber, Paul A.
M/Sgt Graham, Harold L.
WOJG Grant, Gordong H.
Sfc Grant, John W.
Col Graves, Rupert D.
Cpl Gray, Golden L.
1st Lt Gray, Stephen E.
Pfc Graycus, Stanley
Cpl Green, Edward I.
Sgt Green, Francis B.
1st Lt Green, James E.
  1st OLC
  2d OLC

Cpl Greenberg, Bernard
Cpl Greene, Byron D.
1st Lt Greenes, Joseph
  1st OLC
  2d OLC.
  3d OLC
1st Lt Greenfield, Ezra
Sgt Greer, Robert G.
2d Lt Grieve, John D.
Cpl Griffith, George H.
2d Lt Griffith, Joseph
Sfc Griffith, Luther
1st Lt Griffith, Robert J.
Sgt Grigsby, James F.
1st Lt Grinnell, Douglas D.
  (1st OLC)
Capt Grob, Richard H.
Sgt Groom, Cecil W.
Cpl Gross, Anton W.
Capt Gunn, George C.
1st Lt Guynn, Thomas E.
  1st OLC
Pfc Habern, Robert E.
1st Lt Haberman, Carl F.
Capt Hagebocke, John H.
1st Lt Hagerman, David B.
1st Lt Hagman, Carl M.
Cpl Halbrook, Joe E.
Sgt Haley, John P.
Pfc Hall, Dale E.
  (1st OLC)
Pfc Hall, Earl
1st Lt Hall, Harold L.
Major Hall, Robert M.
  (1st OLC)
Cpl Hallums, Tommy M.
Pfc Halverson, Verlin C.
Pfc Hamlin, Boyce D.
Pfc Hammerel, Ambrose B.
Lt Col Hanes, Wallace M.
Sgt Hanley, Jack
Pfc Hanlin, Ernest M.
Lt Col Hannum, Calvin S.
Lt Col Harber, Edward E.
Capt Harbin, Thomas R.
Pfc Hardin, Uncas B.
Sfc Hargrave, Robert W.
Sfc Harper, Lenzy E.
Sfc Harrington, William L.
Pvt Harris, Frank B.
Pvt Harris, Harold E.
Major Harris, John F.
Sgt Harrison, Adamal
Cpl Harrison, Edmund W.
Lt Col Harrison, Fred L.
Sgt Harriss, Myers S.
Sfc Hartman, Charles L.
Cpl Hartsell Robert J.
Sgt Harwood Chester L.
Sfc Hasher, Joseph F.
Pvt Hastings, Wilber D.
Pvt Hawkins, Robert C.
Capt Hawkins, Charles A.
M/Sgt Hawkins, Wesley N.
SFC Hayden, Floyd E.
1st Lt Hayler, Rodney G Jr.
Brig Gen Haynes, Loyal M.
Pfc Hays, James C.
Capt Hayward, Charles W.
Capt Hazelrigg, Charles B.

1st Lt Heady, Charles F.
1st Lt Heath, Mayo S.
Sfc Heath, Wayne D.
Sgt Hebard, Jack E.
Lt Col Hector, John R.
   1st OLC
   2d OLC
1st Lt Hedges, William R.
Pfc Heinlein, Frederick R.
Capt Helsel, Frank E.
Capt Henderson, Oran K.
Pfc Henkel, James H.
Sfc Henry, Gene L.
Cpl Herbert, Anthony B.
Sgt Herbert, Roy C.
Cpl Hermanski, Eugene
1st Lt Hernandez, Derry P.
Cpl Hernandez, Manuel B.
Cpl Herrera, Robert
2d Lt Herring, Edgar L.
Sfc Herron, Robert W.
Cpl Hershberger, Jess S.
   (1st OLC)
Pvt Hicks, Henry L.
Capt Highsmith, Lloyd
Sfc Hicks, Kenneth A Sr.
Pfc Hicks, Saint J.
Capt Hill, David H.
   (1st OLC)
Cpl Hill, Lyle L.
Pvt Hill, William H.
Capt Hillman, Rolfe L.
Cpl Hiltabidel, Homer L.
M/Sgt Hines, Marion M.
Capt Hinton, Reginald J.
1st Lt Hitchings, Aulbry C.
Major Hodges, Warren D.
Cpl Hoffman, Donald W.
1st Lt Hogan, Paul E.
Holbrook, George A.
Sfc Holcomb, Elmer E.
Cpl Holcombe, William A.
1st Lt Hollingsworth, Dale G.
Cpl Holmes, Francis L.
Sfc Holland, Dick
M/Sgt Holt, Cortis A.
   (1st OLC)
Pfc Homen, Joseph L Jr.
1st Lt Hopkins, Paul F.
Capt Hopkins, Paul L.
Sgt Horn, Charles E.
1st Lt Horne, Gerald P.
2d Lt Hornung, Frederick L III.
Pvt Horton, Bill
1st Lt Horton, Max G.
Pfc Houser, Donald A.
Cpl Howard, Joseph C.
M/Sgt Howe, Dwight D.
Cpl Howe, Othel H.
M/Sgt Howell, Claudie
Capt Howell, Edward D.
   (1st OLC)
Sgt Hoyt Paul L.
1st Lt Hoyt, Vernon H.
Pfc Hubbard, John E.
Sfc Hubbel, Philip L Jr.
Cpl Huber, Henry L.
1st Lt Hudson, Dowell B.
M/Sgt Hudson, Harry C.
Cpl Huey, James E.

Cpl Huffman, Gerald L.
1st Lt Hulburt, Charles W.
Sfc Huls, Claude C.
Sfc Hundt, Ernest S.
Pfc Hunley, Harold H.
Capt Hunn, Edward W.
Cpl Hunter, John E.
Ptc Hunter, Raymond, D.
Lt Col Hutchin, Claire E Jr.
Pfc Hurst, Joe W.
Sfc Hurla, Kenneth C.
Sfc Iliff, Harry R.
1st Lt Ireland, Lock W.
   1st OLC
Capt Irving, Kenneth J.
   1st OLC
Pvt Isom, Joseph M.
Capt Isonberg, George M.
Sgt Ivers, James E.
Pfc Jackl, Amel C.
1st Lt Jackson, Clinton H Jr.
Cpl Jackson, Hobson
1st Lt Jackson, Joseph R.
M/Sgt Jackson, William E.
   (1st OLC)
Pfc Jacobo, Malecio
2d Lt Jacobs, John F.
1st Lt Jamerson, Solomon J.
Sgt James, George B.
1st Lt James, Matcher M.
   (1st OLC)
Pfc Jameson, James A.
Sfc Jarman, Cecil L.
Cpl Jarvey, Roland J.
Sgt Jaskowiak, Edmond C.
Sgt Jay, Marvin F.
Pfc Jeffcoat, Elmer N.
Pfc Jeffries, Paul E.
Cpl Jenisch, Frederick H.
M/Sgt Jenkins, Lew
Sfc Jenkins, Rondal E.
Major, Jenson, Lloyd K.
   (1st OLC)
   (2d OLC)
1st Lt Jersey, Donald
Cpl Johnson, Bill D.
Cpl Johnson, Christopher B.
Cpl Johnson, George B.
Sgt Johnson, Leonard F.
Sgt Johnson, Lester H.
WOJG Johnson, Perry J Jr.
Major Johnson, Robert W.
Pfc Johnson, Robert M.
Sfc Johnson, Thomas C.
Pfc Johnston, Herbert N.
Sgt Johnston, Paul E.
2d Lt Jones, Albert E.
M/Sgt Jones, Fulton A.
Pvt Jones, George K.
Sgt Jones, Gordon R.
Pvt Jones, James L.
Pfc Jones, Millard
Sfc Jones, Watt Jr.
Cpl Jordan, Johnny F.
Capt Jordan, William S.
Cpl Jorgenson, Donald J.
Capt Joseph, Edwin M.
1st Lt Juneau, Linus M.
1st Lt Junot, Arthur J.
Sgt Jurkowski, Robert J.

Cpl Justin, Leon P.
1st Lt Kampe, Raymond L.
Pvt Kapfensteiner, Anthony S.
1st Lt Kareiva, Charles T.
   (1st OLC)
Pfc Karschney, Keith C.
Cpl Kasarda, Milton J.
Sgt Kason, Mike M.
Cpl Kaufman, Alfred L.
Pfc Kearney, Paul A.
1st Lt Keathley, Maurice F.
Cpl Keck, William F.
Major Gen Keiser Laurence B.
Cpl Keith, Claude N.
Lt Col Keleher, William P.
   1st OLC
1st Lt Keller, George A.
Sgt Kellison, Charles W.
1st Lt Kelly, Carl L.
Sgt Kelly, William C.
Sfc Kendrick, John G.
2d Lt Kennedy, George E.
Sgt Kennedy, Robert E L.
M/Sgt Kenney, Richard P.
Pfc Kenolio, Arthur
Capt Kerr, Edwin B.
Pfc Kevin, Paul R Jr.
Sgt Kidd, Wallace J.
Pfc Kiger, Ralph T.
Sgt Kilbarger, Norman M.
Lt Col Killilae, Walter
   (1st OLC)
Pfc Kim, Stacy L.
Lt Col Kimbrell, George W.
   (1st OLC)
Capt Kimmel, Louis E.
Pvt Kinder, William L.
Cpl King, Bennie R.
Capt King, George W.
Pfc King, Lee M.
1st Lt King, Raymond F.
   (1st OLC)
Capt King, John H.
Sfc King, Robert L.
Sgt Kinseth, Arlis L.
Sgt Kirpatrick, Joseph
   (1st OLC)
Sfc Kite, Edward J.
Sgt Kiychiro, Tetsuo
Cpl Klauber, Louis A.
Sfc Kluttz, Bill C.
1st Lt Knight, John N.
   (1st OLC)
1st Lt Knight, William F.
Sfc Knudtson, Paul W.
Pfc Kochanski, Paul E.
1st Lt Koebbe, Norvil G.
Sgt Konske, Earl F.
Pvt Kopp, Robert E.
2d Lt Kopscick, George Jr.
M/Sgt Kramsvogel, Charles F.
Pfc Kremer, Daniel L.
Sgt Kreps, Vincent A.
1st Lt Krueger, David P.
1st Lt Krzyzowski, Edward C.
Cpl Kubovitch, Alex H.
2d Lt Kuczynski, Charles P.
Sfc Kuhel, Michael R.
Cpl Kunz, Amos D.
Pfc Kurtz, Robert F.

Cpl Kutsugeras, Peter G.
2d Lt Kuuttila, Harold O.
Capt Kydland, Wallace A.
Sgt Kyzer, Aubrey E Jr.
1st Lt Lacaze, Robert D.
Sgt Lada, Edward
Cpl La France, George A.
1st Lt Lamp, Fred B Jr.
 (1st OLC)
Sfc Landry, Albert R.
Sgt Lane Delbert X.
Cpl Lane, George A.
1st Lt. Lang, Vincent W.
Pfc Langdon, Stanford T.
Pvt Lange, Charles R.
Sfc Langenberg, Lee W.
Pfc Langenfeld, Eugene
Cpl Lanier, Robert L.
Larson, Donald H.
Larkin, Robert A.
Sgt Larue, William L.
Pfc Lashok, Edward R.
Cpl Latham, Harold W.
Pfc Lauderdale, Charles W.
Cpl Laurendine, Caludie B.
Sgt Lawrence, Michael J.
1st Lt Law Kenneth D.
 (1st OLC)
Lt Col Lawrence, O.B.
Sgt Lawson, Ernest C.
LeClair, Lloyd L.
LeClair, Raymond
Sgt Lecomte, Robert F.
Sgt Ledbetter, Stanley K.
Sgt Lee, Elmo D.
Sgt Lee, Everett D.
Pfc Lee, Farrald E.
M/Sgt Lee, Hubert L.
Pfc Lee, Isaac Jr.
Sgt Lee, Nelson H.
Sfc Leggett, Virgil L.
 1st OLC
 2d OLC
1st Lt Lehman, Frederick J.
2d Lt Leighton, Henry P Jr.
1st Lt Le Louer, Roger
Cpl Lema, Antone
Pvt Lemay, Edward F.
Pvt Lemieu, Joseph A.
Sfc Lemoine, Benton B.
Pfc Lenz, Leo L.
Capt Levi, Robert O.
Sfc Lewis, Douglas L.
Pfc Lewis, James A.
Sgt Lewkow, Nicholas
Capt Lieber, Herbert L.
 1st OLC
Sfc Liggett, Ernest A Jr.
2d Lt Ligon, William F. Jr.
Sgt Lillard, Ralph G.
M/Sgt Lilly, Albert C.
2d Lt Lilly, Edmund, J III.
M/Sgt Limerick, Charles W.
M/Sgt Lineham, Edmund, A.
Sfc Lindwuist, Donald C.
1st Lt Lipski, Larue L.
Capt Lively, Richard E.
Sgt Living, Charles W.
Cpl Lobello, Louis V.
Cpl Lockerson, Lewis A.

Sfc Logan, Clifford
Lt Col Londahl, John E.
Pfc Long, George H.
M/Sgt Long William G.
Sgt Lopez, Manuel A.
Cpl Loquiao, Moises G.
Cpl Lorey, John J.
M/Sgt Lotshaw, Byron C.
Sgt Loudin, Gibson Jr.
Cpl Louis, Labello V.
Lt Col Love, Robert W.
Maj Lowry, Leonard
Sfc Loza, Fidel
Pfc Lucas, Pete Jr.
Pvt Lucero, Seferino C.
Cpl Lujan, Alex M.
Cpl Lujan, Benjamin
Pfc Lumb, Norman J.
Sfc Luther, James B.
 1st OLC
1st Lt Lyles, Edward H.
Sfc Lyman, Henry M.
M/Sgt Lynagh, Edmond F.
Cpl Lynch, Joseph M.
 1st OLC
Sfc Lynn, Francis L.
1st Lt Lynn, Otis C.
Pfc Lyons, William W.
 1st OLC
Sgt Lyon, Lindsey D.
Pfc Mabanag, Pacifico
M/Sgt MacDougall, John B.
Pvt Mace, Burl J.
M/Sgt Mace, William M.
 1st OLC
Sfc Mackrall, Blaine E.
Sfc Macedo, Angelo P.
1st Lt Macleod, Duncan A.
Pfc Madara, Charles V.
Pfc Maddox, Bill S.
M/Sgt Magnant, Joseph A.
 1st OLC
2d Lt Maguire, Frank J.
Cpl Mahaffy, Charles A.
M/Sgt Mairich, Mark W.
Pfc Maison, Jack A.
Lt Col Maixner, Harold V.
 1st OLC
 2d OLC
1st Lt Major, William J.
1st Lt Malinowski, Roy
1st Lt Mallard, Charles W.
1st Lt Mallory, Phillip L.
M/Sgt Malone, Herbert E.
1st Lt Malone, James F.
M/Sgt Manipon, Pacual M.
Cpl Manno, Nicolas F.
1st Lt Manto, Joseph V.
Pvt Maple, Lavern E.
Sgt Marek, Thomas D.
Sgt Marez, Joe R.
2d Lt Martin, Carl
 1st OLC
Sfc Martin, Den C.
2d Lt Martin, Gerald H.
Cpl Martin, James F.
Sgt Martin, Vernelle T.
Pfc Martinez, Alexander O.
Sgt Martinez, Guil'aula B.
Pfc Martinez, Ernest L.

M/Sgt Martinez, Herbert
M/Sgt Martis, William J.
2d Lt Mason, George
Cpl Mason, William G.
Sgt Massie, Charles E.
Massie, Charles H.
Cpl Masuda, Kivoshi
Cpl Mattfield, Collie M.
Major Matthews, Myrel O.
Sfc Matyjasik, Walter J.
Sfc Mauritz, Lawrence F.
Capt Maxson, Paul A.
Sgt Maxwell, Henry J.
Capt Maxwell, Raymond B.
Cpl Mayfield, Brit I.
Sgt McAlpine, Douglas B.
Pfc McArthur, George T.
2d Lt McBride, Paul T.
Sgt McCandless, Burley J.
1st Lt McCaslin, John E.
M/Sgt McCelland, Bernice E.
Pvt McClure, Franklin T.
Pfc McClure, Ronnie J.
Sfc McCoig, William L.
Sgt McConnell, Kenneth D.
CWO McCormick, Vane E.
1st Lt McCoy, James R.
Sgt McCoy, John E.
1st Lt McCoy, Joseph
Sgt McCreary, Mark F.
1st Lt. McDade, Robert A.
 1st OLC
1st Lt McDoniel, Raymond J.
1st Lt McDonough, John D.
1st Lt McElroy, Edward R.
Capt McFadden, Charles R.
1st Lt McGee, Paul J.
Pfc McGlothin, Harold W.
Cpl McGovern, Eugene H.
2d Lt McGovern, Jerome F.
Sgt McGregor, Robert J.
2d Lt McGuire, John N.
 1st OLC
Pfc McGuire, John T.
Capt McGuyer, Glenn C.
Sfc McInnis, Thomas
Capt McIntyre, Niles J.
Pfc McMahon, Francis F.
Lt Col McMains, D M.
 1st OLC
1st Lt McManamy, Kenneth E.
 1st OLC
 2d OLC
 3d OLC
 4th OLC
Cpl McMillan, William C.
1st Lt McMullen, James J.
Cpl McMullen, Wayne O
Maj McMar, Joel N.
Sfc McNutt, Billie W.
Sgt McPherson, Carl T.
Cpl McSwain, Charles E.
Pfc Meadows, Merle L.
Sgt Meadows, Tony
Pfc Medeiros, Edmond B.
Maj Mellen, Thomas W.
Sgt Mellinger, John L.
Cpl Melton, Charles S.
2d Lt Mendenhall, Jesse R.
 1st OLC

Cpl Mercer, Edwin R.
Sfc Mercer, George E.
  1st OLC
Cpl Meredith, William T.
Pfc Merrill, Otis H.
Pvt Merritt, William
Col Messinger, Edwin J.
  1st OLC
  2d OLC
Maj Meszar, Frank
  1st OLC
Maj Metts, Albert C Jr.
Pfc Metz, Steve J.
1st Lt Meyer, Edward E.
Col Mildren, Frank T.
  1st OLC
  2d OLC
Pfc Miller, Arnold R.
M/Sgt Miller, Bernard
1st Lt, Miller, Donald O.
M/Sgt Miller, John A.
Pfc Miller, Lawrence E.
Cpl Miller, Norman Jr.
Sfc Miller, Robert E.
Pfc Miller, Thomas M.
Pfc Miller, Vernon R.
Sgt Milligan Joseph F.
Sgt Milligan, Warren E.
  1st OLC
Major Milloy, Albert E.
1st Lt Mills, Charles F.
SFC Mills, Clarence C.
Sgt Miniard, George Jr.
Cpl Mitchell, Donald K.
Sgt Mitchell, William A.
1st Lt Mitchim, Bobbie E.
Sgt Mizerek, Edmund T.
Sfc Moe, Marcus E.
Cpl Molanick, John
Pfc Molins, Val T.
Sgt Moloko, Andrew
Sgt Mondin, August F.
Sfc Monteleone, Thomas
Cpl Montoya, Enriques
Pfc Moralez, Albert P.
Pfc Moran, Donald S.
Cpl Moran, James J.
Sgt Morgan, Ira L.
1st Lt Morris, James R.
Sgt Morrison, Clarence Jr.
M/Sgt Morrison, Clifford O.
1st Lt Morrison, Harry W. Jr.
1st Lt Morrow, Jared W.
Pfc Morse, John H.
1st Lt Mortimer, Frederick
Pfc Mortimer, Thomas J.
Pvt Moruchi, Tetsup
Sgt Mowrer, Robert E.
Sgt Mosier, Leonard L.
M/Sgt Moruicki, Edward
Cpl Muholland, Robert
Cpl Mulder, Laverne C.
Cpl Munhall, George P.
Capt Munoz, Frank E.
Pfc Muntean, Virgil
1st Lt Murdock, Harold R.
SFC Murphy, Paul J.
Cpl Miller, Norman Jr.
Pfc Murray Raymond M.
Pfc Mutersbaugh, Charles

Col Nabors, James F.
  1st OLC
  2d OLC
  3d OLC
SFC Nabozny Eugene L.
Pfc Nace, Harry L.
Pfc Nakata, Shinichi
M/Sgt Nance, Avery M.
M/Sgt Nance, Fleming B.
2d Lt Napier, Leonard
Pfc Napier, Robert W.
Pfc Nappier, John T.
2d Lt Neal, Robert L.
SFC Negamn, John J.
  1st OLC
Sgt Nelson, George W.
Sgt Nelson, William R.
Capt Newell, John H.
  1st OLC
Maj Newman, Charles A.
Pfc Newman, Robert
M/Sgt Newton, George J Jr.
SFC Nicholas, Geither R.
1st Lt Nichols, Willam L.
Pfc Nidiffer, Harold B.
Pfc Nieminski, John
1st Lt Noble, Gus
Pfc Noel, Robert Jr.
  1st OLC
Capt Nolan, John F Jr
Cpl Nord, Donald E.
Cpl Nordwig, Ralph H,
SFC Norton, Floyd E.
Lt Col Norum, Milton G.
  1st OLC
  2d OLC
Sgt Nowlin, Thelbert A.
Sgt Numkens, Lawrence
Sgt Nute, Alfred D.
1st Lt Nutting, Wallace H.
Pfc O'Bannon, Walter W.
Lt Col O'Donnell Robert
SFC Ognas, Max B.
Cpl O'Grady, Clifford,
Pvt Oliver, Russell S,
SFC Oslen, Carl C,
Cpl Olson, Harold M.
Sgt Olson, Paul
Capt O'Neil, Leander W.
Capt O'Neil, William
1st Lt Opoulos, Alexander C.
  1st OLC
  2nd OLC,
Pfc Ortegon, David D.
Pfc Osgood, Leroy G.
Cpl O'shell, Stewart W.
  1st OLC
Cpl Ottesen, Eugene L.
Pfc Ouderkirk, Leonard J.
Pfc Overlease, Samuel
Cpl Owens, Richard K.
Cpl Padello, Alfred
Pfc Paddilla, Timoteo M.
2d Lt Page, Harold R.
Sfc Palamidy, Peter H.
Pvt Palitta, Robert
M/Sgt Palmer, Ranson A.
2d Lt Palmer, Richard A.
Sgt Palsa, Andrew S.
Pfc Papademetrious, John C.

M/Sgt Pappas, John P.
Pfc Pappas, Sam W.
M/Sgt Parker, Clarence A Jr.
Sgt Parker, Emmett V,
Pfc Parker, Ernest
2d Lt Parker, James L.
M/Sgt Parker, Robert E.
Pfc Paschell, Clent D.
Sgt Pascua, Vicente
M/Sgt Pater, John M.
Sgt Patterson, James M.
Pvt Patton, Delmar
1st Lt Payne, Murray L.
1st Payne, Richard M.
Capt Payne, William N.
Pfc Pearl, Gene L.
Pfc Pearson, Gerald L.
Pfc Peace, Jack A.
Pvt Peaver, William E.
1st Lt Pebles, George D.
Sgt Pedigo, George H Jr.
Cpl Peneragast, Joseph D.
Cpl Penrod Rayburn W.
Cpl Pepin, Daniel F.
Col Peploe, George B.
  1st OLC
  2d OLC
1st Lt Perdomo, Jose L.
M/Sgt Perrone, Vito E.
  1st OLC
  2d OLC
Maj Perry, James F.
  1st OLC
Sfc Peterson, Harry J.
1st Lt Peterson, James E.
Capt Petit, Wilfred D.
Sgt Petras, John S.
Maj Petrick, Lawrence R.
Pfc Pettigrew, Roy L.
1st Lt Philipsen, Clifford A.
Sgt Phillips, Alfred N.
Cpl Phillips, Charles A.
Capt Phillips, John J.
M/Sgt Phillips, Joshua M.
Sgt Phillips, Robert
2d Lt Phillips, William E.
  1st OLC
Pfc Phillips, Willie A Jr.
Pvt Pierce, John W.
Cpl Pierce, Raymond O.
1st Lt Pike, John E.
Pfc Pinkerton, William F.
Sfc Piper, Marvin M.
Pfc Pistole, Bobby L.
Sfc Pistulka, William J.
Capt Pittman William F.
1st Lt Planas, Alvin
  1st OLC
  2d OLC
Cpl Platz, Kenneth S.
Sgt Polito, Salvatore
Pfc Polick, Harry
Pvt Pollock, Blaine
Pfc Polus, Louis F.
Pfc Polchroni, Georghias
Capt Pomerene, Robert L.
Lt Col Pope, Harris M.
SFC Porter, Floyd W.
1st Lt Porter, Vernon R.
Capt Poston, Edmund D.

Cpl Powell, Richard
M/Sgt Praska, Donald W.
Sgt Prather, Lawrence H.
Major Pratt, Sherman W.
Sgt Prest, John M.
Pvt Preston, David R.
Sgt Preston, Lewis
2d Lt Price, Blair W.
Cpl Pridmore, Roscoe M.
Pfc Prince, Oscar H.
Pfc Prittz, Jimmie F.
2d Lt Privett, William W.
Sgt Prottas, Soloman W.
Sfc Pruett, Kenneth E.
Cpl Puckett, Charles R.
Cpl Pular, Bernard
Sgt Purcell, Lee T.
Cpl Quasius, Charles H.
1st Lt Quinn, Edward B.
  1st OLC
1st Lt Quinn, John P.
1st Lt Rabe, Lucio R.
Pfc Racey, Maurice D.
Pfc Rackley, Irvin A.
Maj Radow, Sammy E.
Sgt Ragde, Haakon
Cpl Ramirez, Orlando Jr.
1st Lt Ramos, Fred M.
2d Lt Rampendahl, Dieter W.
Capt Ramsborg, John H.
  1st OLC
  2d OLC
Lt Col Raper, John F Jr.
M/Sgt Ray, Howard E.
Pfc Raske, Donald E.
1st Lt Raybould, Lynn R.
Capt Reed, Frank M.
Cpl Reed, Theodore J.
Cpl Register, Harvey L.
Cpl Reid, Harold E.
Pfc Reinhart, Duane C.
2d Lt Reinhardt, Eugene J.
M/Sgt Remilliard, Roger W.
  1st OLC
Pfc Renfro, Johnnie C.
Pfc Reskovac, John Jr.
M/Sgt Rayna, Andrew E
2d Lt Rhodes, Walter R.
Lt Col Richeardson, Beverly I.
SFC Richardson, Joe M.
Pvt Riddick, Gilbert P.
Cpl Riddle, Marvin
Cpl Riggio, John A.
Sgt Rimkus, George
Cpl Riordan, John J.
Sgt Risingsun, Teddy
Pfc Rister, Manuel G.
Cpl Ritter, Bruce M.
Cpl Rivera, Fermin G.
Sgt Robb, Charles L.
Pfc Roberts, Donald R.
Pfc Roberts, Jessie W
Cpl Roberts, Robert O.
Cpl Robinette, Eugene R.
Cpl Robinson, James E.
Cpl Robinson, J B.
Capt Robinson, Ralph R.
Pfc Robinson, William L.
1st Lt Rodgers, Paul C.
2d Lt Rodgers, Walter E.

Pfc Rodriquez, Bonifacio
Cpl Roe, Roy E.
Sfc Rogers, Jack A.
Cpl Rojas, Trinidad
Cpl Roland, Martin
1st Lt Rollins, William
Sfc Rollins, Victor L.
Capt Ronk, Harold F
Sfc Roope, James S.
Capt Roe, William E.
Cpl Rose, Robert C.
1st Lt Rosenbalm, James L.
Pfc Rosenberger, James H.
M/Sgt Roth, James L.
M/Sgt Rowden, Floyd H.
Cpl Rowe, Othel H.
Cpl Rowe, Ralph W.
Cpl Rowe, Willie
Sfc Rowland, Eugene
Pfc Roy, Norbert F Jr.
Pfc Rudder, James E.
Capt Ruggiero, Orlando
  1st OLC
Cpl Ruiz, Abelino
Sgt Ruiz, Jose P
Cpl Rupe, Robert W.
Cpl Russ, George D.
Maj Russell, George H.
  1st OLC
  2d OLC
Pfc Russello, Michael L.
Sgt Ruth, John R.
Cpl Rutherdt, John D.
1st Lt Rutherford, Samuel A.
Capt Sager, Perry A.
  1st OLC
  2d OLC
Pvt Sakamoto, Sadao W.
Sgt Salgado, Frank Jr.
Sfc Samuels, Edward
Cpl Sanchez, Steve
Cpl Sand, Elmer H.
M/Sgt Sander, Boleslow M
Cpl Sanders, John W.
Cpl Sandoval, Leo R.
2d Lt Sanford, William M.
Maj Sanguinetti, John H.
Capt Santoro, Angelo M.
Pfc Santos, Ramon
Sgt Sargent, William R.
Pfc Saroian, Mike
Capt Sawyer, Bickford, E Jr.
Pfc Schafer, Richard L.
Sgt Schafer, Francis J.
Cpl Schaffer, Richard J.
1st Lt Schappaugh, George H.
Cpl Schatz, Richard M
Cpl Schauer, Carl P.
Capt Schauer, Ernest J.
Pvt Scheltens, Frank J.
Cpl Schisler, Donald
Pvt Schmidt, Clarence E.
1st Schmidt, George W.
Pfc Schmidt, Hubert J.
1st Lt Schmitt, Edward
Pfc Schneider, John G.
Pfc Schobloch, Peter H.
Pfc Schoonover, Walter
Pvt Schreieck, Wilford G.
Sfc Schultz, Stanley S.

Sfc Schweer, Donald J.
Sfc Scroggins, James J.
Cpl Scurr, William G
Sfc Seaman, Elmer A.
Cpl Sears, Carl D.
M/Sgt Seeger, Herbert J Jr.
M/Sgt Seeley, Robert J.
Cpl Seay, James T.
M/Sgt Self, Alfred G.
2d Lt Seltzer, Sherman M.
M/Sgt Serna, Francisco
1st Lt Settlew, Alain
Cpl Sever, Aloysius R.
Sfc Shaffier, Frankie W.
Sfc Shanahan, Leo V.
  1st OLC
1st Lt Shannon, Dallas L.
Cpl Shatto, Edward G.
1st Lt Shelton, Irwin D.
Capt Shelton, James E.
Pfc Shelton, Lyle R.
Capt Sheppard, Reginald R.
  1st OLC
Lt Col Sherrard, Robert G Jr.
M/Sgt Shevchenko, John Jr.
M/Sgt Shobe, Joseph H.
1st Lt Shutts, Bion Q.
Sgt Simmons, Joseph W.
2d Lt Simula, Elwood G.
2d Lt. Sines, George T.
Sfc Singletary, Thomas H.
Pfc Sisk, Thomas A.
Sfc Sizemore, Harrell D.
Lt Col Skeldon, James H.
Maj Skelton, Lawrence R.
Sgt Slinn, Grant
Col Sloane, Charles C.
  1st OLC
Pfc Small, John A.
2d Lt Smith, Albert W.
  1st OLC
M/Sgt Smith, Alberton E.
Cpl Smith, Chester E.
Cpl Smith, Darrow O.
M/Sgt Smith, Eugene E.
Cpl Smith, James E Jr.
Pfc Smith, John A.
Pvt Smith, Leonard G.
Cpl Smith, Leonard
Sgt Smith, Merwin E.
1st Lt Smith, Roy B
Capt Smithson, Robert N.
Capt Snell, Maynard J.
  1st OLC
M/Sgt Sobota, John F.
Sgt Sohler, Charles R.
Capt Sokol, Anthony J.
Pfc Sommerfeld, Edward H.
Cpl Soto, Juan C.
Pfc Spann, Joseph F.
Pfc Spear, Spero G.
Pfc Spencer, Charles E.
Pfc Spicer, Orville K.
Sgt Sprinkle, Marion M.
Pfc Srbich, George
Capt Stai, Melvin R.
  1st OLC
Pvt Stamper, Paul
Pfc Srbich George
Sgt Stapf, Rodey D.

Capt Stark, Marshall W.
SFC Stasi, Emilio
Capt Steele, Arthur J.
Capt Staffer, Orville R.
1st Lt Steinberg, William A.
1st Lt Stenmoe, Clarence S.
SFC Stepine, George
Sgt Sterns, James W.
Capt Stevens, Simon J.
Sgt Stewart, Donald E.
Brig Gen Stewart, George C.
  1st OLC
M/Sgt Stewart, Leslie D.
Cpl Stiffler, Francis P.
Maj Stine, Harlan C.
Pfc Stinson, John A.
Pvt Stollberg, Dale R.
Pvt Stone, Harold J.
1st Lt Storrs, Barrie E.
Pfc Stotler, Charles H.
2d Lt Strambler, John A.
Pvt Strandberg, Darold L.
Pfc Strunk, Harold
1st Lt Stryker, Emil J Jr.
Sgt Stuller, Charles E.
Pfc Suit, Wilbur L.
Cpl Suitsev, Kalju
Cpl Sullivan, Andrew
Sfc Summerlin, L D.
Capt Sunde, Carl J E.
M/Sgt Suszko, George D.
Pfc Sutton, George P.
Pvt Svitek, Richard L.
Pfc Swank, Jerry L.
Capt Swanson, Roy W.
Sfc Switala, Richard P.
Pfc Swope, Orvel L.
Sgt Symborski, Henry A.
Sgt Syx, Edward Jr.
Sgt Szymanski, Alfred
2d Lt Szymanski, John V.
  1st OLC
Sgt Taber, Nelson A.
Cpl Tadena, Sinfronio B.
Capt. Tait, Lawrence
Sfc Talotta, Joseph A.
Cpl Tamayori, Patrick S.
Capt Tanghe, Albert L.
Sgt Tarullo, Frank J.
M/Sgt Taschner, Robert
Capt Tassey, George
Sgt Taylor, Ray
Cpl Taylor, Riley S.
Sfc Taylor, Roy L.
Sgt Teague, Herbert L.
  1st OLC
Cpl Tejada, Arthur E.
1st Lt Tennant, Theodore C.
Pfc Terwilliger, William B.
Cpl Theisen, Jack C.
Pvt Thomas, Arnold L.
Sfc Thomas, Eugene P.
Pvt Thompson, Albert
1st Lt Thompson, Benjamin H.
Sfc Thompson, Broadus J C.
M/Sgt Thompson, Denver
M/Sgt Thompson, Edgar Jr.
Pfc Thompson, Ernest C Jr.
Pfc Thompson, Joseph E.
Pfc Thornton, Donald M.

Cpl Tibbs, Clarence E.
Capt Tiffany, Freeman R.
Sfc Tigner, Moses P.
Sfc Tittsworth, Vernon L.
Sgt Todd, Jimmie L.
1st Lt Todd, William R.
Pfc Tomkinson, Tom J.
1st Lt Tomlinson, Maurice
  1st OLC
Capt Totten, John E.
Major Toth, Louis L.
Lt Col Tothacer, Austin J.
M/Sgt Toto, Anthony C.
Pfc Tovar, Candelario
Cpl Tracy, Donald
Cpl Tramel, Tommie G.
Pvt Trapanotto, Lawrence A.
Pfc Travis, Junior
M/Sgt Tromans, Robert D.
M/Sgt Trout, John K.
Pfc Truax, John J.
Pvt Truesdalo, David C.
Sfc Truitt, Warren J.
Capt Truscott, Lucian K III.
1st Lt Tsutsui, Robert S.
M/Sgt Tucciarone, Frank J.
Sgt Tuholsky, Edward J.
Pfc Turcotte, Edmund J.
Pfc Turner, Earnest E.
Cpl Turner, Thomas F.
1st Lt Turner, Tom W.
  1st OLC
1st Lt Turqueza, Arsenio
Pfc Tuttle, Lloyd R.
2d Lt Tworek, George J.
1st Lt Tyree, James H.
Sgt Tyson, Walter L.
Capt Tyrroll, Stanley C.
Sgt Uhrig, Richard A.
Cpl Uyeda, Isamu S.
2d Lt Uzzo, Francis A.
Capt Vails, Maxwell
Capt Valdez, Isidro S Jr.
Cpl Valente, George K.
M/Sgt Valentine, Paul V.
Cpl Valle, Carmelo
Sfc Vance, James E.
Pfc Vandever, Lonnie L.
Pfc Vandorin, Clell E.
Major Van Halbin George R.
  1st OLC
Cpl Van Sciver, George R. III
Cpl Varnell, James O Jr.
1st Lt Vaughn, Guy V.
  1st OLC
M/Sgt Veach, Robert T.
Pfc Verhey, Kenneth J.
Sgt Vessells, John P.
Pfc Vich, Steve
1st Lt Vismor, Alphard R.
Sfc Volk, Virgil H.
Capt Vontom, George E.
  1st OLC
Cpl Wacasey, Ernest E.
Pfc Waem, Richard L.
Capt Waggoner, Cecil C.
Cpl Waite, Rex L.
Capt Wakeman, Paul M Jr.
Pvt Walczak, John G.
Capt Walker, Ansil L.

Capt Walker, Benjamin
Sfc Walker, Jack F.
Sgt Wall ,Paul A.
Sgt Wallace, Jack E.
Sfc Wallin, Gordon L.
Pfc Walls, Claude R.
Pfc Walsh, Robert F.
Sgt Walters, Robert N.
1st Lt Waples, Charles L.
Capt Warden, Robert H.
1st Lt Warnek, Oleg V.
Capt Watson, Charles L.
  1st OLC
Sgt Watt, Leroy J.
Sfc Watts, Royce J.
Sgt Webb, James N.
Cpl Webb, Ralph B.
Pfc Wehinger, John J.
Sgt Weider, Ronald J.
1st Lt Weikel, Thomas E.
Pfc Weissman, Stanley
1st Lt Welch, Earle M.
1st Lt Welcher, James W.
Sfc Wertz, John A.
Pvt Westerman, Kenneth D.
Capt Westfall, William M.
Sfc Weston, Vernon C.
1st Lt Wethered, Theodore J.
M/Sgt Wheeler, Linwood B.
Pfc Whelan, Francis E.
Cpl Whitaker, James E.
Sfc Whitaker, Richard G.
Cpl White, Billie E.
Pvt White, David R.
Sfc White, Donald E.
Capt White, Frank M.
Cpl White, Grover L.
Cpl White. Raymond P.
Capt White, Roger C.
M/Sgt White, Wilber D.
Cpl Whitehead, Thomas J.
Sgt Whitney, Earl S.
Cpl Whitt, Dale E.
SFC Whitten, Thomas K.
  1st OLC
  2d OLC
Cpl Wiggins, Carl W.
Sgt Wilborn, Clyde S.
M/Sgt Wilder, Johnie S.
Maj Wilkins, Wallace W Jr.
M/Sgt Wilkinson, Olin C.
1st Lt Williams, Charles M.
1st Lt Williams, George K.
Pfc Williamson, Henry W.
M/Sgt Wills, Glenn W.
Pfc Wills, Richard R.
M/Sgt Wilson, Floyd R.
Sgt Wilson, Joe J.
Cpl Winder, Charles R.
Pfc Winninger, El Dridge
2d Lt Witherspoon, Don M.
Lt Col Wohlfeil, Carl H.
Pfc Wolfe, Wallace W.
Cpl Wood, Elmer H.
Maj Woodard, Gerald V.
1st Lt Woods, Robert L.
M/Sgt Woolsey, William F.
Pfc Worthy, John N.
1st Lt Wretlind, Clayton L.
Pfc Wright, Earl R.

Cpl Yahiku, Ralph M.
Capt Yamazaki. Alfred A.
Pfc Yancey, Glen R.
Cpl Ybarra. Albert M.
Sgt Ybarra, Mike J.
SFC Yek, Eugene E.
Cpl Yopp, William E.
Pfc York, Melvin D.

Cpl Young, Carroll W.
Maj Young, Jack T.
Pfc Young, Louis G.
1st Lt Young, Raleigh E Jr.
Pfc Young, Tracey H.
Capt Yount, John B.
Cpl Yturralde, Frank
Pfc Zanni, Primo A.

Cpl Zaragoza, Ignacio
Capt Zeper, Philip
Sgt Ziek, Thomas G.
M/Sgt Zielonka, Lavin L.
Sgt Zimmerman, Joyce H.
2d Lt Zinsky, Paul
Sgt Zoeller, John G.
Zurek, Edwin J.

French United Nations Battalion:

Bizet, Andre
Bonnet, Jean
Baxeures, Jacques
Bizieux, Bernard
Bedu, Raymond
Barthelemy, Maurice
Beaurienne, Serge
Bordessoules, Elie
Brabant. Remv
Chasserot, Andre
Croizer, Perre
Callet, Paul
Drieux. Jacques
Durant De Mareuil

De La Croix De Castries
Daudier, Hubert
Girardot, Robert
Garoux, Gustave
Galoux, Jean
Gaudet, Gerard
Gaudre, Marcel
Gallant, Daniel
Goulay, Andre
Huschard, Jean
Jaupart, Claude
Legall. Joseph
Lainel. Pierre
Louvet, Muchel

Lelouer, Robert
Le Merle, De Beauford, Guy
Le Mire, Oliver
Le Beurier, Gildas
Le Mai Tre. Andre
Leroux, Louis
Lebolloch, Jean
PePage, Jean
Leneindre, Yves
Lanet, Alfred
Monclar, Ralph
Ruellan, Henri
Serre, Leon

Netherlands United Nations Ground Forces Korea

Roland, Albert
Ruellan, Renri
Serre. Leon
Bergfurt, Johannes P.

Denouden, Marinus P. A.
Eekhoutm William D H.
Monterie. Coenraad

Van Bolkam, Arnoldus
Gogh, Johannis J.
Van Muers, Alfred J.

Distinguished Unit Citations

*   *   *   *

23d Regimental Combat Team

In the name of the President of the United States as public evidence of deserved honor and distinction the 23rd Regimental Combat Team, 2d Infantry Division, comprised of the following units:

23rd Infantry Regiment
37th Field Artillery Battalion
French Infantry Battalion
"B" Battery, 82d AAA Battalion
"B" Battery, 503d Field Artillery Battalion
"B" Company, 2d Engineer Battalion
2d Clearing Platoon, Clearing Company, 2d Medical Battalion
1st Infantry Ranger Company

is cited for extraordinary heroism in combat near Chipyong-ni, Korea, during the period 13 through 15 February 1951. These units, comprising a regimental combat team, were disposed in a defensive perimeter around Chipyong-ni with the hazardous mission of holding this important communications center and denying the enemy its extensive road net. On 13 February, hordes of Chinese Communist troops launched many determined attacks from every quarter, strongly supported by heavy mortar and artillery fire. Prearranged fire with artillery, tanks and mortars hurled back these fanatical assaults until the morning of 14 February when the enemy separated the 23rd Regimental Combat Team from supporting units to the south, entirely surrounded it, and made resupply possible only by air drop. Because of the encircling force, estimated to be four Chinese communist divisions, the Chipyong-ni perimeter rapidly developed into a "stand-or-die" defense. Fierce hand-to-hand combat engaged the two forces in the evening of the second day of the siege and only one company remained in reserve. With ammunition stocks running low, this one remaining unit was committed on 15 February and waves of attacking Chinese communists again were stemmed. Shortly after noon of 15 February, radio contact was established with a relief force and friendly tanks broke through the enemy encirclement and forced his withdrawal. The dogged determination, gallantry and indomitable spirit displayed by the 23rd Regimental Combat Team when completely surrounded and cut off, the destruction of attacking Chinese communist hordes which enabled the United Nations Forces to maintain their front, resume the offensive, and the steadfast and stubborn refusal to allow a fanatical and numerically superior force to dislodge them are in keeping with the finest traditions of the United States Army and reflect great credit on all members of the units who participated in this historical combat action.

Third Battalion, 23d Infantry Regiment

In the name of the President of the United States as public evidence of deserved honor and distinction the Third Battalion, 23rd Infantry Regiment, 2d Infantry Division, is cited for extraordinary heroism and outstanding performance of duty in action against the armed enemy in the vicinity of Chipyong, Korea, during the period 30 January to 2 February 1951. During this period, the unit was advancing to the north as a part of the 23rd Regimental Combat Team with the mission of locating and engaging the Forty-Second Chinese Army. The Third Battalion, 23rd Infantry Regiment, supported by artillery and tanks, began the attack from the Chongsan-Tanguri assembly area up the Kumdang Chon valley. Advancing to the vicinity of two railroad tunnels which cut through the north-south ridges on each side of the valley, the force halted at darkness. They began organizing and occupying positions around the tunnels. At 0450 hours on 1 February, the Third Battalion, 23rd Infantry Regiment, was attacked by a large force of Chinese infantry, screaming, blowing bugles, and advancing under cover of a heavy barrage of mortar and automatic weapons fire. The Chinese broke through a gap between Companies "I" and "L" of the Third Battalion, but were immediately thrown back by a determined counterattack which the battalion launched at the point of the bayonet. The enemy deployed more forces until the entire 374th Chinese Infantry Regiment was committed. They pressed the attack against the position for eight hours. Many times they reached the crest of the ridges only to meet a hail of hand grenades and point-back fire from the gallant defenders. The crisis came in the early afternoon with the Third Battalion, 23rd Infantry Regiment, still under pressure and no air support available because of heavy ground fog. However, at this time the fog lifted and 24 fighter aircraft strafed and bombed the enemy. Observed mortar and artillery fire was placed on the masses of attacking troops. Under this merciless hail of fire, the enemy broke off the engagement and withdrew at 1800 hours on 1 February, just as a supporting United States battalion arrived from the south. On the next day, more than 600 dead Chinese were counted in front of the positions of the Third Battalion 23rd Infantry Regiment, and many more were known to have been killed or wounded. As a result of the gallant stand of the Third Battalion, 23rd Infantry Regiment, the enemy was prevented from breaking through to the command post rear areas. The position was intact and the 374th Chinese Infantry Regiment was practically destroyed. This action eliminated the 125th Chinese Infantry Division as an effective fighting force and enabled the 23rd Regimental Combat Team to continue its advance. The extraordinary heroism, aggressiveness and determination displayed by the Third Battalion, 23rd Infantry Regiment, 2d Infantry Division, reflects great credit on itself and each courageous soldier, and are in keeping with the fine combat traditions of the United States Army.

72d Tank Battalion

In the name of the President of the United States as public evidence of deserved honor and distinction the 72d Tank Battalion, 2d Infantry Division, is cited for extraordinary heroism and outstanding performance of duty against an armed enemy in the vicinity of Yongsan and Changyong, Korea, during the period 31 August to 3 September 1950. The battalion was assigned the mission of supporting the 9th and 23rd Regiment Combat Teams in their defense zone along the east bank of the Naktong River. On the night of 31 August, the enemy began crossing the river in force at several places and by 0600 hours on 1 September had managed to overrun friendly infantry positions. The 72d Tank Battalion moved forward and engaged the enemy with machine gun and tank-cannon fire in a well-executed delaying action that permitted infantry and artillery units time to establish new defensive positions in the vicinity of Yongsan. Often the tank crews had to actually fire on each other with their small-arms fire to kill the enemy swarming over the tanks. The crisis came that evening at 1700 hours when the Division Commander ordered the battalion to hold at all costs. Stragglers augmented the friendly positions so that at dawn on 2 September when the enemy made repeated banzai attacks into the positions he was repulsed with heavy losses. At dawn the battalion launched an attack into and west of Yongsan and in the Changyong area which forced the enemy to spread out and commit his reserves. The speed, fury and suprise of this attack completely demoralized the enemy causing him to abandon his equipment and positions. By 1400 hours all units were on their assigned objectives. Hurling back repeated attacks made by the enemy throughout the night of 2-3 September, the 72d Tank Battalion was able to hold this position until the next day when reinforcements arrived. The decisive denial to the enemy of the important Changyong-Yongsan-Miryang road prevented him from obtaining his goal, a flanking penetration of the allied perimeter between Taegu and Pusan, which, if successful, could have rolled up the entire allied defense line. This cost the enemy an estimated 1,800 casualties and considerable equipment. The 72d Tank Battalion displayed such gallantry, determination and esprit de corps in accomplishing its mission under extremely difficult and hazardous conditions as to set it apart and above other units participating in the action, and reflects great credit on its members and the military service of the United States.

French Battalion, U. N. Forces

In the name of the President of the United States and as public evidence of deserved honor and distinction the French Battalion, United Nations Forces in Korea, displayed extraordinary heroism in action against an armed enemy in the vicinity of Chipyong-ni, Korea, during the period 30 January to February, 1951. Advancing to the north as a part of the 23rd Regimental Combat Team, 2d Infantry Division, with the mission of locating and engaging the 42d Chinese Army whose position was not known, the French Battalion, together with a battalion of American infantry supported by artillery and tanks, began their attack from the Chongsan-Tanguri assembly area up the Kumdang Chon Valley at 0900 hours, 31 January. Advancing over the rugged, mountainous terrain, the attack progressed slowly until the French Battalion, on the left of the two advancing units, seized Hill 453, a critical terrain feature which not only dominated the area to the south, but also overlooked a northern valley divided by two ridges through which twin railroad tunnels ran on an east west axis. With the French on this hill, the rest of the objective was taken without opposition at 1815 hours and the force immediately began occupation and organization of the high ground around the tunnels. One company of the French Battalion was placed on Hill 453 and the balance of the battalion deployed on the ridges to the north, making up the western half of the perimeter. At 0600 hours on the morning of 1 February, after the American battalion on the eastern half of the perimeter had been under attack for over an hour, the French Battalion was attacked by the 373rd Chinese Infantry Regiment which, by 1020 hours, had employed its entire strength and had reached the crest of Hill 453. The French company on the hill counterattacked with bayonet and drove the enemy back. By noon, elements of another Chinese regiment had gained a high, rocky hill on the northwest corner of the perimeter from which they brought direct machine gun fire down onto the area and the French command post. The French 3rd Company, deploying along the crest, attacked this lodgment under cover of direct recoilless rifle and tank fire, drove the enemy off and restored the lines. The crisis came in the early afternoon with the French 1st and 3rd Companies still under heavy attack and no air support available due to the ground fog which covered the area throughout the entire morning. However, at this juncture the fog lifted. Twenty-four fighter air-craft sorties were brought in, and observed mortar and artillery fire were placed on the masses of attacking enemy. Under this fire power, the enemy broke off and withdrew at 1800 hours, just as a fresh American battalion arrived from the south. The next day, 1,300 dead Chinese soldiers were actually counted in front of the perimeter, the majority of whom were in front of the French Battalion's position. Also, of a total of 225 casualties suffered by the task force, 125 were among the companies of the French Battalion. As a result of the gallant actions of this splendid fighting unit of French volunteers, representing fifty percent of the infantry in the force, the position was held and the 373rd Chinese Infantry Regiment was routed. These actions, coupled with the equally heroic stand of the Third Battalion, 23rd Regimental Combat Team, on the other half of the perimeter where the Chinese 374th Infantry Regiment was destroyed, cost the enemy an estimated 3,600 casualties and put the 125th Chinese Division out of action as an effective unit, thus enabling the 23rd Regimental Combat Team to continue its advance. The extraordinary heroism, aggressiveness and esprit de corps displayed by the French Battalion during this period reflect great credit upon the arms of the Republic of France and the United Nations.

Netherlands Detachment, U. N. Forces

In the name of the President of the United States as public evidence of deserved honor and distinction, the Netherlands Detachment, United Nations Forces in Korea, is cited for exceptionally outstanding performance of duty and extraordinary heroism in combat against the armed enemy at Hoengsong and Wonju, Korea, during the period 12-15 February, 1951. On the early morning of 12 February, the enemy launched an offensive with two divisions aimed at splitting the central front. Against this onslaught the Netherlands Detachment had the mission of maintaining blocking positions on the out-skirts of the strategically important communication center of Hoengsong. The purpose of this was to permit two American battalions, supporting artillery, and remnants of the 5th and 8th ROK Divisions to withdraw from their exposed positions where surrounded. The Netherlands Detachment deployed astride the main axis of hostile advance. Large groups of hostile forces approached along the high ground from the west and on the ridges to the north. A small enemy group penetrated to the positions of the defenders but was quickly repulsed. By noon of 12 February, the enemy had concentrated a large force in the vicinity of Hoengsong and was delivering small-arms automatic weapons and mortar fire on the gallant defenders. All during the afternoon, the troops of the Netherlands Detach-ment supported the withdrawal of the United Nations Forces by delivering accurate and effective fire. After darkness had fallen, a company of enemy troops infiltrated with the withdrawing Republic of Korea forces. They succeeded in passing around the open right flank of the detachment's positions and reaching the location of the command post. Recognizing the enemy and shouting warning to his troops, the commander of the Netherlands Detachment rallied his headquarters personnel and led his small group against the treacherous foe until he fell mortally wounded. His gallant example and self-sacrifice so inspired the staff personnel that they repelled the enemy and killed many of them in fierce hand-to-hand combat. The battered and courageous troops withdrew to successive blocking positions until the last of the friendly forces broke through the enemy lines. The enemy meanwhile had infiltrated to the southwest and established a road block on the main supply route to Wonju. Once more the valiant troops of the Netherlands Detachment were ordered to fight a rear-guard action and hold the enemy until the road block could be eliminated. They fought tenaciously against overwhelming odds, and gained time for friendly forces to open the road. Utilizing 13 February to establish new defensive positions, the Netherlands Detachment dug in and waited for the next onslaught, which came against "B" Company early on the morning of 14 Feruary. The company was forced back until friendly mortar and artillery fire could be brought to bear on the Chinese attackers. The situation became critical by the evening of 14 February. The enemy was in full control of Hill 325, a dominate terrain feature overlooking the friendly position. Communications were disrupted, losses heavy and the situation fluid. At this time, "A" Company, so understrength that it had to be reinforced by a platoon from both "B" Company and the Heavy Mortar Company, was ordered to retake the hill. Launching their first counterattack at 0230 hours on the morning of 15 February, they were beaten back by heavy machine gun fire from the top of the hill. They moved up again at 0345 hours. This time they advanced to within 300 yards of the crest, only to be repulsed for the second time. At 0600 hours, after two set-backs and three sleepless nights of fighting, this noble band of heroic men, short of ammunition and out of communications, snatched victory from defeat by fixing bayonets and storming the hill. Shouting their famous "Van Heutz" battle cry, they slashed their way to the crest of the hill through the last of the remaining enemy. The inspiring and determined actions of the brave soldiers of the Netherlands Detachment withstood the enemy offensive and enabled allied forces to withdraw and regroup. The Netherlands Detachment displayed such gallantry, determination and esprit de corps in accomplishing its mission under extremely difficult and hazardous conditions as to set it apart and above other units with similar missions. The individual and collective heroism displayed by the soldiers of the Netherlands Detachment in their valiant stand against great odds reflect the highest credit on themselves, their homeland, and the Armed Forces of the United Nations.

Company "A", 72d Tank Battalion

In the name of the President of the United States as public evidence of deserved honor and distinction, the Third Battalion, Royal Australian Regiment; Company A, 72d Tank Battalion 2d Infantry Division; and Second Battalion, Princess Patricia's Canadian Light Infantry are cited for extraordinary heroism and outstanding performance of combat duties in action against the armed enemy near Kapyong, Korea, on 23 and 24 April 1951. The enemy had broken through the main line of resistance and penetrated to the area north of Kapyong. These units were deployed to stem the assault. Early on 24 April, the Third Battalion, Royal Australian Regiment, moved to the right flank of the section and took up defensive positions north of the Pukhan River. The Second Battalion, Princess Patricia's Canadian Light Infantry, defended, in the vicinity of Hill 677, on the left flank. Company A, 72d Tank Battalion, 2d Infantry Division, supported all units to the full extent of its capacity and, in addition, kept the main roads open and assisted in evacuating the wounded. Troops from a retreating division passed through the sector which enabled enemy troops to infiltrate with the withdrawing forces. The enemy attacked savagely under the clangor of bugles and trumpets. The forward elements were completely surrounded going through the first day and into the second. Again and again the enemy threw waves of troops at the gallant defenders and many times succeeded in penetrating the outer defenses but each time the courageous, indomitable and determined soldiers repulsed the fanatical attacks. Ammunition ran low and there was no time for food. Critical supplies were dropped by air to the encircled troops, but still they stood their ground in resolute defiance of the enemy. With serene and indefatigable peristence, the gallant soldiers held their defensive positions and took heavy tolls of the enemy. In some instances, when the enemy penetrated the defenses, the commanders directed friendly artillery fire on their own positions in repelling the thrusts. Toward the close of the second day, 25 April, the enemy break-through was stopped. The seriousness of the break-through on the central front was changed from defeat to victory by the gallant stand of these heroic and courageous soldiers. The Third Battalion, Royal Australian Regiment; Second Battalion, Princess Patricia's Canadian Light Infantry; and Company A, 72d Tank Battalion, 2d Infantry Division; displayed such gallantry, determination and esprit de corps in accomplishing their missions under extremely difficult and hazardous circumstances as to set them apart and above other units participating in the campaign, and by their achievements they brought distinguished credit on themselves, their homelands, and all freedom loving nations.

DECORATIONS PENDING APPROVAL

CONGRESSIONAL MEDAL OF HONOR

Pfc Dillon, William K.
  Med Co, 23d Inf Regt

Cpl Edwards, Junior D.
  Co E, 23d Inf Regt

Sgt Griego, Simon
  Co C, 38th Inf Regt

1st Lt Hartell, Lee R. (P)*
  Hq Btry, 15th FA Bn

2d Lt Harvey, George W. (P)*
  Co E, 38th Inf Regt

Sfc Hollaway Jimmie
  Btry A, 15th FA Bn

Capt Krzyzowski, Edward C. (P)*
  Co B, 9th Inf Regt

Sgt Long, Charles R.**
  Co M, 38th Inf Regt

Pfc Martin, Robert L.
  1st Ranger Inf Co

Pfc Nakamura, Wataru
  38th Inf Regt

Sfc Sitman, William S.
  Co M, 23d Inf Regt

Pfc Smith, David M.
  Co E, 9th Inf Regt

    * Posthumous
    ** Verbal Authority, EUSAK (not official)

DISTINGUISHED SERVICE CROSS

Pfc Anderson, Clyde T.
Lt Col Barsanti, Olinto M.
M/Sgt Brown, Jack P.
1st Lt Brumet, Chester C.
Cpl Carter, Raymond C.
M/Sgt Castonguay, Romeo
Pfc Cooper, Donald D.
Sgt Craug, Charles D.
2d Lt Curtis, Robert W.
Brig Gen De Shazo, Thomas E.
1st Lt Dunn, John H.
Cpl Graham, William E.
1st Lt Hall, Harold D.
Pfc Haycock, Joseph Jr.
Capt Jackson, Chester T.

1st Lt James, Hatcher M. Jr.
1st Lt Lacaze, Robert D.
Pfc Lederer, Edward R.
Maj Lowery, Leonard
M/Sgt Lyle, Ned
Capt Mallard, Charles W.
Pvt McGraw, Daniel E.
Lt Col McMain, D. M.
Sgt Mettner, Rodney G.
Pfc Morivama, Fumio
Capt Mulcahy, Merlin M.
Pfc Nayock, Joseph Jr.
Sgt Palmer, David M.
Cpl Payne, D. F.
Sgt Perez, Jessie F.

Capt Reed, Frank M.
Pfc Reeder, Jack N.
2d Lt Rhodes, Walter R.
Lt Col Richardson, Geverly T.
Pfc Rodgers, Franklin
1st Lt Sakowski, John M.
Cpl Sawickis, John J.
Sgt Sayles, Curtis O.
Cpl Shaffer, Raymond F.
Col Sloane, Charles C. Jr.
2d Lt Smith, Albert W.
Capt Tate, John A.
1st Lt Trenen, William P.
1st Lt Westerman, Samuel V.
2d Lt Wilde, David G.

SILVER STAR

1st Lt Abbott, Basil G.
Pfc Abbott, Melvin G.
Pfc Amezcua, Frank J.
Cpl Anderson, Laurence F.
Pfc Araiza, Celso M.
Sfc Armentrout, Howard D.
Sfc Auer, Myron C.
Sgt Bales, Russell J.
Sgt Baptista, Benjamin D.L.S.
Cpl Barto, Clifford A.

Sgt Berlett, Billie M.
1st Lt Biehl, John F. Jr.
1st Lt Binkoski, Joseph F.
Pfc Blunk, Robert M.
Major Boatright, Robert L.
1st Lt Bonnett, George M.
Cpl Breedlove, Gordon N.
1st Lt Brooks, John R.
Cpl Burris, Tony K.
Cpl Burtness, Curtis

Pvt Cavanaugh, James H.
Sgt Cena, Librado
1st Lt Chamblin, William W.
Pvt Chapman, Arthur
Pfc Chavez, George
Pfc Childress, Lindsey
Cpl Collins, James R.
1st Lt Cook, Donald E.
Lt Col Craven, Virgil E.
Lt Col Daniels, Henry F.

Pfc Davis, Alfred E.
Pfc Davis Howard J.
Cpl DeBoer, Arend
1st Lt Dent, Austin, D.
Cpl Delmont, James L.
1st Lt Deveau, Jack T.
Pfc Devor, William F.
Pvt Diaz, Phillip R.
Capt Dick, James
Sgt Donaldson, Samuel C. E.
1st Lt DuBois, Robert H.
Major Duncan, James R.
Pfc Dunphy, Thomas M.
Major Eliasson, Arne H.
Pfc Escobar, George J.
Pfc Fadie, Auguste J.
Pfc Foggin, David C. Jr.
Sgt Foglesong, Oliver O.
Pfc French, Joel F.
1st Lt Gannon, Rodney E.
Sfc Garcia, George
Sgt Gibson, John T.
Cpl Godeaux, Lionel
M/Sgt Goodman, Harry A.
Pfc Goyer, David W.
1st Lt Griscom, Charles W. Jr.
Lt Col Gurfein, Joseph I.
Pfc Gwin, James D.
Capt Harding, Robert R.
Sfc Hartman, Charles L.
Sfc Heltzel, Earl G.
M/Sgt Hergert, Anthony B.
Sgt Hernandez, Joe B.
Pfc Herzer, Milton D.
1st Lt Hudson, Dowell B.
Sgt Humkey, John E.
Pvt Hurley, Robert G.
Pvt Ikenoyama, Hideo

M/Sgt James, George B.
Sgt Jamca, Louis E.
Lt Col Keleher, William P.
Sgt Kennedy, Charles J.
Pfc Khula, Paul D.
Cpl Koszi, Victor S. Jr.
Sfc Kurfman, Richard O.
Capt Larkin, Martin J.
Cpl Lauffer, Richard P.
Sfc LeBow Joseph F.
2d Lt Lewis, Jeremiah
Pfc Lehnhart, Paul A.
Sgt Linn, Charles R.
Sfc Little, Robert E.
Sgt Lujan, Tim M.
Sfc Luke, Walter J.
Col Lynch, John M.
Sgt Mahue, Aurius J. Jr.
M/Sgt Manuel, Webster C.
Sfc Marks, Ira L.
Cpl Martin, Joseph W.
1st Lt Marx, Ralph J.
M/Sgt Mattila, Henry E.
Sgt McArthur, George T.
Pfc McCarthy, Joseph B.
Col Mildren, Frank T.
Capt Moody, Douglas M.
2d Lt Morgan, Hunton L.
1st Lt Mormino, Salvatore C.
Sgt Morrison, Clarence Jr.
Cpl Muse, Howard J.
1st Lt Nagle, Francis C.
Pfc Neelon, Jack
Cpl Novak, Martin T.
Pfc Olson, David J.
Pfc O'Neil, George E.
Pfc Orlandi, Anthony G.
Sgt Patterson, James M.

1st Lt Payne, Lloyd G.
Pfc Plessis, Joseph H.
2d Lt Pritchett, William Jr.
Sgt Puckett, Charles R.
Cpl Rapine, Lonnis D.
Pfc Reeg, Edwin F.
Sgt Roach, William D.
Cpl Robertson, Lynn E.
Sfc Romain, John M.
Cpl Roth, Donald R.
Sfc Runions, Avery H.
Cpl Sambuco, Louis
Cpl Sanders, Paul W.
Sgt Sanders, Robert J.
Sfc Sandoval, Leo R.
Sfc Scales Zeb S.
Pfc Scalia, Robert
Cpl Sharp, Clement J.
Sfc Sleppy, Jay
Pfc Stanley, Elmer V.
M/Sgt Sun, Herbert C. Y.
Sfc Swango, George L.
Pfc Tarantino, Daniel S.
Sgt Turland, William C.
Capt Tyree, James H.
Cpl Uejo, Seibo
Sgt Underwood, Floyd
Sfc Walker, Jack M.
M/Sgt Wallace, Billy J.
Pfc Wallgren, Willard P.
Cpl Wells, Charlie F.
Major Williams, George H. Jr.
2d Lt Wills, William L.
Sgt Wing, Charles L.
Pfc Yamamoto, Robert S.
Capt Yamazaki, Alfred A.
Cpl Yun Ke Yong

SUMMARY OF DECORATIONS

Outstanding performance in combat by men of the 2d Infantry Division in Korea was recognized by presentation of the following medals:

Congressional Medal of Honor	8
Distinguished Service Cross	81
Silver Star	1,538 (thru 15 Nov)
Bronze Star	2,940
Purple Heart	22,880

Outstanding performance in combat by units of the 2d Infantry Division in Korea was recognized by presentation of the Distinguished Unit Citation to the following organizations and attachments (only attachments organic to the Division are included):

2d United States Infantry Division

23rd Regimental Combat Team (Second Decoration for all)
    23rd United States Infantry Regiment
    French Infantry Battalion, United Nations Forces
    37th Field Artillery Battalion
    1st Ranger Company
    "B" Battery, 82d AAA Battalion
    "B" Battery, 503d Field Artillery Battalion
    "B" Company, 2d Engineer Battalion
    2d Clearing Platoon, Clearing Company, 2d Medical Battalion

72d Heavy Tank Battalion (Second Decoration)

Netherlands Detachment, United Nations Forces (Second Decoration)

Third Battalion, 23rd United States Infantry Regiment (Third Decoration)

French Infantry Battalion, United Nations Forces (Third Decoration)

"A" Company, 72d Heavy Tank Battalion (Third Decoration)

...And now shall mine head be lifted up above mine ene[mies] round about me...